This book provides an accessible and comprehensive account of the field of Equity, Diversity and Inclusion (EDI). The practical examples and case studies demonstrate the outcomes of dedicated and persistent commitment to EDI. This will be a very useful book for school leaders, teachers and practitioners actively pursuing equitable practice in their institutions.

Emerita Professor Vini Lander, *Leeds Beckett University*

This book provides a significant resource for ED&I educators, offering comprehensive, accessible, and research-informed guidance on key issues and challenges. It includes useful tabular syntheses and case studies examples of practice. There is so much to learn from the grounded experiences and ideas captured in this book.

Professor Heather Jane Smith, *Newcastle University*

Equity, Diversity and Inclusion in Schools

Are you struggling to implement meaningful Equity, Diversity and Inclusion (ED&I) practices in your school? Are you uncertain where to begin or how to navigate the complexities of ED&I work as a teacher or school leader? This exciting book explores what it means to lead on ED&I to ensure all staff and students feel they belong and can thrive. It provides guidance on embedding ED&I in the wider school strategy and shows how a culture of belonging can be created through a carefully crafted ED&I curriculum and the creation of safer spaces within training, coaching and mentoring as well as in the classroom.

Raheem and Rothery reveal how leaders and teachers can adopt an ED&I lens to create a school environment where all belong. They share practical strategies and recommendations for ED&I-specific interventions, including guidance around how to incorporate them into School Improvement Plans. They also reflect on the challenges of leading on ED&I, including having courageous conversations and overcoming resistance. Features include:

- Actionable strategies adaptable to your specific school context
- Real-world case studies from diverse schools across England
- Practical solutions that work within existing financial and time constraints
- Guidance on listening to and learning from your school community
- Frameworks for embedding ED&I into school strategy and daily practice as a teacher or leader

Providing readers with a deep understanding of what it means to lead on ED&I, this book will empower school leaders and ED&I educators so they are confident and intentional in working towards a school culture where everyone belongs.

Natasha Raheem has been teaching English in inner city schools for over 18 years. As a senior leader, she has experience leading on coaching and mentoring, literacy, teaching and learning, teacher training and professional development focusing on areas such as ED&I and leadership. She is currently an Assistant Vice Principal for Dixons Academies Trust and has always had a personal and professional interest in helping all staff and pupils to belong.

Funmilola Rothery is Trust Assistant Principal at Dixons Academies Trust, where she leads on anti-racism and ED&I. Her work has included national contributions to curriculum and professional development, and she is committed to embedding equitable practices at all levels of school leadership and classroom teaching. She is dedicated to developing inclusive environments where all staff and students feel seen, heard and valued. Passionate about social justice and belonging, Funmilola's leadership is rooted in empowerment, advocacy and meaningful change.

Equity, Diversity and Inclusion in Schools

A Practical Guide for Creating a Culture of Belonging

Natasha Raheem and Funmilola Rothery

LONDON AND NEW YORK

Designed cover image: © Getty Images

First published 2026
by Routledge
4 Park Square, Milton Park, Abingdon, Oxon OX14 4RN

and by Routledge
605 Third Avenue, New York, NY 10158

Routledge is an imprint of the Taylor & Francis Group, an informa business

© 2026 Natasha Raheem and Funmilola Rothery

The right of Natasha Raheem and Funmilola Rothery to be identified as authors of this work has been asserted in accordance with sections 77 and 78 of the Copyright, Designs and Patents Act 1988.

All rights reserved. No part of this book may be reprinted or reproduced or utilised in any form or by any electronic, mechanical, or other means, now known or hereafter invented, including photocopying and recording, or in any information storage or retrieval system, without permission in writing from the publishers.

For Product Safety Concerns and Information please contact our EU representative GPSR@taylorandfrancis.com. Taylor & Francis Verlag GmbH, Kaufingerstraße 24, 80331 München, Germany.

Trademark notice: Product or corporate names may be trademarks or registered trademarks, and are used only for identification and explanation without intent to infringe.

British Library Cataloguing-in-Publication Data
A catalogue record for this book is available from the British Library

ISBN: 978-1-032-95207-9 (hbk)
ISBN: 978-1-032-95199-7 (pbk)
ISBN: 978-1-003-58365-3 (ebk)

DOI: 10.4324/9781003583653

Typeset in Melior
by SPi Technologies India Pvt Ltd (Straive)

For Mia and Elise, my strong, kind, brave and curious daughters who inspire me to be better every day and see the world as they do. (N.R.)

For my wonderful niece, Maya. You inspire me to hope for a better world - may you always know the power you hold to shape it. (F.R.)

And for all the children who we've had the great privilege to teach.

Contents

Acknowledgements	x
Introduction	1
1 The current ED&I landscape in England	8
2 Developing an ED&I strategy	34
3 Raising awareness of self and developing person-centred knowledge	55
4 Adopting an ED&I lens to create an inclusive school culture	78
5 Creating an ED&I training curriculum for staff and pupils	98
6 Creating a safer space during ED&I training	127
7 Coaching and mentoring with an ED&I lens	146
8 Creating a positive action programme	167
9 Actions to take after ED&I training to enable lasting change	178
10 Protecting yourself as an ED&I educator	190
11 Final thoughts	204
Index	206

Acknowledgements

To Alfie, writing my first book, with our new-born, Elise, and our joyous 3-year-old, Mia, was never going to be easy. I could never have done it without your constant championing, support and love – thank you for always believing in me. To my mum, Ruma, and dad, Rashid – you moved to England from Mauritius and encountered racism for the first time. You have taught me courage, strength and compassion. Without your utter commitment to providing myself and Ria with a better life, we would not be where we are today. (N.R.)

To Ash, thank you for your unwavering love and support, always, but especially throughout the writing of this book. Thank you for every moment you reminded me I could do this, even when I doubted myself. To my mum, Sarah, and my sister, Moji, thank you for always believing in me, for encouraging me to be proud of who I am, and for the countless conversations in which we set the world to rights. We have faced many challenges together and I am forever grateful to have had such phenomenal women to learn from and look up to throughout (F.R.)

We are grateful to Dixons Academies Trust for providing us with the opportunity to lead on and showcase this work. To Luke Sparkes, we value your commitment to ED&I and recognise the significance of this being a priority for Dixons. To Jenny Thompson and Judith Kidd, we are especially grateful for your constant support, your invaluable wisdom and for amplifying our voices. To Shirley Watson – thank you for starting the conversation and for giving us the space to be our authentic selves.

One of the joys of writing this book was getting to listen to and learn from a range of educators engaging in transformational ED&I work across the country. Thank you to everyone who wrote a case study; we truly appreciate your intellectual generosity.

To Vini Lander and Heather Smith, thank you for taking the time to endorse our book and for your endless commitment to this work.

Thank you to Louise Ishani and Florence Olajide for reminding us of our value and encouraging us to see that this book could be a reality.

Thank you to Dr Aisling Cowan, Verity Howorth, Omena Osivwemu, Dr Sam Sims and Hannah Wilson for using your platforms to elevate this book and enabling us to draw upon a range of voices for our case studies.

To the many people who have shared their lived experience with us and trusted us with its care, we tread this path with you in mind.

Introduction

Why do equity, diversity and inclusion matter to us?

We'll begin by sharing our experiences of the education system and the times in which our sense of belonging has been diminished. Although we focus on our time in education. Such experiences have unfortunately, also marked our personal lives.

Experiences in primary school

During primary school, Natasha went on a residential and, whilst there, she was singled out and was the victim of numerous microaggressions from the residential leader. This was not noticed by her teachers and she did not have the language to describe what was happening and why it was wrong. She still remembers shrinking back into herself, avoiding answering questions, or asking them, to avoid being mocked. She was already used to using silence as a safety mechanism due to numerous instances of overt racism outside of school, most often by strangers and mainly by adults. Natasha and her sister were the only two racially minoritised children in her primary school and, even though she has fond memories of primary school, it is also marked by a complete absence of discussion of race or racism.

Funmi is mixed Nigerian and White British and was brought up by her mum, who is White British. Funmi has one sister with the same ethnicity as her and two brothers who are White British. Funmi and her sister were minorities in primary school and experienced racism, along with assumptions that they *must* be adopted. When Funmi's mum raised the racism with the school staff, she was asked, "Are you sure the racism isn't coming from home?" Funmi's mum removed both her and her sister from the school soon after, but these experiences impacted Funmi's sense of identity and made her feel almost ashamed of her mixed heritage. Thankfully, Funmi's mum was dedicated to challenging this.

Experiences in secondary school

Natasha went to a secondary school with a large South Asian population. In a lesson, the teacher asked students to raise their hands if their parents or grandparents were from South Asia. The teacher in front of the entire class laughingly asked Natasha why her hand was not raised. Natasha responded with, "My parents are from Mauritius." She remembers the teacher's complete lack of apology and dismissal of her answer. In future lessons with that teacher, she felt uncomfortable and uncertain about how much she should participate in their lessons.

During secondary school, Funmi reported racism that she had experienced from some other pupils. A staff member's response was to create a 'racist list' to which the names of 'perpetrators' would be added. Funmi was not made aware of any other response to the pupils involved. When other pupils became aware of the list, it was made into a joke with comments such as, "Be careful, Funmi will get you added to the racist list." Following this, Funmi lost her confidence to report incidents and even began to see racism as something she should accept. It is only in adulthood that she has regained confidence to challenge and report racist incidents.

Experiences in higher education

Natasha received a late diagnosis of epilepsy and was still coming to terms with managing this condition whilst undergoing her teacher training. During the early stages of her teaching career, no school leaders ever spoke about the additional support that some people may need in the workplace and Natasha did not have the knowledge to know what would help or what to ask for. It is only in recent years that Natasha has had the confidence to engage in self-advocacy and know precisely what can help her to feel safe in school. Admittedly, this knowledge is not fixed and, during Natasha's pregnancies, she had to think more carefully about how to manage triggers as her body was changing. Natasha, while she still experiences racism, feels that having a hidden disability has more of a significant impact on her day-to-day life: the fear of having a seizure is something that Natasha carries constantly. This is not to undermine racist experiences; rather, it highlights how intersectionality adds layers of competing challenges on a person's lived experience.

Having had very low exposure to Black teachers in her primary and secondary school experience, Funmi hoped this experience would change during her time at university. This was not the case. This had an impact on Funmi's career choices – her love of history made her think about going into teacher training, but her experiences of racism as a pupil, along with the lack of representation at every stage of her education, made her feel like this was not a safe choice to make. It was years later, when working for an educational charity, that Funmi realised that she herself could support young people to have a better experience than hers.

Based on our names on the front cover of this book, assumptions may have already been made about our identities. To really engender change, we must face these assumptions head-on, no matter how uncomfortable this might be. Consequently, before we've even explained our intentions, assumptions might be made about whether our commitment is to equity, diversity and inclusion (ED&I) or solely to race. We are committed to both. If we failed to talk about race, a significant part of our lived experience, we would not present ourselves authentically. This is something we do not feel we should have to apologise for because we have been forced to feel self-conscious about this element of our identity for the majority of our lives. For any readers that have ever felt a lack of belonging, this is likely to resonate with you.

We've begun our book by sharing our lived experience to attempt to explain why ED&I matters to us. Our experiences of being marginalised have resulted in a commitment to ensuring the children in our care are not denied a sense of belonging. We have both been saddened when recognising the parallels between our own childhood experiences and the experiences of many pupils in schools today whether this is known to staff, and believed, or not. For us, taking the time to understand the experiences of those around us is central to seeing people for who they are, rather than defining them by their characteristics and assuming a lived experience and identity that is not their own. Working in the ED&I space has enlightened us to the huge variety of challenges that colleagues from underrepresented groups face, as well as their strength and commitment to young people despite this. We hope to ensure that those within school communities show solidarity and school staff feel equipped to know how to create a culture of belonging, ensuring a more positive experience of education for future generations.

Why have we written *Equity, Diversity and Inclusion in Schools: a Practical Guide for Creating a Culture of Belonging?*

To acknowledge the realities of the work

Our book aims to provide our readers with a deep understanding of what it means to lead on ED&I, including the realities of this role. ED&I work can be incredibly challenging for many reasons. Various aspects of the work can be contentious due to a lack of widespread understanding of purpose. Additionally, the wide range of stakeholder feedback in this area can make it difficult to decipher what is the 'right' approach to take. When we first started ED&I work in schools, we struggled to know where to start and how we could do this, step by step, in a school context. Often, education in the sphere of ED&I focuses on key concepts. However, we know that real-life application can be challenging, particularly with the financial and time constraints faced by the education system, local contextual priorities and limiting and/or non-existent legal and statutory frameworks.

To encourage listening and learning

Impactful ED&I work begins with listening and learning in order to raise awareness of self and others, especially of those within the school community. It then moves on to providing high-quality training to all necessary stakeholders in response to these contextual priorities. ED&I interventions have to meet the needs of the school community; there is not a defined and established route for all schools to replicate.

To provide practical solutions and adaptable advice

Within the ED&I space, it is essential to draw upon a range of experiences. Hearing from experts is a useful starting point, and it is also important to be receptive to learning from those we interact with on a daily basis. We have endeavoured to include a wide range of case studies from schools across England to showcase the different ways schools approach belonging and to promote a diversity of voices. We hope that seeing where schools have made progress in this area will support readers in demonstrating that change is possible, as well as providing insights into the thought process that school leaders have undertaken.

With in our book, we aim to share practical strategies for implementation in every chapter with the acknowledgement that this is context-dependent. We also reflect on challenges that may be encountered and suggest potential solutions. We are not aiming to provide a rigid blueprint for approaching ED&I-related change and hope to provide ideas that can be implemented in a way that suits your specific school setting.

Disclaimer – inclusion

We fully appreciate that a book of this scope cannot truly provide a comprehensive guide to each protected characteristic. Our focus is more on implementation than developing in-depth knowledge of any one characteristic, although we do reference ways to develop this knowledge.

Throughout the book, we avoid overemphasising the policies and practices that are currently in place and aim to encourage readers to broaden their horizons to move beyond statutory obligations especially as, at the time of writing, the ED&I landscape is swiftly changing.

How to use this book

Our book is aimed at ED&I educators and by this we mean any staff member with additional responsibility to lead in this area – this may be part of a standalone role or embedded within an existing role. We recognise that, depending on your local context, such a role may not exist. If this is the case, ED&I educators also refers to school leaders with an interest in this area and staff who may be adopting an ED&I lens through their curriculum adaptations, leading on enrichment or cultural events or through daily interactions with those within the school community.

While our book does lend itself towards those who are decision-makers in schools and can embed ED&I in school strategy, the book is still useful for those seeking to adopt an ED&I lens across their various roles and responsibilities in school. You may prefer to read the book in its entirety, or read specific chapters based on your role, experience, or particular areas of interest.

Our use of language

We realise that there is not always one shared agreement on the best language to use in the ED&I space and that identity and descriptors are highly personal. Here, we will outline the language we will use, but we urge readers to ask individuals rather than assuming preferences when referring to characteristics in daily life.

Race

We are aware that people have different individual preferences for terminology related to race. Where we are not referring to specific groups, we have used the following range of terms interchangeably and this is a reflection of how we self-describe and the research we have drawn upon.

- Ethnic minority
- Global majority
- People of colour
- Racialised minority
- Racially minoritised

Sexuality

- We use the acronym LGBTQ+ in line with Stonewall, who affirm that people define their sexuality in a variety of different ways and that language is ever-evolving (Stonewall, n.d.).

Gender Identity

- Where we use the terms 'women' and 'men' this is inclusive of any person whose gender identity this reflects.

Disability

- We recognise that some people may prefer person-first language when referring to disability whereas others prefer identity-first language. We use the terms flexibly, alternating between the two to reflect this range of preferences (Dunn & Andrews, 2015 cited in Best, Mortenson, Lauzière-Fitzgerald, Smith, 2022).

Reclaiming 'woke'

'Woke' is an interesting political term and it was first used in America. It originally referred to the need to wake up to the lived experience of Black people in America and the systemic oppression they faced (Smith, 2021). The term is used more generally now and refers to a raised awareness of social injustice against all underrepresented groups. We first came across the term on social media where the original meaning has been usurped. 'Woke' is used as a weapon to criticise and demean those who are committed to ED&I; it's seen as political correctness that's out of control and those with a 'woke' agenda are portrayed as easily offended. Research from YouGov suggests that 'among people who use the term, the vast majority do so in a pejorative sense – 73% use it in a disapproving way, compared to only 11% who employ it approvingly' (Smith, 2022).

We want to reclaim this term. We encourage ourselves and our readers to be proudly 'woke' because, by doing so, you are awake to the discrimination faced by those from underrepresented groups, awake to personal change needed and awake to changes needed within your school and society as a whole. To be 'woke' is to be aware: aware of injustice; aware of privilege; and aware of how you act in solidarity with those from underrepresented groups. We should all be willing to reimagine schools as places where all can belong without fear or isolation.

In the world we live in now, we need now more than ever to embrace being 'woke'. We need to acknowledge the impact of lockdown on our lives and how dangerous views about underrepresented groups were able to fester because they were not diluted by school culture and wider interactions in society. We need to acknowledge that the internet, bots, negative algorithms, the unrelenting impact of social media and performative bullies as influential figures are spreading harmful dominant narratives and extremist violent ideologies. Within the education sector, we have a duty both to our young people and to ourselves to counter increasingly dangerous and damaging views by: raising awareness of self; developing person-centred knowledge; encouraging critical thinking; and noticing, naming and addressing prejudicial incidents unabashedly. For an ED&I lens to be adopted by all within the school community, consistent and high-quality training for staff is needed. It is only then that children will see and appreciate what it means to be truly human in a digital world.

ED&I is not a temporary fad, nor is it a naive utopian vision of a better world. Schools are microcosms of society and having ED&I as a strategic priority forms the foundation for social cohesion where people feel safe to be their authentic selves and value the experiences of others. Together, let's reclaim the meaning of what it is to be 'woke' because, in these uncertain and troubling times, it is a sign of hope and a manifestation of the commitment of many to truly creating a culture of belonging.

References

Best, K. L., Mortenson, B. W., Lauzière-Fitzgerald, Z., Smith, E. M. (2022). *Language Matters! The Long-Standing Debate between Identity-First Language and Person First Language.* Available at: https://www.tandfonline.com/doi/full/10.1080/10400435.2022.2058315 [Accessed 17 April 2025].

Smith, M. (2021). *What Does 'Woke' Mean to Britons?* Available at: https://yougov.co.uk/politics/articles/35904-what-does-woke-mean-britons [Accessed 15 April 2025].

Smith, M. (2022). *Most Britons Now Know What 'woke' Is.* Available at: https://yougov.co.uk/politics/articles/43645-most-britons-now-know-what-woke [Accessed 15 April 2025].

Stonewall (n.d.). *List of LGBTQ+ Terms.* Available at: https://www.stonewall.org.uk/resources/list-lgbtq-terms [Accessed 17 April 2025].

1 The current ED&I landscape in England

In this chapter we highlight some significant aspects of the ED&I landscape that directly affect schools and trusts across England. We reiterate that the information presented is not exhaustive but rather provides a foundational overview of the themes, duties and frameworks that underpin discussions throughout this book.

Due to our focus on practical implementation of ED&I, we acknowledge that we are unable to present an equivalent picture of the ED&I landscape in other countries. This is due to the variation of ED&I practices and the extent to which they are embedded. For example, at the time of writing, the Inclusiveness Index shows that New Zealand is the most inclusive with UK ranking in 20th position (Othering and Belonging Institute, 2024). However, this can change quickly if we consider the dismantling of ED&I interventions in the US. We encourage readers in other countries to consider:

- The strengths and limitations of any legal frameworks related to ED&I (if available).
- National and local ED&I priorities.
- Cultural norms and any opportunities arising from this or any challenges to ED&I interventions.
- Any risks if engaging in ED&I work.
- Differing socio-economic contexts as this will affect how much additional resource and capacity can be given to ED&I.
- Opportunities available in schools to diversify the curriculum and provide the necessary training for staff and pupils.

Many of the policies and statutory duties that we will reference offer a useful starting point for schools embarking on their ED&I journey. However, it is crucial to view them as a starting point. The chapters that follow will offer practical guidance to help readers to cultivate equitable practices that extend beyond compliance and foster meaningful, lasting change.

What is Equity, Diversity and Inclusion (ED&I)?

Equity, Diversity and Inclusion (ED&I) may be described differently depending on context and the name of this work benefits from thoughtful consideration based on the vision and values of your setting. Some may refer to these important values in a different order with Diversity, Equity and Inclusion (DEI), whilst other organisations substitute equality for equity or refer to DEIB (Diversity, Equity, Inclusion and Belonging) or EDIJ (Diversity, Equity, Inclusion and Justice). We are not proposing that our choice of values and the order in which we list them is the answer. Whatever values are selected to define and describe an organisation's strategy, it is important that there is a clear rationale for each value and that the same language is used consistently by all.

Equity

The 'E' in ED&I is sometimes used to refer to equality; for us, however, it is equity that must be placed at the forefront. Whilst both equality and equity have connotations of fairness, they cannot be used interchangeably. Equality is based on the notion that to be fair is to ensure people are not treated differently. Striving for equality means ensuring that all people and groups are provided with the same opportunities and resources to enable them to achieve the same outcomes. Although treating people in the same way may feel like the just thing to do, assuming that everyone requires the same treatment fails to acknowledge the fact that people come from a range of different starting points.

Equity, by contrast, acknowledges individual difference and ensures that necessary adjustments are made to ensure nobody is prevented from reaching the same outcomes. A simple analogy may support in understanding here: imagine that you are faced with two people – one that has the means to eat three meals a day and another that lives in poverty, is malnourished and has not recently eaten a meal. *Equal* treatment here involves offering both individuals the exact same meal. *Equitable* treatment, however, involves offering the first individual a meal, whilst offering the second person a meal to eat immediately as well as providing them with food to take home. This acknowledges that, for the first person, a meal may be a welcome treat, whereas for the second person, the food is a necessity for survival. Sometimes, equitable treatment can involve providing resources to those that need it without offering anything additional to those that are not facing barriers. In the previous analogy, for example, if only one meal was available, it would be equitable to offer this to the malnourished individual only. This would acknowledge that the malnourished individual's need for food is urgent and life-sustaining, whereas the other person is not in immediate need. In this context, equity means directing the limited resource to the person whose survival depends on it.

In society, there are various historical, systemic and structural disadvantages that impact different groups. Equity acknowledges this and strives to adjust the allocation of resources to dismantle the barriers faced by some. In schools, this is most commonly recognised in relation to SEND. For example, a student with dyslexia may have extra time or use a word processor in exams; these are examples of an equitable process. Whilst these examples are things that schools are legally obliged to fulfil, not all situations where equity is needed are covered by law. In such cases, there is a need to go beyond simple compliance, to act independently and proactively to identify potential barriers and to be intentional in removing them. For example, many schools set homework using online platforms. Treating pupils *equally* would mean setting the exact same homework, with the exact same deadline, with no further considerations. An *equitable* approach, however, would mean recognising that not all students have the same access to the homework task. Some may not have internet access at home, or may only have limited access due to living across multiple households. Here, equity may involve extended deadlines or facilitating specific times for the work to be completed in the school building. Equity does not mean allowing some people an easier experience than others. It means acknowledging and addressing the challenges faced by some that are not experienced by all. It would not be equitable, for example, to excuse some students from the homework altogether, since this may disadvantage them further if they make less progress in class than their peers as a result.

For us, equity leads the way in ED&I because it places emphasis on organisational change through an interrogation of current practices. It acknowledges that fairness involves enabling access for all to the same resources and opportunities as those in dominant groups.

Diversity

Diversity in itself refers to 'the fact of many different types of things or people being included in something' (Cambridge Dictionary, n.d.) In the ED&I space, diversity is often used to refer to the variety of human differences, including but not limited to gender identity, sexual orientation, race, ethnicity, religious belief, age, socio-economic background, physical ability, life experience and much more. Diversity is something that naturally exists in society (although some contexts are less diverse than others in various ways) rather than a standalone goal to 'achieve'. We believe that what truly matters is *embracing* and *valuing* that diversity.

A physical manifestation of diversity comes in the form of representation, that is, the physical presence of people with a range of characteristics and from a range of demographic backgrounds. Representation is important in schools for staff and pupils alike and can refer to being able to see themselves reflected in areas, such as the staff body, the curriculum and the school environment. For pupils, seeing themselves reflected in the staff body is important in providing examples of what academic success can look like for people they identify with (Gibbs, 2021). Research suggests that there are academic benefits for students from ethnic minority backgrounds who are taught by a teacher from the same background and where their school represents different ethnicities equitably (Donlevy, Meierkord & Rajania, 2015; Villegas and Irvine, 2010). In terms of the curriculum, Pearson (2023) found that 64% of students agree that they learn better if they see people from their background reflected in what they learn at school and Elliot et al. (2021) found that studying a more diverse English curriculum supported students in developing increased empathy and understanding. Further research demonstrates that a lack of curriculum diversity and role models can act as a significant barrier to achievement (YMCA, 2020).

Many teachers that we have worked with have explained that a lack of diversity in the staff body and leadership has impacted their sense of belonging. Research indicates the prevalence of this, and Davidson et al. (2005) found that ethnic minority staff 'felt more comfortable in schools where they were not identified because of their "difference" and hence preferred to work in schools that were culturally diverse'. Representation is just as important for individuals whose identities may not be immediately visible or who may not feel fully comfortable disclosing key aspects of who they are. In these cases, it becomes more complex, as representation goes beyond visible characteristics. When identities are hidden or undisclosed, ensuring meaningful representation through the presence of role models or shared experiences can feel challenging. This is where the school environment becomes incredibly important. for example, Cawley (2020), identified the need for representation for LGBTQ+ teachers in schools, indicating that displays of support such as 'wearing LGBT lanyards, flying the Pride flag outside and inside their school, having displays around school that celebrate diversity and LGBT issues' can have an impact on perceptions and feelings of acceptance. This demonstrates that representation will not always come from physical human presence alone.

Inclusion and belonging

Although physical representation clearly has an impact on a sense of belonging for staff and students, it is essential that schools act to *value* diversity, making it meaningful. This links directly to the 'I' in ED&I, which stands for inclusion. Within a school context, inclusion is commonly associated with SEND, but the broader framework of ED&I both encompasses this and goes beyond it. Throughout our book, we use inclusion to refer to how all staff and students experience being part of a school and/or wider trust and how much the school culture enables them to thrive due to feeling respected and valued as their authentic selves.

Inclusion acts as an important part of the process in developing a sense of belonging for all. Whilst a diverse staff body, curriculum and school environment can support the school community in feeling *represented*, any efforts to achieve this will be undermined if this does not also translate into wider practices and policies. Additionally, being part of a diverse team does not automatically ensure that everyone can *belong* as their authentic self. When researching the experiences of student teachers undertaking teacher training, for example, Åkesson (2024) found that their sense of belonging was impacted by the failure of their training programme's ability to 'provide a sense of belonging for students who do not conform to an able-bodied, white, middle-class, male norm'.

Cawley (2020) explains that many LGBTQ+ teachers can feel unsafe in the school environment and may feel unable to disclose their sexuality to colleagues as they are uncertain as to what the reaction will be and Lee (2019) indicates that this level of uncertainty may prevent LGBTQ+ teachers from applying for promotions or moving on to different schools. Lee also identified differences in the experiences of LGBTQ+ teachers who worked through the discriminatory era of Section 28, noting they had markedly different workplace experiences compared to those who entered the profession after its repeal in 2003, with those who lived through the legalised prejudice being less inclined to view their personal and professional identities as compatible.

Each of these examples makes clear that the physical presence of diversity alone is not enough to generate a sense of inclusion in the school environment. No matter what someone's characteristics are, if they do not feel safe in the school building, have to hide elements of their identity, or feel unable to share their thoughts, diversity is superficial. Where this is the case, it can mean career progression is limited and, for an organisation, it means that there may not be awareness of where there is systemic bias. Consequently, this means that staff talent from underrepresented groups is not developed and nurtured.

Belonging is the outcome of the complex and interwoven threads of ED&I so members of the school community 'feel personally accepted, respected, included, and supported by others' (Smith and Culbert, 2024). It cannot occur without being part of a whole-school strategy or without consistent leadership commitment. Belonging is not present just because there is visible diversity or because certain ED&I interventions are in place. Developing a sense of belonging for all involves being intentional in developing person-centred knowledge (see Chapter 3) and making a commitment to providing an equitable experience for all. Without doing this, ED&I interventions will remain surface-level rather than ensuring that all members of a school community feel seen and heard. Throughout this book we will explore the ways in which behaviours, systems, policies and procedures can be adapted through the lens of ED&I to ensure that schools and trusts are inclusive places for all.

Statutory duties for schools

It is essential for everyone working in schools to understand their legal responsibilities around equality. For ED&I educators especially, a solid grasp of these duties is crucial to effectively support and educate others. In this section, we outline key statutory duties relevant to schools. This is not an exhaustive list and we focus primarily on the legislation that we go on to reference throughout the book. For a deeper understanding, further research into each specific duty and beyond is strongly recommended. It is important to note that we are writing this book in late 2024 to early 2025 and that equalities law is subject to change across the globe. The Labour government have announced a 'call for evidence to break down barriers to opportunity at work' which 'will help shape the measures included in the draft Equality (Race and Disability) Bill which will be published this session' (Office for Equality and Opportunity, 2025). This means there are likely to be new considerations at the time of publishing and we encourage readers to remain alert to these.

The Equality Act, 2010

To truly understand the necessity of ED&I work in schools, and the barriers that can work to disadvantage specific groups, it is important to understand the Equality Act (2010) and the protected characteristics it outlines. In England, Scotland and Wales, the Equality Act makes it illegal to discriminate against a person based on the grounds of nine protected characteristics which are:

- age
- disability
- gender reassignment
- marriage and civil partnership
- pregnancy and maternity
- race
- religion or belief
- sex
- sexual orientation.

The Equality Act then outlines specific definitions of discrimination: direct discrimination; indirect discrimination; harassment; and victimisation (EHRC, 2019). It is important for all school staff to have a thorough understanding of the protected characteristics so that everyone is wholly equipped to prevent and challenge discrimination. Training in this area often simply shares the list of characteristics without any further explanation. It is essential to go further than this to ensure that lived experiences are not reduced to a single word on a PowerPoint slide.

Here, we will provide information linked to each protected characteristic and, where data is available, will link this to the education system. This will include implications linked to representation, discrimination and belonging. It is important for us to acknowledge the limitations of the examples shared – this does not amount to a comprehensive account of each characteristic and we do not want to encourage assumptions of homogeneity. Whilst reading, it is important to consider the different types of discrimination as well as remembering that discrimination by perception and association apply to each protected characteristic. If you would like to find out more about each characteristic, we would highly recommend reading the Diverse Ed Manifesto.

We invite readers to use this section to develop their awareness. The following questions may be helpful to consider:

- Who is represented within your context? Who isn't?
- Are there any examples of discrimination that you can personally relate to?
- How does/might discrimination manifest itself in your school context?
- Are your school policies and practices procedures inclusive and representative of the range of protected characteristics? What, or who is missing?

Age

Age discrimination is when a person is treated differently because of their age. In schools, pupils are not protected by age discrimination. Examples of age discrimination may include:

- Not shortlisting someone for a job based on the number of years they had been teaching, unless the decision can be justified by the employer.
- Selecting a teacher or education professional for redundancy based on their age.
- Younger colleagues being promoted over older colleagues, with various reasons stated, but the older colleague may sense that it is due to age.
- Older colleagues being denied access to Continuing Professional Development (CPD) opportunities, whilst younger colleagues are encouraged to attend.

In schools where experienced teachers are seen as problematic due to cost or their views, such teachers 'are likely to feel – at best – unappreciated and, at worst, actively targeted and aggressively managed out' (Brighouse, 2022). In some of the examples outlined, and without direct proof, it can be hard to challenge decisions. This can cause feelings of helplessness, isolation and discontent in the individuals, as well as making them question their worth.

Facts and figures: age

- Now Teach canvased the views of several hundred teachers and found that one-third had experienced age discrimination in school, though none of them had seen it fit to complain (Kellaway, 2024).
- In the 2023/4 academic year, the percentages of teachers by age group were as follows (DFE, 2024a)
    - ☐ 4.5% under 25
    - ☐ 14.1% 25 to 29
    - ☐ 33.1% 30 to 39
    - ☐ 27.9% 40 to 49
    - ☐ 17.6% 50 to 59
    - ☐ 2.8% 50 and over.
- Flexible working is the number one workplace practice the over-50s say would support them to work for longer (Thomson, 2018 cited in Thomson 2022).

Disability

The Equality Act (2010) defines a person as disabled if they have 'a physical or mental impairment that has a "substantial" and "long-term" negative effect on your ability to do normal daily activities' (Gov.UK, n.d.-a). Schools (and all employers) must make reasonable adjustments to make sure that staff and pupils with disabilities, or physical or mental health conditions, are not disadvantaged and discriminated against. Hidden disabilities are protected under the Act. There is no legal requirement for someone to notify their employer of their disability, and many employees may not be aware or may not have been diagnosed with a disability. However, for reasonable adjustments to be made, individuals are likely to need to disclose their disability and work with their employer to outline what is needed.

Schools also have a duty to make 'reasonable adjustments' to make sure disabled students are not discriminated against. These changes could include providing extra support and aids like specialist teachers or equipment (Gov.UK, n.d.-b) Reasonable adjustments must not be considered a 'favour' or as though schools are going out of their way to support staff and students with disabilities: 'If you are suspicious as to whether they need reasonable adjustments or if you are questioning why additional support is given, then you are holding an ableist perspective' (Golding, 2022).

Examples of discrimination may include:

- Discrimination arising from a disability e.g. if a disabled pupil is prevented from going outside at break time because it takes too long to get there.
- Harassment e.g. if a teacher/line manager shouts at a disabled student/staff member for not paying attention when their disability stops them from easily concentrating.
- Victimisation e.g. suspending a disabled student or disciplining a staff member because they have complained about harassment.

Facts and figures: disability

- Young people with autism or social, emotional and mental health (SEMH) difficulties were more likely (71%) to report having experienced bullying than those with other SEND needs (Anti-Bullying Alliance, n.d.).
- Over 1 in 3 people with a learning disability said that being bullied is one of the things they worry about most when they go out (Mencap, 2019).
- Many schools are not including disability when collecting staff diversity data (Belger, 2023) and in the 2021 School Workforce Census disability status was not obtained for 52% of teachers (DFE, 2023a).
- The DFE (2024a) did not publish data on disability in their report on the school workforce in England.

Gender reassignment

Under the Equality Act (2010), gender reassignment refers to anyone 'proposing to undergo, undergoing or having undergone a process to reassign your sex'. Legal protection against gender reassignment discrimination applies regardless of whether someone has had medical procedures or surgery. Individuals are protected at any stage of their transition, whether they are planning, undergoing, or have completed the process. Possessing a Gender Recognition Certificate is not necessary for this protection (EHRC, updated 2023).

Examples of discrimination may include:

- Refusing to appointment a person to a post due to fear of reactions from parents and carers (NEU, n.d.-a).
- In absence procedures: being treated less favourably for taking time off due to gender reassignment, compared to how others are treated when absent due to illness or injury.

- Indirect discrimination through any policy or way of working that puts people with the protected characteristic of gender reassignment at a disadvantage. For example, being criticised for not sharing a childhood photo during a planned team activity, where the requirement disproportionately disadvantages trans staff.

- Through harassment e.g. being repeatedly and deliberately misgendered by colleagues (EHRC, updated 2023).

- Through victimisation e.g. being treated badly because you have made a complaint about transphobic discrimination.

In 2024, as part of a process of consultation, the Conservative government published draft non-statutory guidance for schools regarding the response to what they refer to as 'gender questioning students', as well as draft statutory guidance on teaching sex education in schools. The guidance published has been criticised as being discriminatory and non-compliant with the Equality Act (Birketts LLP, 2024; TES, 2024). Stonewall (2023b) described the guidance as 'legally unworkable and contrary to existing equality law and the government's own guidance on safeguarding' with the view that 'it would inevitably lead to real harm being caused to trans children and young people across England'. We will avoid going into significant detail about the guidance here as the current government are yet to announce the action that will be taken going forwards.

Facts and figures: gender reassignment:

- Nearly 64% of trans pupils overall are bullied for being LGBT at school (Stonewall, 2017).
- Just 41% of LGBT students report that their schools say transphobic bullying is wrong (Stonewall, 2017).
- 77% LGBT pupils have never been taught about or discussed gender identity and what 'trans' means and just 10% of LGBT pupils (10%) have learnt about where to go for help and advice about being trans (Stonewall, 2017).
- Half of trans and non-binary people have hidden or disguised the fact that they are LGBT at work because they were afraid of discrimination (Stonewall, 2018).
- Data on the sexual orientation and trans status of young people who are not in education, training or work is not routinely collected at national or local levels. This means that there is no accurate figure or estimate of the number of LGBT young people who are not in education, training or work in the UK today (Stonewall, 2023a).

Marriage and civil partnership

Direct marriage and civil partnership discrimination is when you are treated less favourably because you are married or in a civil partnership. Examples of discrimination may include:

- Not being promoted because you are in a civil partnership.
- Being dismissed from a role upon being married due to the perception that your obligations should be in the home.

Discrimination can be challenging to evidence here in the absence of any clear and direct comments or judgements. Where discrimination is perceived, it can be useful to consider how this can be evidenced. This may involve seeking support from witnesses but may also include things like messages and emails from the time the discrimination took place. For this reason, it can be useful to keep a paper trail and to document interactions that have taken place. This may involve following up meetings and conversations by email, or even sending personal messages that describe the discriminatory event at the time it has taken place (Monaco Solicitors, n.d.).

Pregnancy and maternity

Employees are protected from pregnancy discrimination as soon as pregnancy is known or suspected. There is no obligation to tell an employer that you are pregnant until 15 weeks before the baby is due to be born. However, where pregnancy has not been disclosed and your employer is not aware, you will not be protected from pregnancy discrimination when treated unfavourably. This can be particularly challenging, as many people choose to keep the news private until after the first trimester, when the risk of miscarriage reduces. However, the first trimester can often be physically challenging and plagued with anxiety, especially if you have undergone fertility investigation or treatment or have experienced pregnancy loss. Examples of discrimination may include:

- Refusing to recruit a candidate who is pregnant, is on maternity leave, has just taken maternity leave, or is about to go on maternity leave.
- Refusing to allow pregnant employees to take reasonable paid time off to attend antenatal appointments or criticising an employee for taking time off to attend antenatal appointments.
- Refusing to consider a pregnant employee for promotion, not informing them of promotion opportunities or discouraging them from applying.
- Disciplining a pregnant employee or subjecting them to performance or capability management procedures for reasons related to pregnancy including pregnancy-related sickness.
- Ignoring a pregnant employee or making hurtful comments about the pregnancy or maternity leave.

> **Pregnancy and maternity facts and figures**
>
> - Research suggests that women aged 30–39 are the largest demographic to leave teaching every year and that women's career progress slows when they become mothers, comparative to fathers and to both men and women who do not have children (Sheppard and Campbell, 2023).
> - 50% of mothers described a negative impact on their opportunity, status or job security. This included: requests for flexible working leading to negative consequences; being given unsuitable work or workloads; or feeling treated with less respect or that their opinion was less valued (Adams et al., 2016).

Race

The Equality Act defines race as a person's colour, nationality (including citizenship) and ethnic and national origins. It is important to note that a person's race may not be immediately determined, or inaccurate judgements about a person's race may be made. Where less favourable treatment takes placed based on this, it is an example of discrimination by perception. Examples of discrimination may include:

- Refusing to employ or promote someone based on their race.
- Indirect discrimination, such as English as a first language being a requirement for a job role and resulting in people from being turned away despite being otherwise suitably qualified (Davidson Morris, 2025).
- Harassment through being subjected to racist slurs from colleagues, under the guise of 'banter'.
- Victimisation through being treated badly in work due to a formal complaint being made in relation to racism that has been experienced.

There are important exceptions when it comes to different treatment based on race. For example, where employers introduce positive action programmes for racial groups that are underrepresented (see Chapter 8).

Not only are employers under statutory duty not to discriminate against employees or potential employees based on race; they are also responsible for taking reasonable steps to prevent and respond to racism by other employees. This involves having clear policies in place from the outset. Employers must also review all workplace policies and practices to ensure they are not indirectly discriminative (Davidson Morris, 2025). We will explore how to enact and move beyond this in Chapter 4.

> **Facts and figures: race**
>
> - In the 2023/24 academic year, 83.8% of classroom teachers were White British with 37% of students coming from an ethnic minority background (DFE, 2024a).
> - In the 2021/22 academic year, 92.5% of headteachers were White British, along with 90.8% of deputy headteachers, 87.8% of assistant headteachers and 84.2% classroom teachers (DFE, 2023c).
> - Despite being overrepresented in ITT applications, ethnic minority groups have lower acceptance rates at every stage from enrolment to ITT to headship (NFER, 2024).
> - 95% of young Black people have heard and witnessed the use of racist language in school, with 75% claiming this was of a higher frequency as they heard or witnessed racist language 'sometimes', 'regularly' or 'all the time'. 49% of young Black people surveyed deemed racism the biggest barrier to them achieving at school (YMCA, 2020).
> - White Gypsy or Roma and Traveller of Irish heritage pupils had the highest permanent exclusion rates in the 2022 to 2023 school year, followed by Mixed White and Black Caribbean and Black Caribbean students (DFE, 2024c).

Religion or belief

Religion or belief discrimination is when a person is treated differently because of their religion or belief or lack or religion or belief. Expressing faith may be a visible or invisible characteristic based on the individual's personal preferences Notably, discrimination can occur even where both the discriminator and the person being discriminated against hold the same religious or philosophical belief. Examples of discrimination may include:

- Using someone's religion as a reason to avoid employing them.
- Failing to promote someone due to them requesting time off for religious worship or pilgrimage (NEU, n.d.-c).
- Policies and practices that apply to everyone but disadvantage specific religious groups. For example, meetings that require all staff attendance being scheduled on the dates of Eid.
- Harassment through disparaging comments repeatedly being made about religious practices in the staff room.

Conversations with some Muslim women in our network have revealed perceptions that assumptions have been made about their career aspirations, resulting in them feeling as if their career is at a standstill or that they must demonstrate extra determination to be able to progress.

Sex

Sex discrimination is where a person is treated differently because of their sex. Sex can also refer to a group of people, such as women and men or boys and girls. Examples of discrimination may include:

- Appointing a man, rather than a woman with superior qualifications and more experience, to a senior post leading on behaviour and attitudes on the assumption that a woman may not have the gravitas to lead on this (NEU, n.d.-d)
- Refusing to appoint the best-qualified applicant to a teaching post in an infant school, on the grounds that he is a man and that a woman would be preferred (NEU, n.d.-d)
- An employer's failure to treat an employee's menopause in the same way as other medical conditions under its performance management policy (NEU, n.d.-d)
- Comments made to suggest men should be promoted over women due to the perception that women will leave to have children, even where this is not directed to any individual woman.
- Sexual harassment, such as sexual comments, 'jokes', touching or assault.

The Equality Act also imposes into all employment contracts a sex equality clause which states that women doing equal work as a man in the same employment are entitled to equal pay and contractual terms that are no less favourable than the man's (NEU, n.d.-d). However, this is difficult to ensure when people don't disclose salaries and when a person may take on additional work without asking (or knowing to ask) for an honorarium or additional time.

At the time of writing, there has been a significant change in how sex is defined in UK law. When first drafting this chapter, we drew upon the Equality and Human Rights Commission (EHRC) (2020) guidance on sex and sex discrimination, which stated 'under the [Equality] Act, a person's legal sex is the sex recorded on their birth certificate or their Gender Recognition Certificate (GRC)'. However, in April 2025, the UK Supreme Court ruled that the terms 'woman' and 'sex' in the Equality Act refer only to a 'biological woman' and to biological sex (Carrell, 2025). This means that a transgender woman with a GRC will no longer be legally defined as a woman and that only cisgender women are protected under the characteristic of sex. This decision has been described as 'incredibly worrying for the trans community' (Blake, 2025), and has been deemed as a mechanism 'to exclude trans people wholesale from participating in UK society'. Some perceive that the ruling "may also have broken the Equality Act beyond repair"

(Belcher, TransActual, 2025). Updates are to be expected to the code of conduct for services, particularly involving single-sex spaces (O'Hare, 2025); at the time of writing, however, we are unable to comment on what the exact outcome will be. We urge readers to stay alert to future changes. We stand in solidarity with the transgender community and urge individuals and employers to remember that gender reassignment continues to be a protected characteristic, rendering discrimination unlawful. This is incredibly important in keeping the trans community safe in schools.

> **Facts and figures: sex**
>
> - Boys are twice as likely to be in the growing number of school exclusions than girls (CSJ, 2025).
> - Polling suggests that 41% of sixth-form boys and girls have been taught in school lessons that boys are a problem for society (CSJ, 2025).
> - 92% of girls, and 74% of boys, said sexist name-calling happens a lot or sometimes to them or their peers (Ofsted, 2021).
> - Women make up 76% of the teacher workforce, but are less likely to be in leadership positions than men (DFE, 2022).
> - Research shows that, within a workplace, a white male is assigned higher-status characteristics and thus has more prestige and influence whereas women may not be perceived legitimately as leaders (Agarwal, 2020).

Sexual orientation

Sexual orientation discrimination is where a person is treated differently because of their sexual orientation. This includes how individuals choose to express their sexual orientation. Examples of discrimination may include:

- A person not being appointed to a faith school because of their sexual orientation (NEU, n.d.-b).

- A person who is gay being denied the right to take time off to look after a sick partner if a person who is heterosexual would be allowed this time off (NEU, n.d.-b).

- Imposing a more severe disciplinary penalty on a bisexual worker than a straight worker for similar conduct in similar circumstances (NEU, n.d.-b).

Some may prefer not to disclose this aspect of their identity due to fear of discrimination, meaning there may not always be awareness of a person's sexual orientation. This may impact on their wellbeing and sense of identity through the individual feeling they must hide this part of themselves. They may also hear discriminatory comments about others based on their sexual orientation and feelings of isolation may increase.

Facts and figures: sexual orientation

- 40% of LGBT pupils had never been taught about LGBT issues in school (Stonewall, 2017).
- Nearly half of lesbian, gay, bi and trans pupils (45%) are bullied for being LGBT at school (Stonewall, 2017).
- 52% of pupils hear homophobic language 'frequently' or 'often' at school and more than 36% hear biphobic language 'frequently' or 'often' (Stonewall, 2017)
- 29% of bullied LGBT pupils say that teachers intervened when they were present during the bullying (Stonewall, 2017).
- 53% of LGBT pupils say that there isn't an adult at school they can talk to about being LGBT (Stonewall, 2017).

The problem with protected characteristics

The Equality Act (2010) was made necessary due to the historic discrimination faced by underrepresented groups. However, questions can be raised as to whether the legislation truly protects the range of characteristics. For example, Mos-Shogbamimu (2018) criticised the Act's lack of acknowledgement of intersectional experiences, an example being that there are 'multiple complexities in relation to discrimination experienced by women'. This means that where a woman with multiple protected characteristics experiences discrimination, it may not be possible to reduce this to a single discrimination claim. If the law does not promote an understanding of intersectionality (see Chapter 3), there is a risk that organisations such as schools may not see this as a necessary consideration. This risks key aspects of people's identities being rendered invisible.

Further to this, there is a strong argument for the language of the Equality Act to be updated to be more inclusive and explanatory. For example, under the protected characteristic of sexual orientation, the Act only explicitly names 'heterosexual, gay, lesbian or bisexual'. In reality, the spectrum of sexual orientation is much broader, yet the Act's wording does not explicitly require organisations to recognise or understand identities beyond those listed. Additionally, the Act lacks clarity regarding protections for individuals who identify as non-binary. In *Taylor v Jaguar Land Rover Limited* (2020), an Employment Tribunal ruled that the definition of gender reassignment under section 7 of the Act includes non-binary and gender-fluid individuals (Cooke and Davies, 2020). However, this was an individual tribunal ruling; it does not set a legally binding precedent (EHRC, 2021) and non-binary identities remain absent from the Act's official guidance. It should not be the case that individuals must experience discrimination and take legal action before progress is made. Updating the legislation to reflect evolving understandings of identity is both necessary and overdue. Please also refer to the recent ruling surrounding the protected characteristic of 'sex', as previously outlined.

Finally, whilst the law offers protection from maltreatment in the workplace, its emphasis is primarily on mitigating harm, rather than actively promoting inclusivity. It may be easy for schools to fall into the trap of believing that by adhering to the requirements of the Equality Act they are naturally supportive of all employees and students alike. However, it is important to avoid homogenising the experiences of all with protected characteristics, and to recognise that even characteristics that do not currently hold legally protected status can have a significant impact on the daily experiences of individuals. Whilst the protected characteristics are a starting point, staff and children alike may face discrimination due to other characteristics such as ability, accent and dialect, appearance, socio-economic background, body size, education, family, health, income, language, name, organisational role, political beliefs and more. For schools to truly cultivate a culture of belonging for all, they must endeavour not only to meet the minimum expectations outlined in law, but to move above and beyond these by truly committing to adapting to the needs of the entire school community.

The Public Sector Equality Duty (PSED)

The Equality Act (2010) also states that all public authorities, including schools, must comply with the Public Sector Equality Duty (EHRC, 2022a). The purpose of the PSED is to hold organisations to account in considering and reviewing how they are promoting equality in:

- decision-making
- internal and external policies
- procuring goods and services
- the services they provide
- recruitment, promotion and performance management of employees

Legally, schools must comply with the three aims of the general duty, which make sure that public authorities have due regard to the need to:

1. Put an end to unlawful behaviour that is banned by the Equality Act 2010, including discrimination, harassment and victimisation.

2. Advance equal opportunities between people who have a protected characteristic and those who do not.

3. Foster good relations between people who have a protected characteristic and those who do not. (EHRC, 2022b)

To comply with the PSED, schools must publish at least one public-facing equality objective which should be 'clearly defined', 'specific and measurable', 'agreed with the school's governing body or academy trust board' and 'reviewed and published every four years' (EHRC, 2022b). This responsibility means that, to an extent, schools must be proactive in promoting fairness and inclusivity, as well as aiming to reduce discrimination.

However, it is important to note that schools are not required to publish an action plan to demonstrate how their equality objectives will be met, nor is there any mention of distributing roles and responsibilities for the practical administration of these objectives. The PSED's requirement for public facing equality objectives may allow schools to present to the public as though they are taking meaningful action without them pragmatically doing so, enabling them to make claims within outward-facing policies that may not be wholly representative of their internal practices. We explore ways to develop an ED&I implementation plan in Chapter 2.

Keeping Children Safe in Education (KCSIE)

Keeping Children Safe in Education (KCSIE) is the framework that outlines the expectations for all school staff to safeguard students in schools and colleges in England. The document directs schools on how to identify and respond to potential risks and concerns surrounding the safety of students. Significantly, the guidance includes sections on safeguarding students with specific protected characteristics and is another key mechanism for equitable practice in schools. It is positive that a range of protected characteristics are referred to explicitly throughout the documentation. For example, sexuality and gender are referenced in the document, although there have been some explicit adaptations between 2023 and 2024. The 2023 document had a section titled 'Children who are lesbian, gay, bi, or trans' (DFE, 2023, p. 51), which has now been replaced with a draft section with the heading 'Children who are lesbian, gay, bi, or gender questioning'. DFE (2023b, p.51) noted that 'there is a range of support available to help schools counter homophobic, biphobic, and transphobic bullying and abuse', which has now been replaced with comments in relation to the aforementioned guidance in relation to 'gender questioning children'. It is notable that, despite the latter guidance being non-statutory at the time of writing, the previous government included it in a statutory document, stating that 'schools should' refer to this when making decisions surrounding support for pupils (DFE 2024b).

Despite the obvious shift in the section on sexuality and gender, the nuanced experiences of students with a range of protected characteristics are recognised. By including explicit detail surrounding this in the statutory guidance, it ensures that this cannot be overlooked by school staff without them being in direct breach of statutory safeguarding duties. There are, however, clear omissions from the statutory guidance. KCSIE does not provide any insight into the impact of race and racism. In fact, the term 'racism' is mentioned only twice within the 185-page long document.

KCSIE defines safeguarding as involving 'protecting children from maltreatment', 'preventing the impairment of children's mental and physical health or development' and 'taking action to enable all children to have the best outcomes' (DfE, 2024, p. 7). An exploration into the impact of racism demonstrates that it meets this definition in its entirety. The UK Trauma Council (2022) and Mind (2021) have found that racism can lead to decreased self-esteem and confidence, anxiety disorders and severe mental health issues such as depression, PTSD, and suicidal thoughts. The NSPCC (2022) explicitly outlines racism as a safeguarding issue and recognises that 'for children and adults from Black, Asian and minoritised ethnic communities there may be additional barriers to asking for help' … highlighting that there is 'systemic silence and reticence' in addressing and confronting issues surrounding race, ethnicity and culture in safeguarding practice (Child Safeguarding Practice Review Panel, 2025). There have been consistent calls for racism to be deemed a safeguarding issue in schools (Weale, 2022; Davis, 2022; Agboola, 2024) but this has not yet been recognised in detail in KCSIE.

Through raising awareness of the experiences of other protected groups, whilst simultaneously overlooking those of racially minoritised children, a hierarchy of protected characteristics may be established. Whilst all staff are explicitly aware of the legal duty to safeguard other groups of children, they may remain uninformed as to necessity of safeguarding racially minoritised children. This may be less problematic in schools where staff have high levels of racial literacy and are well informed on the prevalence and impact of racism. However, where this is not the case, the lack of detail may prevent adequate responses. For this reason, to hold staff to account in responding effectively to racism in schools, there is a necessity to develop a specific policy on prejudicial incidents (see Chapter 4).

Initial Teacher Training

Initial Teacher Education and Training (ITE/ITT) has been criticised for the extent to which it effectively educated trainee teachers in valuing diversity. Smith and Lander (2022) outline that the Core Content Framework (CCF), which all ITT training providers must adhere to, 'contains no reference to race, racism, anti-racism, or even the terms prejudice or discrimination'. Without race, prejudice and discrimination being focal points of the CCF, it is difficult to understand how training provision can wholly prepare teachers to know how to create a culture of belonging in their classrooms.

Smith and Lander's (2022) work drew our attention to evidence that supports this notion. In 2017, the DFE conducted a survey of newly qualified teachers (now known as Early Career Teachers) on their perceptions of teacher training. Only 53% of respondents felt that their ITT prepared them to teach across all ethnic backgrounds, with only 39% feeling prepared to teach students with English as an Additional Language (EAL). Since then, the Early Career Framework (DFE, 2019) has been introduced after recognition that many new teachers had 'not enjoyed the support they need to thrive, nor have they had adequate time to devote to their professional development'. The ECF 'underpins what all early career teachers should be entitled to learn about and learn how to do based on expert guidance and the best available research evidence'. It is problematic, therefore, that the framework includes no specific reference to knowledge of different races, cultures, religions and so on. Although the ECF encourages adaptive teaching, requiring new teachers to 'understand pupils' differences' which is positioned directly in relation to SEND, some aspects of the framework, such as behaviour management, have been criticised as not being appropriate for all SEND pupils, with calls for updates to be made (UCET, 2023).

The CCF and ECF do not explicitly prevent providers from including in-depth training on the range of pupils' characteristics, but the problem lies in the fact that it does not ensure that they do. As a result, some providers may choose to take positive action in these areas, whilst others may not. Consequently, many ITTs and ECTs will remain unprepared to teach in a diverse and multicultural society. Even where providers do aim to develop training in this area, the absence of a framework or consensus for what constitutes good-quality ED&I training, the frequency at which this should take place and what should be avoided means that the nationwide impact may be limited. There is also the potential for harmful ideas to be embedded where providers are not given appropriate guidance. Smith and Lander have developed an anti-racism framework for ITE/ITT and hope to 'encourage space in ITE courses for critical and informed reflections upon race, racism, and anti-racism, countering, for example, narratives of colour-blindness, meritocracy and assumptions/discourses of deficit as explanatory factors for education disparities'. However, without this framework being compulsory, only some trainee teachers will benefit from this essential knowledge, impacting the reach of this powerful work.

Teachers' Standards: personal and professional conduct

Here, we refer to an extract from the 'personal and professional conduct' section in the Teachers' Standards for teachers in England. The expectations for teachers include:

- showing tolerance of and respect for the rights of others

- not undermining fundamental British values, including democracy, the rule of law, individual liberty and mutual respect, and tolerance of those with different faiths and beliefs. (DFE, updated 2021)

While the expectations around teachers' personal and professional conduct are sound, it is worth considering how actively they promote a sense of belonging for all pupils.

The problematic term 'tolerance' appears twice in this section and it can be defined as 'willingness to accept behaviour and beliefs that are different from your own, although you might not agree with or approve of them'. This implies that a child may simply be allowed to be present in the classroom and that the teacher should not actively dismiss their lived experience. As an expectation, this is not enough. As teachers, we should be intentional in considering what we need to do to accept the whole child, allowing them to feel safer and confident in their own identity. Most adults would agree that we deserve more than just to be tolerated, and children should be given the same right. Tolerance also, 'intrinsically carries within it the power dynamic that something/someone enjoys the privilege of being reflective of the norm, and there is something/someone now *disrupting* that norm' (Vansant, 2018). In this sense, to 'tolerate' a person from an underrepresented group positions them negatively.

Next, we consider the reference to 'fundamental British values'. The values themselves are positive, but their positioning as values that are 'fundamental' and uniquely 'British' is something that has been critiqued. Yildiz (2021) suggests that the values depict a single national identity which overlooks the diversity of British society and may alienate those from racially minoritised groups who may not see themselves as British at their core. This may be due to individual preference, but also to the way they have been included or excluded by their local communities. Taylor and Soni (2017) indicate that the authorities' rhetoric surrounding fundamental British values and the Prevent duty can generate fear. Crawford (2017) refers to the perception of a 'disjuncture between white British values and that of Islam' in British policy, with Muslims being positioned as a threat. We do not dispute that teachers should uphold their duty in promoting these values, especially when they are framed as qualities of being a compassionate human. However, given the current social and political landscape, the framing around fundamental British values needs to be careful and considerate. This is essential to avoid the othering of specific groups.

Questions

- Consider the statutory responsibilities required by teachers in your country with an ED&I lens, what could be problematic?
- What opportunities are available in your school to put in place ED&I interventions?
- Consider your role, how could you raise awareness of this and what change is needed?

References

Adams, L., Winterbotham, M., Oldfield, K., McLeish, J., Large, A., Stuart, A., Murphy, L., Rossiter, H., Selner, S. (2016). Pregnancy and Maternity-Related Discrimination and Disadvantage: Experiences of Mothers. *Equality and Human Rights Commission and Department for Business, Innovation and Skills.* Available from: https://www.equalityhumanrights.com/sites/default/files/mothers_report_-_bis-16-146-pregnancy-and-maternity-related-discrimination-and-disadvantage-experiences-of-mothers_1.pdf [Accessed 15 April 2025].

Agarwal, P. (2020). *Sway: Unravelling Unconscious Bias.* London: Bloomsbury Sigma.

Agboola, J. (2024). *Protecting young Black lives, celebrating Black professionals.* [Online]. Berkshire: Cumberland Lodge. Available from: https://www.cumberlandlodge.ac.uk/resource/protecting-young-black-lives-celebrating-black-professionals-report/ [Accessed 27 May 2024].

Åkesson, E. (2024). The Longing to Just Be – A Belonging Body in Teacher Education. *European Journal of Teacher Education*, 1–18. Available from: [Accessed 15 April 2025].

Anti-Bullying Alliance (n.d.). *Disabled Young People and Bullying.* Available from: https://anti-bullyingalliance.org.uk/tools-information/all-about-bullying/at-risk-groups/sen-disability#:~:text=Disabled%20young%20people%20and%20those,autism%20are%20particularly%20at%20risk [Accessed 15 April 2025].

Belger, T. (2023). DfE Told to Fix Disability Data Gaps for Half of Teachers. *Schools Week.* Available from: https://schoolsweek.co.uk/disabled-staff-teachers-disability-data-dfe-guidance-reporting/ [Accessed 15 April 2025].

Birketts LLP (2024). *Gender Questioning Children: A Summary of the Legal Position for Schools.* Available from: https://www.birketts.co.uk/legal-update/gender-questioning-children-a-summary-of-the-legal-position-for-schools/#:~:text=Gender%20questioning%20children%3A%20a%20summary%20of%20the%20legal%20position%20for%20schools&text=As%20part%20of%20its%20consultation,questioning%20children%20(the%20Guidance) [Accessed 16 April 2025].

Blake, S. (2025). *Stonewall Responds to Today's Supreme Court Ruling.* Available from: https://www.stonewall.org.uk/news/stonewall-responds-to-todays-ruling-form-the-supreme-court [Accessed 17 April 2025].

Brighouse, J. (2022). The Crimes of Miss Jean Brodie: Why Are Experienced Teachers No Longer Valued?. In Wilson, H., Kara, B. (eds.) *Diverse Educators: A Manifesto.* London: University of Buckingham Press

Cambridge Dictionary (n.d.). *Diversity.* Available from: DIVERSITY | English meaning – Cambridge Dictionary [Accessed 2 April 2025].

Carrell, S. (2025). Legal Definition of Woman Is Based on Biological Sex, UK Supreme Court Rules. *Guardian.* 16 April. Available from: https://www.theguardian.com/society/2025/apr/16/critics-of-trans-rights-win-uk-supreme-court-case-over-definition-of-woman [Accessed 17 April 2025].

Cawley, J. (2020). My Wellbeing as a LGBT Teacher. *Diverse Educators.* Available from: https://www.diverseeducators.co.uk/my-wellbeing-as-a-lgbt-teacher/ [Accessed 14 April 2025].

Centre for Social Justice (2025). *Lost Boys: Restoring Hope for Britain's Boys and Young Men.* Available from: https://www.centreforsocialjustice.org.uk/library/lost-boys [Accessed 14 April 2025].

Child Safeguarding Practice Review Panel (2025). *"It's Silent": Race, Racism and Safeguarding Children.* Available from: https://assets.publishing.service.gov.uk/media/67cb0a9d5993d41513a45c5b/Race_Racism_Safeguarding_March_2025.pdf [Accessed 30 March 2025].

Cooke, A., Davies, O. (2020). A Substantive Review of the Landmark Decision in Taylor v Jaguar Land Rover Limited and the Protection It Provides for Those Who Identify as Non-Binary and Gender Fluid under the Equality Act 2010. *Lamb Chambers*. Available from: https://www.lambchambers.co.uk/latest-news/taylor-v-jaguar-land-rover-limited/ [Accessed 15 April 2025].

Crawford, C. (2017). Promoting "Fundamental British Values" in Schools: A Critical Race Perspective. *Curriculum Perspectives*, 37(2), 197–204. Available from: https://www.researchgate.net/publication/320022852_Promoting_'fundamental_British_values'_in_schools_a_critical_race_perspective [Accessed 30 March 2025].

Davidson Morris (2025). *Racial Discrimination at Work*. Available from: https://www.davidsonmorris.com/racial-discrimination-at-work/ [Accessed 15 April 2025].

Davidson, J., Powney, J., Wilson, V., Hall, S., Mirza, H. S. (2005). Race and Sex: Teachers' Views on Who Gets Ahead in Schools? *European Journal of Teacher Education*, 28(3), 311–326. Available from: https://doi.org/10.1080/02619760500269459 [Accessed 14 April 2025].

Davis, J. (2022). *HM Inspectorate of Probation: Adultification Bias within Child Protection and Safeguarding*. Available from: https://www.justiceinspectorates.gov.uk/hmiprobation/wp-content/uploads/sites/5/2022/06/Academic-Insights-Adultification-bias-within-child-protection-and-safeguarding.pdf [Accessed 13 January 2024].

Department for Education (2019). *Early Career Framework*. Available from: https://assets.publishing.service.gov.uk/media/60795936d3bf7f400b462d74/Early-Career_Framework_April_2021.pdf [Accessed 16 April 2025].

Department for Education (2021). *Teachers' Standards Information Sheet*. Available from: https://assets.publishing.service.gov.uk/media/60795936d3bf7f400b462d74/Early-Career_Framework_April_2021.pdf [Accessed 16 April 2025].

Department for Education (2022). *School Leadership in England 2010 to 2020: Characteristics and Trends*. Available from: https://assets.publishing.service.gov.uk/media/626950bfe90e0746c0a7b057/School_leadership_in_England_2010_to_2020_characteristics_and_trends_-_report.pdf [Accessed 14 April 2025].

Department for Education (2023a). *Disability Data Collection in Schools Workforce*. Available from: https://assets.publishing.service.gov.uk/media/63f3966cd3bf7f62e8c349cd/Disability_data_collection_in_schools__workforce.pdf [Accessed 15 April 2025].

Department for Education (2023b). *Keeping Children Safe in Education 2023 Statutory Guidance for Schools and Colleges*. Available from: London: Department for Education.

Department for Education (2023c). *School Teacher Workforce*. Available from: https://www.ethnicity-facts-figures.service.gov.uk/workforce-and-business/workforce-diversity/school-teacher-workforce/latest/#by-ethnicity-and-role [Accessed 14 April 2025].

Department for Education (2024a). *Reporting Year 2023: School Workforce in England*. Available from: https://explore-education-statistics.service.gov.uk/find-statistics.school-workforce-in-england/2023#dataBlock-a7db4189-36a3-4ff4-a96f-be3f632d4234-tables [Accessed 14 April 2025].

Department for Education (2024b). *Keeping Children Safe in Education 2024 Statutory Guidance for Schools and Colleges*. Available from: London: Department for Education.

Department for Education (2024c). *Permanent Exclusions: Ethnicity Facts and Figures*. Available from: https://www.ethnicity-facts-figures.service.gov.uk/education-skills-and-training/absence-and-exclusions/permanent-exclusions/latest/

Donlevy, V., Meierkord, A., Rajania, A. (2015). *Study on the Diversity within the Teaching Profession with Particular Focus on Migrant and/or Minority Background*. Luxembourg: Publications Office of the European Union. Available from: https://migrant-integration.ec.europa.eu/sites/default/files/2016-03/teacher-diversity_en.pdf [Accessed 14 March 2025].

Elliott, V., Nelson-Addy, L., Chantiluke, R., Courtney, M. (2021). *Lit in Colour: Diversity in Literature in English Schools*. Available from: https://litincolour.penguin.co.uk/assets/Lit-in-Colour-research-report.pdf

Equality Act (2010). London: HMSO.

Equality and Human Rights Commission (2019). *Direct and Indirect Discrimination*. Available from: https://www.equalityhumanrights.com/equality/equality-act-2010/your-rights-under-equality-act-2010/direct-and-indirect-discrimination [Accessed 15 April 2025].

Equality and Human Rights Commission (2020). *Sex Discrimination*. Available from: https://www.equalityhumanrights.com/equality/equality-act-2010/your-rights-under-equality-act-2010/sex-discrimination [Accessed 17 April 2025].

Equality and Human Rights Commission (2021). *Jaguar Land Rover Ltd Signs a Legal Agreement with EHRC*. Available from: https://www.equalityhumanrights.com/media-centre/news/jaguar-land-rover-ltd-signs-legal-agreement-ehrc [Accessed 16 April 2025].

Equality and Human Rights Commission (2022a). *The Public Sector Equality Duty (PSED) | EHRC*. Available from: https://www.equalityhumanrights.com/guidance/public-sector-equality-duty-psed [Accessed 13 April 2025].

Equality and Human Rights Commission (2022b). *Publishing Equality Objectives: Guidance for Schools*. Available from: https://www.equalityhumanrights.com/guidance/public-sector-equality-duty/public-sector-equality-duty-guidance-schools/publishing-0#:~:text=To%20comply%20with%20the%20Public [Accessed 13 April 2025].

Equality and Human Rights Commission (updated 2023). *Gender Reassignment Discrimination*. Available from: https://www.equalityhumanrights.com/equality/equality-act-2010/your-rights-under-equality-act-2010/gender-reassignment-discrimination [Accessed 16 April 2025].

Gibbs, R. (2021). Why Representation Matters in Primary Schools. Foundation Stage Forum. Available from: https://eyfs.info/articles.html/primary/why-representation-matters-in-primary-schools-r366/ [Accessed 2 September 2025].

Golding, R. (2022). The Protected Characteristic of Disability: An Introduction. In Wilson, H., Kara, B. (eds.) *Diverse Educators: A Manifesto*. London: University of Buckingham Press.

GOV.UK (n.d.-a). *Definition of disability under the Equality Act 2010*. Available from: https://www.gov.uk/definition-of-disability-under-equality-act-2010 [Accessed 15 April 2025].

GOV.UK (n.d.-b). *Your Rights as a Disabled Person: Education*. Available from: https://www.gov.uk/rights-disabled-person/education-rights [Accessed 17 April 2025].

Kellaway, L. (2024). The Frontline of Age Diversity. *Now Teach*. Available from: https://nowteach.org.uk/advice-and-insight/blog/the-frontline-of-age-diversity/ [Accessed 15 April 2025].

Lee, E. (2019). Fifteen Years on: The Legacy of Section 28 for LGBT+ Teachers in English Schools. *Sex Education*, 19(6), 675–690. Available from: https://doi.org/10.1080/14681811.2019.1585800 [Accessed 14 April 2025].

Mencap (2019). *New Research from Mencap Shows Bullying of People with a Learning Disability Leading to Social Isolation*. Available from: https://www.mencap.org.uk/press-release/new-research-mencap-shows-bullying-people-learning-disability-leading-social [Accessed 15 April 2025].

Mind (2021). *Not Making the Grade: Why Our Approach to Mental Health at Secondary School Is Failing Young People*. Available from: https://www.mind.org.uk/media/8852/not-making-the-grade.pdf [Accessed 15 April 2025].

Monaco Solicitors (n.d.). *Marriage and Civil Partnership Discrimination*. Available from: https://www.monacosolicitors.co.uk/discrimination/marriage-civil-partnership [Accessed 15 April 2025].

Mos-Shogbamimu, S. (2018). UK Equality Act Is Not Fit for Purpose: It's Time for the Law to Recognise Multiple Discrimination. *Fawcett Society*. Available from: https://www.fawcettsociety.org.uk/blog/uk-equality-act-is-not-fit-for-purpose-its-time-for-the-law-to-recognise-multiple-discrimination [Accessed 15 April 2025].

National Education Union (n.d.-a). *Transgender Discrimination*. Available from: https://neu.org.uk/advice/your-rights-work/discrimination-and-harassment/transgender-discrimination [Accessed 16 April 2025].

National Education Union (n.d.-b). *Sexual Orientation Discrimination*. Available from: https://neu.org.uk/advice/your-rights-work/discrimination-and-harassment/sexual-orientation-discrimination [Accessed 16 April 2025].

National Education Union (n.d.-c). *Religion or Belief Discrimination*. Available from: https://neu.org.uk/advice/your-rights-work/discrimination-and-harassment/religion-or-belief-discrimination [Accessed 16 April 2025].

National Education Union (n.d.-d). *Sex Discrimination*. Available from: https://neu.org.uk/advice/your-rights-work/discrimination-and-harassment/sex-discrimination [Accessed 16 April 2025].

NSPCC (2022). Safeguarding Children from Black, Asian and Minoritised Ethnic Communities. *NSPCC Learning*. Available from: https://learning.nspcc.org.uk/safeguarding-child-protection/children-from-black-asian-minoritised-ethnic-communities [Accessed 15 April 2025].

O'Hare, P. (2025). Supreme Court Ruling 'Has Dire Consequences for All Trans People'. *BBC News*. 17 April. Available from: https://www.bbc.co.uk/news/articles/cy8q55d27lgo [Accessed 17 April 2025].

Office for Equality and Opportunity, Disability Unit (2025). Government Launches Call for Evidence to Break Down Barriers to Opportunity at Work. Available from: https://www.gov.uk/government/news/government-launches-call-for-evidence-to-break-down-barriers-to-opportunity-at-work [Accessed 17 April 2025].

Ofsted (2021). *Review of Sexual Abuse in Schools and Colleges*. Available from: https://www.gov.uk/government/publications/review-of-sexual-abuse-in-schools-and-colleges/review-of-sexual-abuse-in-schools-and-colleges [Accessed 30 March 2025].

Othering and Belonging Institute (2024). *Inclusiveness Index Results*. Available at: https://belonging.berkeley.edu/inclusiveness-index/index-results [Accessed 20 April 2025]

Pearson (2023). *Pearson School Report 2023*. London: Pearson Education Ltd. Available from: https://www.pearson.com/content/dam/global-store/en-gb/files/Pearson-School-Report-2023.pdf [Accessed 30 March 2025].

Sheppard, E. and Campbell, G. (2023). We're on a Road to Nowhere: Women Aged 30–39 – Why Are They the Largest Demographic to Leave Teaching Every Year?. *Impact, Chartered College of Teaching*. Available from: https://my.chartered.college/impact_article/were-on-a-road-to-nowhere-women-aged-30-39-why-are-they-the-largest-demographic-to-leave-teaching-every-year/ [Accessed 15 April 2025].

Smith, P., Culbert, C. (National Children's Bureau) (2024). School Belonging A Literature Review. Available from: https://www.ncb.org.uk/sites/default/files/uploads/attachments/School%20Belonging%20-%20A%20Literature%20Review%202024_2.pdf [Accessed 17 April 2025].

Smith, H., Lander, V. (2022). Finding 'Pockets of Possibility' for an Anti-Racism Curriculum for Student Teachers: From Absence to Action. *The Curriculum Journal*, 34(1), 22–42. Available from: https://bera-journals.onlinelibrary.wiley.com/doi/10.1002/curj.177 [Accessed 14 April 2025].

Stonewall (2017). *School Report: The Experiences of Lesbian, Gay, Bi and Trans Young People in Britain's Schools in 2017*. Available from: https://files.stonewall.org.uk/production/files/the_school_report_2017.pdf?dm=1724230520 [Accessed 16 April 2025].

Stonewall (2018). *LGBT in Britain: Trans Report*. Available from: https://files.stonewall.org.uk/production/files/lgbt_in_britain_-_trans_report_final.pdf?dm=1724230505 [Accessed 16 April 2025].

Stonewall (2023a). *Shut Out: The Experiences of LGBT Young People Not in Education, Training or Work*. Available from: https://files.stonewall.org.uk/production/files/shut_out_2020.pdf?dm=1724230513 [Accessed 16 April 2025].

Stonewall (2023b). *Not Fit for Purpose: Stonewall's Response to the Draft Trans Guidance for Schools in England*. Available from: https://www.stonewall.org.uk/news/not-fit-purpose-stonewalls-response-draft-trans-guidance-schools-england [Accessed 16 April 2025].

Taylor, L., Soni, A. (2017). Preventing Radicalisation: A Systematic Review of Literature Considering the Lived Experiences of the UK's Prevent Strategy in Educational Settings. *Pastoral Care in Education*, 35(4), 241–252. Available from: [Accessed 30 March 2025].

TES (2024). DFE Urged to Rethink School Transgender Proposals. *Tes*. Available from: https://www.tes.com/magazine/news/general/dfe-urged-rethink-school-transgender-proposals [Accessed 16 April 2025].

Thomson, P. (2022). Towards Age-Inclusive, Sustainable Careers in the Education Sector. In Wilson, H., Kara, B. (eds.) *Diverse Educators: A Manifesto*. London: University of Buckingham Press.

TransActual (2025). *Response by TransActual to Supreme Court ruling on Equality Act*. Available from: https://transactual.org.uk/blog/2025/04/16/response-by-transactual-to-supreme-court-ruling-on-equality-act/ [Accessed 17 April 2025].

Universities' Council for the Education of Teachers (2023). *CCF and ECF Refresh: Call for Evidence*. Available from: https://www.ucet.ac.uk/14978/ccf-and-ecf-refresh-call-for-evidence [Accessed 16 April 2025].

VanSant, G. (2018). *Focusing Language: Inclusion versus Tolerance*. Available at: https://www.gwendolynvansant.com/home/2018/4/13/getting-precise-inclusion-versus-tolerance [Accessed 8 April 2025].

Villegas, A. M., Irvine, J. J. (2010). Diversifying the Teaching Force: An Examination of Major Arguments. *Urban Review*, 42(3), 175–192. Available from: [Accessed 15 March 2025].

Weale, S. (2022). Racism in English Education Should Be Seen as Safeguarding Issue, Says Author. *Guardian*. 5 June. Available from: https://www.theguardian.com/education/2022/jun/05/racism-england-schools-education-safeguarding-issue-jeffrey-boakye [Accessed 13 January 2024].

Yildiz, U. (2021). An Anti-Racist Reading of the Notion of 'Fundamental British Values'. *PRISM: Casting New Light on Learning, Theory and Practice*, 3(2). Available from: https://openjournals.ljmu.ac.uk/prism/article/view/493/358 [Accessed 30 March 2025].

YMCA (2020). *Young and Black: The Young Black Experience of Institutional Racism in the UK*. Available from: https://ymca.org.uk/wp-content/uploads/2024/08/ymca-young-and-black-2020.pdf?utm_source=chatgpt.com [Accessed 12 April 2025].

2 Developing an ED&I strategy

Before embarking on an ED&I journey, an organisation must first consider its rationale for doing so. It is true that ED&I work correlates with desirable outcomes, such as greater innovation, higher-performing teams and enhanced reputation (Dixon-Fyle et al., 2020). However, it is important to recognise these benefits as secondary outcomes, rather than primary drivers. A fixation on material gain for the organisation may lead to a desire for shortcuts and quick fixes, neither of which are conducive to lasting change. Additionally, an emphasis on economic gain can remove the human nature from ED&I and research shows this can lead to disillusionment from underrepresented groups (Ely and Thomas, 2020).

Schools may also move to prioritise ED&I due to research that highlights belonging as a key driver of attendance (ImpactED, 2024) or due to expectations from Ofsted, who assess how well schools equip children to "gain an understanding of the world they are growing up in, and learn how to live alongside, and show respect for, a diverse range of people' (Ofsted, updated 2023). For ED&I work to generate authentic, long-term and significant transformation in schools, its primary intention must be to foster a deep sense of belonging in the school community as a whole.

A sense of belonging is highly personal and does not happen by chance. An effective ED&I strategy should be tailored to the unique needs of a school's community. This section will focus on how leaders can begin to develop their knowledge of the lived experience of the school community, which should be the foundation of an effective ED&I strategy.

Listening and learning

From national data

Reviewing national and educational data can be a valuable starting point for gathering ED&I-related insights which could then form the main strands of an ED&I strategy. Some schools might explore data based on a hypothesis around experiences of belonging whereas other settings might review data to better define and clarify the priority. Data may focus on characteristics of particular relevance to the school community or on insights that will allow pupils to understand the experiences of people they may encounter later in their lives. This data helps to illustrate the broader factors that shape people's experiences and can be especially helpful when trying to deepen understanding of the protected characteristics. The list below outlines some organisations that provide datasets:

- Department for Education: for data on educational outcomes, attainment gaps, school demographics, and exclusions which can help to analyse disparities related to race, disability, gender, and socio-economic background.

- The National Foundation for Educational Research (NFER) – for research on educational trends, student attainment, teacher workforce data, and social mobility, offering insights into inequalities affecting various protected characteristics.

- Diverse Educators – for information surrounding representation and inclusion in education, offering data and resources across the range of protected characteristics.

- The Maternity Teacher/Paternity Teacher Project (MTPT) – for insights into gender equality in education, particularly around parental leave, career progression, and flexible working policies for teachers and school leaders.

- Stonewall – for information surrounding LGBTQ+ inclusion, offering data on experiences of LGBTQ+ students and staff in education, as well as guidance on creating inclusive school environments.

- MENCAP – for information on the experiences and rights of people with learning disabilities, providing data on accessibility, inclusion and barriers faced by students and staff with disabilities in education.

- Runnymede Trust – focuses on race equity and social justice, offering valuable data for addressing racial disparities in education.

From the school community

Exploring national data is not a means to an end and a school or trust's ED&I strategy must be focused on its people and existing provision. Audits based on an ED&I focus are helpful in ascertaining next steps (see Chapter 4 for an example based on diversifying the curriculum). Additionally, leaders should be authentic in listening to the school community and this means being receptive to feedback. By doing this, there is the opportunity to increase buy-in for ED&I because people feel heard and involved in any organisational change.

The barriers faced by those from underrepresented groups can make it challenging for individuals to speak openly about their experiences for fear of negative repercussions. One barrier that can immediately be removed is the need for individuals to establish their own independent mechanisms for speaking out. Instead, leaders should invite such conversation and make it clear that honesty is not only welcome but also essential for their own development. Chartered Management Institute (2024) found that in companies in which ED&I was seen as critical, 61% of employees surveyed felt that they had opportunities to feed into the creation and review of organisational policies and practices. In contrast, in companies without ED&I at their core, only 29% felt this way. When leaders intentionally take the interests of their people into account, allowing them to influence thinking and processes, there is a shift in power which can transform perceptions and give people a sense of agency that may previously have been diminished (Ely and Thomas, 2020).

It is important to note, as with all ED&I interventions, there may be an element of fear where people disclose aspects of their lived experience and there can be many reasons for this, as explored in Chapter 3. When gathering data of this nature, it is important to provide an introduction that provides reassurance of the purpose of the data, who will see it and how the results will be shared. This transparency is important in generating trust and strengthening connection. In this section, we will outline useful mechanisms for gaining feedback from the school community.

Case Study

Susie Weaver, Education Director, Cabot Learning Federation

Over the past five years, we have invested in developing a strong strand of pupil participation across the trust. Our curriculum statement of intent outlines a focus on children developing their sense of self, of place and of agency, and strengthening pupil voice and active engagement are central to our commitment to all of our children.

Our investment in pupil voice forms part of our wider work to connect pupils across the trust. Through establishing pupil participation groups at both trust and school level, we aim to ensure that all pupils feel valued and can directly contribute to the organisation's future policy and direction. The creation of our Pupil Parliament formed the basis of this approach, and in the early stages of formation, the Executive team worked alongside the Pupil Parliament to consider areas of focus for the group. Together, they identified two significant issues that they were keen to prioritise: Looking after the world – through Climate Action, and Looking out for each other – through embracing Equality, Diversity and Inclusion. This has developed through charity action work, campaign groups for change and collaborations with local policy makers.

Surveys and questionnaires

Questionnaires can be useful to gather data on lived experience. As with any data collection method, the questionnaire format must allow for results to be filtered

Table 2.1 Some example survey questions

	Question	Optional responses	Additional detail
Example 1	Do you see aspects of your culture, background or identity celebrated within school?	• Yes • No	
Example 2	Where do you see aspects of your culture, background and identity celebrated within school?		
Example 3	How often do you see aspects of your culture, background or identity celebrated within school?	• Very often • Often • Sometimes • Never	Please provide further detail if you wish to do so.

through multiple characteristics so that trends across and between groups can be identified. Formulating appropriate questions requires some hard thinking. Questions need to be carefully crafted to avoid the survey leading employees in any specific direction, or restricting their responses in any way. Although closed questions may be appealing to allow for easily filterable quantitative data, including opportunities for lengthier comments is important in allowing colleagues to be open in their lived experiences. Table 2.1 demonstrates how small tweaks to a question can have a significant impact:

In the first example in Table 2.1 the binary nature of the question limits the depth of the response. Respondents must choose between 'yes' or 'no', without any room for nuance or elaboration. This approach oversimplifies their experience and may not capture the full extent of their feelings. The second example assumes that respondents do see aspects of their culture, background and identity celebrated in school, which may not be the case. It is a leading question in the sense that it subtly encourages respondents to think of examples, rather than allowing for the possibility that they do not see any representation at all, limiting the accuracy of the data collected. Additionally, because the responses to the question would be entirely qualitative, they would require more extensive analysis, such as coding and categorisation, to extract patterns or trends. Whilst this is likely to provide valuable insights, it would also be time-consuming and may lead to inconsistencies in interpretation. In contrast, the third example improves upon this by asking *how often* aspects of a respondent's culture, background or identity are celebrated in school. This phrasing allows for a more nuanced response, acknowledging that representation is not always absolute but can vary in frequency. Additionally, the inclusion of an open-ended section invites respondents to expand on their answers, providing specific examples or highlighting specific aspects of their identity in which they feel either seen or overlooked. Richer data can offer more meaningful insights for those analysing the responses.

> **Case study**
>
> Bobbie Mills, Head of Research and Analysis at Lift Schools, shares how Lift Schools are starting to measure belonging
>
> Our decision to measure belonging stems from the strategic goals for our schools. Our flagship goal is around radically improving outcomes by 2028 and, to provide balance, we also have a goal focusing on student wellbeing. We recognise that students' sense of belonging is an upstream driver of wellbeing, attendance and achievement. Belonging as a concept is often used without clear definition in our sector – so we have closely adhered to the literature that defines 'sense of belonging' as a mindset. It is the student's belief that they are respected and valued in the classroom context – both by their peers and by their teachers (Mindset Kit, n.d.). This mindset can be developed in the classroom by specific teacher practices. To begin to measure this, we have drawn on Cultivate, a survey tool designed by the UChicago Consortium on School Research (Farrington et al., 2012). Whilst this influenced our design, we adapted questions so they are more relevant for our context and students and staff understand how the data will be used, with particular reassurances around accountability. We have invested in this so the data presented to our school principals is in a more accessible form and, as we are a large trust, it enables us to benchmark. This is part of a multi-year research programme to explore links between culture, belonging, and outcomes.

Focus groups

Another way to collect school-specific data is through focus groups with key stakeholders such as staff, pupils and families. Focus groups could be facilitated by an ED&I educator, with the discussions allowing for a deeper understanding of a range of experiences and the participants being able to elaborate more candidly on their responses. Feedback from our networks suggests that discussing experiences in a group – where some experiences are shared – can help reduce feelings of risk and isolation that may arise when disclosing personal aspects of lived experience. Focus groups require the creation of safer spaces, which are explored in detail in Chapter 6. As with questionnaires, carefully crafted questions are essential here, and participants must be given permission to opt out, without judgement, of answering anything that makes them feel uncomfortable.

Ofsted's (2021) report on a rapid review of sexual abuse in schools exemplifies the benefits of using focus groups:

In the focus groups, many children and young people talked about teachers not 'knowing the reality' of their lives, or being 'out of date'. In general, they reported much higher incidences of sexual harassment, online sexual abuse and bullying behaviours than teachers and leaders tended to be aware of.

Running focus groups with multiple stakeholders is important for validity in information gathering. In this example, conversations with leaders and students revealed entirely contrasting perspectives to those of teachers. Through cross-referencing this information, a recommendation on teacher training was able to be made.

Employee resource groups (ERGs)

Employee resource groups (ERGs) are usually comprised of a group of staff who have shared characteristics or interests. They are becoming increasingly prevalent in organisations, with 90% of Fortune 500 companies having ERGs (Catalino et al., 2023). When ERGs are managed effectively, they can boost feelings of inclusion for those from typically underrepresented groups, attract new talent, retain current staff and increase representation (Catalino et al., 2023). The work of an ERG should advance the ED&I policy of the school and it is important participants are aware of this, so their expectations are managed. For example, if recruitment is part of the EDI strategy, an ERG could focus on this through the lens of their characteristic, providing diversity of thinking and practical strategies for their school moving forwards. Though an ERG tends to focus on one characteristic, a range of lived experiences are likely to be brought forward. For example, the category of disability is very broad and the needs of someone with mental health conditions may differ to a person with physical disabilities. ERGs should work closely with the organisation to ensure activity isn't duplicated and that work from each group enhances the work of others, ensuring strategic alignment (Catalino et al., 2023).

Case study – Dixons Academies Trust

In 2020, Dixons Academies Trust founded an Anti-Racism Group. The group was established by an executive leader who hoped to establish an anti-racist action plan but was conscious of the lack of diversity within senior leadership teams. Seeking to understand the experiences of racially minoritised staff was important to ensure any actions were based on lived experiences as opposed to assumptions. Both Funmi and Natasha were involved in this group and the following things were instrumental in establishing a safer environment for participants:

- The first few meetings were dedicated to allowing participants to share their own experiences. This was important in developing raised awareness of lived experience and the specific challenges faced by racially minoritised groups.

- For many participants, this was the first time they had shared such experiences in a professional environment. This proved to be liberating as it made participants realise that they were not alone and that their experiences did not have to remain hidden.
- Nobody was put under pressure to share before they were ready. For Funmi, in particular, this was important. As the least 'senior' member of the group, Funmi felt incredibly cautious about how she was perceived. Gentle questions such as 'Is there anything you would like to add?' supported her in being open.
- The executive chair was aware of her position of power and ensured this did not act as a barrier. It was made clear that honest opinions and perceptions were incredibly important and that there would be no repercussions surrounding this. Our feedback was kept anonymous.
- Although the space to listen and learn was important, it was also significant that we were able to see where our feedback was making a difference. For example, after many of us shared our experience of microaggressions, the co-chair worked with us to develop training in this area that was rolled out in all schools.

Making use of existing mechanisms for change

Collecting and collating data requires the use of appropriate context-specific tools based on the size of the organisation and the resource available. In cases where it is not immediately feasible to develop data collection mechanisms that are specific to ED&I, existing systems can be adapted. For instance, many schools conduct annual employee solely experience surveys. By adapting existing surveys and incorporating ED&I-related questions, these surveys can serve as an initial means of data collection. Additionally, schools already possess various datasets that can support this work. For example, absence monitoring is already compulsory in schools and registers are taken multiple times a day. Attendance records could be analysed through the lens of ethnicity, gender and SEND, with any trends being explored in detail. Similarly, recruitment data can be examined to assess which demographic groups apply for teaching positions and how successful they are in securing roles.

Case study

Here, Julie Kettlewell, Assistant Director of Huntington Research School and Assistant Headteacher, shares how they've adopted an ED&I lens through their work on understanding students' sense of belonging in extra-curricular activities.

We want our socio-economically disadvantaged students, eligible for Pupil Premium, to feel like they are part of our school community. We want them to find something that they enjoy and something that provides them with a sense of achievement to support their sense of belonging. To enable this, we have focused on increasing participation in extra-curricular activities to improve attendance and behaviour, which, in turn, will improve student outcomes. This has required a comprehensive review of data, beyond registers of who attends extra-curricular activities. For example, through stakeholder surveys, we have examined the barriers in place for those not attending. We have also started to consider the impact of lunchtime detentions on attendance at extra-curricular activities and whether this creates more of a sense of belonging for pupils in this sub-group as opposed to the whole school community. Admittedly, there have been challenges with tracking this data as we don't want the completion of a register to be a barrier to those running a club, but it has enabled us to see which clubs benefit those who feel like they don't belong in the school community. Discussing extra-curricular opportunities has become a key part of the conversation with school refusers; for example, those who have an interest in our new Darts Club may choose to come to that as the first experience of returning to school. It's not only improving school attendance but also providing pupils with opportunities they may not have access to outside of school as well as a safer space in school for them.

Utilising data

Although gathering data may feel like a significant piece of work, it is not a means to an end. CMI (2024) found that 90% HR decision-makers say they collect at least one type of pay data, yet a far smaller percentage use this data to identify barriers to progression (55%), to identify and address training needs (54%) or to identify recruitment process improvements (57%) and refer to this as a significant underutilisation of valuable data. The same applies in schools – simply having the data does not generate change – the next step is to see the data as valid and use it to set deliverable targets.

Designing a data-informed strategy for ED&I is the first step to generating meaningful and long-term transformation. This may be part of a school's self-evaluation and improvement plan or may be an additional document that succinctly in addition to this that succinctly summarises the school's commitment to ED&I and outlines its areas of focus.

Case study

Saima Akhtar, Inclusion and Diversity Co-ordinator, Cabot Learning Federation

Each of our academies has an Academy Improvement Plan (AIP). The Equality, Diversity, and Inclusion (EDI) statement established by each academy includes objectives that align with and support the AIP, and vice versa. Integrating these objectives with a commitment to EDI practices formalises our efforts and facilitates ongoing review and monitoring. Additionally, all policies undergo an Equalities Impact Assessment (EQIA) process, with designated working groups overseeing this review depending on the specific policy under consideration.

> Example objectives: King's Oak Academy in South Gloucestershire
>
> Communication
>
> Ensure communication method has clarity for staff and families and is accessible. This will ensure communications are able to reach all members of the KOA community and allow stakeholders from all groups to engage with the academy.
>
> Curriculum
>
> Raise awareness and understanding of EDI within subject and wider contexts with curriculum opportunities, within and beyond the KOA community identified.
>
> Celebration
>
> Create a sense of belonging for all members of our community by reflecting our community in the assemblies, curriculum, events and activities we provide.
>
> This year EDI at King's Oak Academy will be focused through the lens of racial literacy.

Dedicating time to mapping out an approach to ED&I reduces the likelihood of relying on ad-hoc interventions that are difficult to monitor and inconsistent leadership support. An implementation plan can then be used, based on an area within the strategy, to ensure that any action is integrated within the school and/or trust so ED&I is not seen as a short-term or tokenistic project.

Creating an ED&I implementation plan

The Education Endowment Foundation (EEF)'s 'A School's Guide to Implementation' provides several recommendations so new approaches and practices have an impact on the day-to-day work of staff in schools. The EEF's three main areas that enable effective implementation are: recommendations are as follows:

1. 'Adopt the behaviours that drive effective implementation.
2. Attend to contextual factors that influence implementation.
3. Use a structured, but flexible implementation process.'

We have drawn on the EEF's implementation plan template (2024) to consider the implementation of one ED&I intervention. This serves two purposes. Firstly, it enables school leadership to provide feedback on plans, so change is more likely to be navigated effectively. Secondly, it showcases the intervention and the rationale for it, developing person-centred knowledge and gaining buy-in from those in leadership, especially in contexts where there may be backlash to ED&I interventions. The timeframe may be longer than one academic year and a longer timeframe means the necessary training and stakeholder feedback can obtained. We would recommend starting with the problem and then final outcomes and then working through the columns as this ensures strategies links to outcomes. The overall ED&I implementation plan is essentially a simplified document that outlines the problem, summarises the main actions and states the final outcomes. After the implementation plan has been completed, we would also recommend using a task management tool so it is clear: who is responsible for specific actions; when key actions will take place; and what additional actions are needed.

This example plan (Table 2.2) is based on having an ED&I lead in role and already having permission from school leadership to create a prejudicial incidents policy – they know this is a problem based on data and staff and pupil voice drawn from whole-school surveys and focus groups. For further information based on training as part of this implementation plan, please go to Chapter 5 and refer to Chapter 10 for guidance about monitoring and evaluation.

Table 2.2 is a strong model of an implementation plan for a strand of ED&I work because it includes:

- A clear objective: the plan sets out a specific, measurable area for development which has been informed directly from contextual data in the form of student voice. It focuses on student confidence in staff, specifically in responding to prejudicial incidents, rather than a vague or overly broad measure of trust in staff.

- Clearly defined roles and responsibilities: the plan ensures accountability by assigning clear roles. Senior leadership takes responsibility, with the principal directly involved, demonstrating that EDI is a priority. This example acknowledges where schools may not have a dedicated ED&I lead. Here, external expertise is integrated where needed. There is also an acknowledgment that senior leaders require training to support staff effectively, rather than assuming they have the necessary expertise already.

- A comprehensive approach: instead of relying on a single action, the plan outlines a range of interventions. These interventions are designed to be monitored for consistency.

- Consideration of buy-in: research suggests that buy-in is important in ED&I and it can be shown through: advocacy; resources to support activity that promotes ED&I; and by holding people to account (CIPD, 2019). By considering this during the implementation stages, it means strategies are in place to minimise resistance e.g. the establishment of a business case for an intervention or ED&I as part of appraisal and a commitment to time for necessary changes from school leadership.

- Timeframes for accountability: while specific dates are not included, there are milestones that allow progress to be measured. This, combined with more specific project planning, prevents the work from losing momentum. These timelines

Table 2.2 Example ED&I implementation plan linked to prejudicial incidents in a school

Problem (Why?)	Intervention description (What?)	Implementation strategies (How?)	Progress (How well?) **Short term**	Final outcomes (And so?)
Student voice reveals lack of confidence in staff responses to prejudicial incidents so they are less likely to speak to a trusted adult.	Policy in place based on responding to prejudicial incidents	**Policy** Research similar policies Draft a policy with a consultant and discuss with trust leadership link and headteacher – make clear the difference between prejudicial incidents and behaviour incidents and the need for learning conversations rather than an immediate punitive responses Discuss the management of any reputational risk. Get stakeholder feedback on this to increase buy-in. Present to SLT and relevant pastoral staff to get further feedback. Present to staff as part of training on prejudicial incidents Share policy with pupils in assembly with a member of SLT and raise awareness about the importance of speaking up.	Provisional dates mapped out in PD calendar and protected time in PSHE and RSHE. Draft policy created Relevant participants receive training.	Pupils feel safe and able to speak-up about prejudicial incidents in school because they know it will be 'dealt with quickly, consistently and effectively whenever they occur' (Ofsted, 2023)
Staff do not feel confident addressing prejudicial incidents and feel they lack the skills to do so. They are unsure of what language to use.		Provide safer spaces for pupils who want to talk to a trusted adult about any concerns and ensure staff leading the safer spaces are trained appropriately to support pupils with dealing with this (they feel seen and heard and reminded of their worth)		Staff feel confident noticing and tackling prejudicial incidents based on regular training where learning is revisited. Regular training is embedded based on prejudicial incidents

Developing an ED&I strategy 45

		Medium term	
Prejudicial incidents are perceived as being the same as behaviour incidents with sanctions given.	ED&I curriculum in place based on prejudicial incidents for pupils and staff.	To promote buy-in, time for this is provided in the professional development calendar for staff and through PSHE and RSHE or the equivalent opportunity in your country's setting	Monitoring of data reveals consistency in response, demonstrating a speak-up culture – expect a 'spike' in incidents due to increased understanding
		Focus group with pupils from different year groups to ascertain contextual priorities in relation to prejudicial incidents.	
Pastoral data does not include explicit logging of all prejudicial incidents.		ED&I lead works with the PSHE and RSHE lead to look for opportunities to adopt an ED&I lens within existing curriculum plans	Prejudicial policy distributed so it is available to all key stakeholders.
		Lessons on the protected characteristics/contextual priorities are reviewed and/or created so pupils understand what prejudicial incidents look like in practice.	School management systems adapted to record prejudicial incidents.
Higher number of teachers raising concerns about prejudicial incidents in class.		To promote buy-in, key stakeholders are informed of changes and know who to contact with concerns (guiding principal of transparency).	Mechanisms to get stakeholder feedback on prejudicial incidents are in place.
		Designated Safeguarding Leads to review changes to ensure the primacy of safeguarding.	
		SLT to review potentially contentious lessons to ensure they are age-appropriate and to manage any reputational risk.	
		Staff reflect on learning after teaching prejudicial incidents related content and pupils provide feedback.	
		Further changes made to curriculum plans following stakeholder feedback.	

(Continued)

Table 2.2 (Continued)

Problem (Why?)	Intervention description (What?)	Implementation strategies (How?)	Progress (How well?)	Final outcomes (And so?)
	Curriculum plans in other subjects are reviewed to explore opportunities to discuss prejudice and how prejudice is overcome (negative and positive experiences)	Whole-school survey to ascertain contextual priorities in relation to prejudicial incidents. Training with curriculum leads. Time in professional development calendar for staff to work on this Set as an agenda in line management meetings for subject leads to discuss planned opportunities Staff reflect on learning after teaching prejudice related content and this feedback informs future planning. Pupils feedback, further changes made to curriculum plans based on most urgent priorities.	**Long term** Policy is embedded and all key stakeholders are aware of it. Prejudicial incidents data dashboard created with data reviewed three times in an academic year. Staff training at the start of every academic year has an explicit focus on prejudicial incidents to address ever changing contexts.	

Developing an ED&I strategy

Staff trained on how to address prejudicial incidents.	Review survey data based on prejudicial incidents to identify patterns in pupil and staff experience.	Responsive staff training in place e.g. tackling prejudicial incidents while on duty.
	Meet with focus groups to learn more.	
	Engage in wider research and literature to develop some ideas about training content.	Specialist safer spaces are in place in school so all pupils feel they have a trusted adult they can talk to.
	Work with an ED&I consultant to discuss a training outline for: SLT, and behaviour and attitude leads; all staff and all pupils.	
	Confirm planning and facilitation teams for the different training sessions (facilitating in pairs) with SLT.	
	Set aside time to co-plan.	
	Organise a briefing with facilitators to address any concerns	
	Time arranged for participants to talk to facilitators about any concerns following training.	
School management system e.g. Bromcom/SIMS and CPOMS enables tracking of different prejudicial incidents	Discuss changes needed and feasibility with data and planning team, refer to new data logs during training for staff and distribute a guidance sheet, discuss who is responsible for monitoring consistency in staff responses and repeat incidents from pupils and where this additional capacity can come from. Ensure this is embedded into specific supervision for DSL and behaviour and attitudes teams	Curricula plans provide opportunities for prejudicial incidents to be discussed sensitively and in an age appropriate way.

should remain flexible, allowing for updates if there are setbacks and as progress evolves over time.

- Ongoing progress monitoring: the plan includes mechanisms for tracking progress over time, ensuring that interventions remain effective and can be adjusted as needed.
- Defined outcomes: clearly stated desirable outcomes help stakeholders understand what success looks like. Importantly, the plan commits to revisiting student feedback to measure progress, ensuring that the impact of interventions is measurable.

Please note that this is just one example and there is no specific blueprint of the exact interventions that an ED&I strategy or implementation plan should include. Remember – the most effective plans will be based on data and context. Academy trusts may focus on overarching examples that impact all of their schools. In order for progress to be made, however, schools should have individual plans to address the trust's overarching goals.

Distributing responsibility

Any school-based initiative requires strong leadership to ensure effective implementation. In the same way that senior leaders are deployed to oversee quality of education, behaviour and culture, it is essential for someone to take ownership of ED&I. This applies when launching an ED&I strategy in one school or across a trust. To ensure ED&I leaders are heard, it is essential for them to be seen as credible and with necessary authority. Individuals are often assigned ED&I responsibilities on top of their existing roles without being provided with the resources or time necessary to lead on this important work. This is problematic for many reasons. Like any role that is not adequately funded or resourced, significant limits are placed on what is possible to achieve, with any outcomes lacking in depth and consistency. It may be that an individual is passionate and insightful about the role and has plans for a wide range of interventions, but without being granted time to dedicate to these, they are likely to last only in the short term.

ED&I work requires consistent data collection, analysis and adaptation and, where the person in post is not adequately supported to do this, they are likely to be forced into generating only limited outputs, such as statements, policies and one-off training sessions. Not only does this prevent any meaningful organisational change to take place, but it is also likely to be detrimental to both internal and external perceptions. For any marginalised groups that had become hopeful at the newfound focus on ED&I, the disappointment at any perceived tokenism is likely to contribute to disillusionment with the organisation (Katara and Verma, 2023). Ideally, an ED&I role should be considered as a TLR or formal leadership position, with additional remuneration in salary and/or dedicated time.

It would be unfair for us to ignore the pressures faced by many schools financially, as well as in staff shortages. Where such constraints make the establishment of an individual ED&I leadership position impossible, it may be necessary for ED&I responsibilities to be divided and distributed across existing positions. For example, most organisations already have colleagues responsible for key areas such as recruitment, meaning that implementing an ED&I approach does not necessarily require appointing someone new. Instead, existing staff can integrate ED&I into their current practice. For example, a colleague responsible for recruitment can use their data analysis skills to analyse the recruitment process through an ED&I lens through tracking how many people with protected characteristics apply to the organisation, are successful at interview, and how long they remain in the profession. Similarly, curriculum leadership positions could be adapted to include responsibility for ensuring that the school curricula are representative of the diversity within society, and behaviour and safeguarding roles could include an expectation for the consistent monitoring and responding to the prevalence of incidents linked to protected characteristics. In order to provide people with the expertise to do so, comprehensive ED&I training would be required (see Chapter 5).

The role of governors

It is important for a governing body to 'have the knowledge, skills, and tools they need to take action in promoting diversity, equity, and inclusion in the school community' and the diversity of the board itself is necessary to consider.

Here Omena Osivwemu (a Governor, Education Policy Officer and former Teacher) and Aisha Sanusi (a MAT Trustee and Co-Founder and Director of ACEN) draw upon their experiences of working towards anti-racism in education in a wide range of state, grammar and independent schools across the UK. They share reflections on the role of school governors in the whole-school journey towards anti-racist practice:

To consider the role of school governors in the whole-school journey towards anti-racist practice, we draw upon a hypothetical school.
School A:

- *Part of a multi-academy trust*
- *In a diverse area of England*
- *The majority of the student body are from racially minoritised backgrounds*
- *The senior leadership team, governors and trustees are predominantly white British*

Creating a governing board that reflects the school community is a positive step towards better understanding the needs of the school and the community it serves. School governors are one

> *of the largest voluntary services in the UK, yet 52% of those making strategic decisions for our young people are aged 60 or older (NGA, 2024), with only 9% of governors under the age of 40 and 1% under 30. Of this, only 4% of governors are from ethnic minority groups (Hackney.gov.uk, 2025) representing 18% of the population of England and Wales and 3% of school pupils (GOV.UK, 2025). There is a real need for governors from diverse ethnic backgrounds and younger generations. Schools like School A may seek to diversify their governing board to address the lack of diversity in their leadership team. However, optical representation alone does not result in diversity of thought and leaders must first establish a culture and environment that is open to learning (for all including leaders), critique, and change. Without taking steps to build an inclusive culture, governing boards have the potential to be a hostile environment in which questions posed by racially minoritised governors are brushed over and their input muted or silenced.*
>
> *Governors are responsible for reviewing school policy and those with an understanding of anti-racism should prioritise areas where ethnic disparities are most prevalent. Recognising the significance of data, School A has employed an external ED&I company to measure and track progress towards creating equitable cultures. This is done by identifying patterns, proposing interventions, and benchmarking against national standards. Despite this, School A's data continues to expose ethnic disparities in attainment, exclusions, behavioural rewards and sanctions, and pupil experience (through pupil voice). Governors' role here is to challenge these systemic issues by questioning and monitoring the Head's reports, conducting listening sessions with the school community, and reviewing and critiquing policy. Governors at School A also hold senior leaders to account through visits focused on equalities in a similar vein to the SEND-link governor visits to examine SEND provisions and inclusion.*

Although this case study refers specifically to anti-racist governance, similar methods and principles could be applied by governors to advance equity, diversity and inclusion more broadly. Once schools and trusts have gathered ED&I-related data, governors can support in monitoring progress and upholding accountability.

Cascading ED&I training – who should be trained and when?

Training is essential for the success of any ED&I action plan and, throughout this section, we will explore recommendations for embedding and cascading training.

Here, Omena Osivwemu and Aisha Sanusi return to School A to explain the importance of training in racial literacy for staff at all levels.

> *Developing racial literacy within the governing board and senior leadership team is an ongoing process. Without this understanding, policy changes and targeted interventions aimed at dismantling barriers faced by minoritised staff and pupils will likely encounter resistance. Racially literate leaders are better equipped to make informed decisions that consider the impact on*

> *diverse communities, leading to policies and practices that are more equitable and inclusive. Effective anti-racism must be owned across the school, driven by leadership, and embedded within a long-term strategic plan. At School A, a senior leader has been appointed to lead the whole-school DEBI strategy, and one year all teaching staff received unconscious bias inset training. However, a key barrier to an effective anti-racist strategy is the narrow understanding of what racism is. Training in this area should be extended to all school staff, including support staff and administrators, as systemic racism occurs on an institutional level. Training must be revisited continuously to deepen and consolidate learning and must go further to develop the collective racial literacy of the school.*

Training is essential in all areas of ED&I and must be delivered to staff at all levels. If your school is part of an academy trust, there is an opportunity to train executive leadership teams and principals before senior leaders in school. This allows principals and other trust leaders to engage in self-reflection and then lead by example in training (Beijbom, 2022). There is real power in school and executive leaders facilitating training, if they feel confident with the content and in demonstrating vulnerability, as it demonstrates a genuine commitment to ED&I. If this isn't an option, senior leadership teams should ideally have this training before staff so training can be adapted to be more context-specific. For example, when training school leaders on raising awareness, they could consider which protected characteristics or other relevant characteristics should be an area of focus in future training.

Middle leaders should be next in the training cascade because to support their teams they also need to model the behaviours needed during training. We know time is a luxury in schools and, where it is not possible for leaders to be fully trained separately to staff, the slides could be shared in advance. This would allow leaders to familiarise themselves with the content, to offer critique by considering the potential response of their teams and to provide support during training. It is helpful for training facilitators to have a group of informed leaders to disperse between groups, to sense check the tone of conversations and to support in facilitation at a smaller group level.

Teachers and teaching assistants should then receive the training. We have already mentioned that training should be part of a wider school strategy and, if the training is planned before an ED&I intervention, staff then are provided with an opportunity to rehearse techniques and receive feedback. For example, where teachers have adapted the curriculum to ensure it is representative of a range of groups, they will also need to consider how the content is framed for students. The training could prepare teachers with planning time and provide examples and non-examples of framing so teachers can begin to script and consider what they will say in a way that is authentic to them and suitable for the students they teach.

Training should also form part of new staff induction, so they understand its importance and relevance to the school context. In Chapter 1, we identify some of shortfalls in statutory teacher training, where there may be limited explicit content on ED&I. Therefore, there should be separate sessions or breakout groups for any training aimed at trainees and ECTs so they can discuss specific challenges they may face.

Demonstrating a commitment to change

Schools and trusts may make the decision to publish equalities policies and statements that are available to the public and outlining a public commitment to ED&I can influence the perception of key stakeholders. Heath (2023), for example, found that the inclusion of equality and diversity information in job advertisements can positively impact the perceptions of job applicants from racially minoritised backgrounds and that the absence of such information can lead to scepticism. For parents and families, identifying that a school has a commitment to equalities may encourage them to apply for a place for their child, particularly those with protected characteristics.

However, it is important to avoid confusing publishing a policy or statement with generating meaningful change. If a policy is not paired with an implementation plan (see Table 2.2), it is unlikely to materialise into anything of substance. Ahmed (2007) argued that policies designed to promote [racial] equity may play a significant role in sustaining inequalities, rather than overcoming them. This is because of the reputational shift that institutions can achieve through bold statements, even where there is minimal accountability to ensure that the policy is enacted in practice. Bell (2003, p. 215) defined this as 'performativity' which 'produces opacity rather than transparency as individuals and organizations [sic] take ever greater care in the construction and maintenance of fabrications'. There is a high risk that public acknowledgements may create the illusion that equitable practice is an institutional priority, without specific changes being made to support marginalised groups. In this sense, change is depicted without being actualised. Ultimately, whether it is an equality statement, policy or objective, a mechanism must be put in place for it to manifest into meaningful and concrete action. Where the latter does not exist, words is all that statements are.

> **Questions**
>
> 1. How can you listen to and learn from your school community? Who will be prioritised first?
> 2. How can you distribute responsibility for ED&I?
> 3. What leadership support is needed to enable you to be able to complete an ED&I implementation plan based on one strand of activity in your ED&I strategy?

References

Ahmed, S. (2007). You End Up Doing the Document Rather Than Doing the Doing: Diversity, Race Equality and the Politics of Documentation. *Ethnic and Racial Studies*, 30(4), 590–609. Available from: https://doi.org/10.1080/01419870701356015 [Accessed 25 January 2024].

Beijbom, M. (2022). *Striving for Equity, Inclusion, and Safer Spaces at Work: A Review of the Literature*. Guelph, ON: Live Work Well Research Centre, University of Guelph.

Bell, S. J. (2003). The Teacher's Soul and the Terrors of Performativity. *Journal of Education Policy*, 18(2), 215–228. Available from: https://doi.org/10.1080/0268093022000043065 [Accessed 29 January 2024].

Catalino, N., Gardner, N., Goldstein, D., Wong, J. (2023). *Effective Employee Resource Groups Are Key to Inclusion at Work – Here's How to Get Them Right*. Available from: https://www.mckinsey.com/capabilities/people-and-organizational-performance/our-insights/effective-employee-resource-groups-are-key-to-inclusion-at-work-heres-how-to-get-them-right [Accessed 30 March 2025].

CIPD (2019). Diversity Management that Works an Evidence-Based View. Available at: https://www.cipd.org/globalassets/media/knowledge/knowledge-hub/reports/7926-diversity-and-inclusion-report-revised_tcm18-65334.pdf [Accessed 22 April 2025].

CMI (2024). *Walking the Walk? Managers, Inclusivity and Organisational Success*. Available from: https://www.managers.org.uk/wp-content/uploads/2024/07/Walking-The-Walk-Report.pdf [Accessed 30 March 2025].

Dixon-Fyle, S., Dolan, K., Hunt, D., Prince, S. (2020). *Diversity Wins: How Inclusion Matters*. Available from: https://www.mckinsey.com/featured-insights/diversity-and-inclusion/diversity-wins-how-inclusion-matters [Accessed 8 February 2025].

Education Endowment Foundation (2024). *A School's Guide to Implementation: Build Your Own Implementation Plan*. Available at: https://educationendowmentfoundation.org.uk/education-evidence/guidance-reports/implementation [Accessed 15 March 2025].

Ely, R., Thomas, D.A. (2020). Getting Serious About Diversity: Enough Already with the Business Case. *Harvard Business Review*. Available from: https://hbr.org/2020/11/getting-serious-about-diversity-enough-already-with-the-business-case [Accessed 8 February 2025].

Farrington, C.A., Roderick, M., Allensworth, E., Nagaoka, J., Keyes, T.S., Johnson, D.W., Beechum, N.O. (2012). *Teaching Adolescents to Become Learners. The Role of Noncognitive Factors in Shaping School Performance: A Critical Literature Review*. Chicago: University of Chicago Consortium on Chicago School Research.

GOV.UK, 2025. https://explore-education-statistics.service.gov.uk/find-statistics.school-pupils-and-their-characteristics/2024-25

Hackney.gov.uk, 2025. https://education.hackney.gov.uk/content/become-school-governor

Heath, A. J., Carlsson, M., Agerström, J. (2023). What Adds to Job Ads? The Impact of Equality and Diversity Information on Organizational Attraction in Minority and Majority Ethnic Groups. *Journal of Occupational and Organizational Psychology*, 96, 872–896. Available from: https://doi.org/10.1111/joop.12454 [Accessed 30 March 2024].

ImpactEd (2024). *Report 1 – Understanding Attendance: Findings on the Drivers of Pupil Absence from over 30,000 Young People in England*. Available from: https://www.impactedgroup.uk/research-campaigns-and-resources/understanding-attendance-4e8e8 [Accessed 30 March 2025].

Katara, A., Verma, M. K. (2023). Perceived Tokenism and Its Impact on Employee Morale and Job Satisfaction: A Study in Corporate Workplaces. *BPAS*, 43(2), 20519–20534. Available from: https://bpasjournals.com/library-science/index.php/journal/article/view/2782/2493 [Accessed 30 March 2025].

Mindset Kit (n.d.). *What Is Belonging?* Available at: https://www.mindsetkit.org/belonging/about-belonging/what-is-belonging. [Accessed 29 April 2025].

National Governance Association (2024). *Interested in Becoming a School Governor or Trustee?* Available from: https://www.nga.org.uk/about/become-a-governor-or-trustee [Accessed 23 April 2025].

Ofsted (2021). *Review of Sexual Abuse in Schools and Colleges.* Available from: https://www.gov.uk/government/publications/review-of-sexual-abuse-in-schools-and-colleges/review-of-sexual-abuse-in-schools-and-colleges#to-what-extent-do-schools-know-about-sexual-abuse-when-they-do-know-how-do-they-respond [Accessed 30 March 2025].

Ofsted (2023). *Inspecting Teaching of the Protected Characteristics in Schools.* Available from: https://www.gov.uk/government/publications/inspecting-teaching-of-the-protected-characteristics-in-schools/inspecting-teaching-of-the-protected-characteristics-in-schools [Accessed 20 April 2025].

Raising awareness of self and developing person-centred knowledge

ED&I threshold concepts

It can be challenging to know where to begin when raising self-awareness as identity is incredibly complex. When embarking on our ED&I journey, it was essential for us to develop our knowledge of significant ED&I threshold concepts. Threshold concepts are key to transforming the way students understand a whole subject, allowing them to move on in their learning (Cousin, 2006; Meyer & Land, 2003 in Olaniyi, 2020). Although engaging with these concepts can be challenging initially, they are instrumental in understanding the complex nature of ED&I. Such concepts also allow an intelligently sequenced ED&I curriculum to be developed with learning revisited meaningfully and intentionally in training (see Chapter 5).

Identity

Identity refers to our sense of who we are as individuals (personal identity) and as members of social groups (social identity) (Facing History, 2021). A person's identity is established through a combination of things which can and cannot be controlled. It is formed through childhood and adult experiences, relationships, external characteristics, beliefs, attitudes and values (Psychology Today, n.d.-a). Some aspects of identity are fixed and unchanging, whereas others are more fluid. In this sense, identity is often viewed as a social construct, as it is informed through the social contexts we inhabit, the interactions we engage in, the expectations we encounter and the aspects of all of this that we adopt and resist along the way (Easy Sociology, 2024). Identity is essentially a combination of labels that an individual uses to define themselves. These labels may be shared with others and, where this occurs, you may be perceived as belonging to the same identity group.

Lived experience

Lived experiences are 'the things that someone has experienced themselves, especially when these give the person a knowledge or understanding that people who have only heard about such experiences do not have' (Cambridge Dictionary). Every individual has a lived experience and, although we may share similarities with others, they are unique only to ourselves. Lived experiences can also transcend generations and manifest in the form of intergenerational trauma which is 'the apparent transmission of trauma between generations of a family' (Psychology Today, n.d.-b). This can occur when the children or grandchildren of people who have experienced significant trauma continue to experience emotional, psychological or behavioural effects even if they didn't directly experience the trauma themselves (Marschall, 2024), especially where the effects of the original trauma are continually witnessed (Lee et al., 2023). Intergenerational trauma can stem from many different experiences, including racial discrimination, long-term oppression, or exposure to abuse – even as a witness. These traumatic events can influence a person's behaviours, beliefs and ability to form relationships and, over time, these effects can be passed down, shaping how future generations think, feel and relate to others (Embark, n.d.)

The concept of lived experience can cause debate. Some might argue that 'lived' denies the person's experience in the present or that it encourages the individual to feel they have expertise in a certain area and that this expertise cannot be challenged. It can also be an alienating concept for people who are not from a historically marginalised group who may feel that their experiences are incomparable or insignificant. Moreover, a focus on lived experience can dangerously narrow representation if assumptions of homogeneity are made and this misconception is not challenged.

Whilst we acknowledge these critiques, there is power in defining and exemplifying the concept of lived experience before engaging in structured self-reflection. Lived experience allows us to understand, from the outset, that there are limits to our understanding of those around us. We might assume we have detailed knowledge of people because we encounter people throughout our lives, but this knowledge can be superficial when based on assumptions and harmful stereotypes. Lived experience allows us to understand that we don't automatically fully understand the nuances and complexities of any individual situation unless we have been through it personally and that, even then, intersectionality can lead to differences.

Intersectionality

Intersectionality is central to seeing the whole person rather than merely singular characteristics. The term was first used by Professor Kimberlé Crenshaw to describe how Black American women were doubly discriminated against – because of their gender and because of their race. It is important to understand that people who hold several, intersecting protected characteristics can be particularly affected by prejudice and discrimination and Crenshaw describes intersectionality as 'a prism, for seeing the way in which various forms of inequality operate together and exacerbate each other' (Steinmetz, 2020). Without a strong understanding of intersectionality, we might be prone to one-dimensional interpretations of those around us, rendering it impossible to understand people as their authentic selves.

Unconscious bias

Bias is when a person has a particular tendency, feeling or opinion, especially one that is without reason or evidence. Bias can be conscious, meaning that you're very clear about your biased feelings and attitudes. By contrast, unconscious bias refers to the associations that are made between different qualities and social categories such as race, gender or disability and judgements that are made without conscious awareness (Diverse Educators, n.d.) It influences behaviours and decisions made by individuals.

Dr Pragya Agarwal (2020a) explores how unconscious biases are formed and attributes this to cognitive shortcuts. These cognitive shortcuts are useful because it means we don't need to relearn how to do everyday tasks, such as brushing teeth, but it also means that it results in people 'defaulting to making judgements about people different than us' (Tulshyan, 2022). We will summarise Agarwal's discussion of cognitive shortcuts here and we highly recommend reading *Sway: Unravelling Unconscious Bias* for a more in-depth exploration.

Agarwal (2020a) comments on error management theory, where judgements about opportunities and threats tend to lean towards an extreme response, resulting in people being cautious. This might include avoiding action or not selecting the best action out of different options; the intention here is to keep people safe from danger. Agarwal then examines artefact theory, where biases are a product of applying the wrong strategies in the wrong context i.e. what was helpful for our ancestors in ensuring survival and reproduction is not necessarily suited to modern needs. Whilst Agarwal (2020a) explores these reasons for unconscious bias, she also mentions that the 'evolutionary basis of cognitive biases does not give us permission to act in a discriminatory way', especially as gender and race are social constructs. There are questions to be raised as to whether describing bias as unconscious removes accountability for the individual and Tulshyan (2022) limits her use of the term because she feels it can be used to 'justify repeated harmful behaviours of prejudices because they were not perpetuated consciously'.

As educators, we must realise that, despite good intentions, bias may affect our interactions with both pupils and colleagues, especially in the context of a busy school environment. Agarwal (2020a) states that:

> taking our time with important decisions can help us de-automatise. This means that we do not fall back on our unconscious biases but instead activate our logical and rational thinking and actively bust any biases that can affect our decision.

As humans, we have self-awareness and consequently can take responsibility and address our biases to avoid discriminatory behaviour, but only if we choose to. It is impossible to eliminate all our unconscious biases but by raising self-awareness, we can at least strive to disrupt them. Nevertheless, a focus solely on the individual cannot lead to organisational change. For this to occur, a systemic review of bias at all levels is needed and, for this, organisational commitment is required.

Why is it important to raise awareness of self?

Harvard Business Review identified key behaviours demonstrated by inclusive leaders: striving for authenticity rather than leadership presence; redefining rules and removing exclusionary practices; embracing active learning; ensuring equal opportunities and equitable outcomes and promoting inclusion as everyone's responsibility (Zheng et al., 2023). Leaders cannot expect to develop these behaviours within their teams if they do not themselves exhibit them. Self-reflection and moving beyond their comfort zone can support leaders in contributing to safer workplaces for all (Beijbom, 2022). Any ED&I work must begin with self-reflection because we cannot attempt to understand others without truly understanding ourselves. Taking the time to reflect on our own identities, lived experiences, and biases can remind us of the complexities within ourselves, which can, in turn, help us understand the multifaceted nature of others.

Self-reflection involves thinking of past events, interactions and experiences, reflecting on how one's own point of view is informed and considering alternate views of an experience. Research suggests that for self-reflection to be effective in training, it needs to be critical and should involve questioning how our lived experiences and privileges affect action and inaction (Nicolaides & Poell, 2020 cited in Beijbom, 2022). This is especially crucial for individuals who are part of more privileged identity groups as they:

> are most likely to have an unconscious and taken-for-granted experience of their organisation's culture (which often include White, masculine, heterosexual values) and how it reflects their identity and norms at the expense of others. It is not that they will never face challenges, but that these challenges will not be directly related to or compounded by virtue of the identities they hold. Therefore, they may be relatively unaware of what challenges are present for people with identities different than their own. Becoming aware of these gaps in their understanding that is an important step towards creating safer and more inclusive workplaces.
> (Wong, 2019 cited in Beijbom, 2022)

Engaging in structured self-reflection requires individuals to be humble – in acknowledging where their awareness needs to be raised – and vulnerable – in speaking out and sharing their own experiences. With busy lives, we don't often allow ourselves the time and space to reflect on aspects of our identity and ask the hard questions which allow for critical self-reflection. Even if we try, it can be difficult to know what to ask and how far to engage in the thinking process. It is hard to dig deep, and self-reflection can incite strong emotions – both positive and negative. Therefore, the beginning of anyone's ED&I journey should begin with intentional and structured self-reflection in a safer space.

How to raise and encourage self-awareness

In this section, we share some strategies that can be used to raise self-awareness. They can either be used during a period of independent reflection or shared with staff and students during training. Here, we narrate how this would be delivered in training with staff, but this structure can also be used for independent self-reflection. As our identities and lived experience are ever-evolving, it is helpful for this task to be revisited.

Bennie Kara (2021, p. 25) uses a circular diagram to encourage teachers to map out their awareness of different cultural, racial, gender-based and physical identities. She does this through encouraging reflection into:

- My identity
- Identities in my life
- Identities within my classroom
- 'Unknown and unexperienced identities', suggesting that readers identify where they are less familiar and make a deliberate plan to deepen their knowledge.

We were inspired by Kara's (2021) model and have utilised what we have coined as 'awareness circles' in our own professional development sessions. We have made the following adaptations:

- Instead of asking individuals to reflect on their identity as a whole, we ask them to consider both 'visible characteristics' and 'invisible characteristics'. Our aim here is to encourage participants to reflect on the complexities of identity, how they see themselves and how they are seen by others. Both impact identity formation and this also allows for discussion of intersectionality and its impact.
- We extend the consideration of identities within the classroom to identities within classrooms, schools and teams to ensure the activity includes all staff working within a school context.

Explanation and framing

Before asking participants to complete the awareness circles, we always explain the purpose of the activity. We acknowledge that the activity may feel unfamiliar and challenging and, importantly, explain that there will be no expectation or pressure for anyone to share aspects of their identity that they do not feel comfortable in doing so.

Providing tools for completion

To support participants in completing the activity, we display the protected characteristics. We also display other characteristics like ability, accent and dialect, appearance, socio-economic background, education, English as an additional language, family, health, income, language, name, organisational role, political beliefs, work experience and many more. This is particularly important because our experience demonstrates that some people may feel reluctant to participate in the activity where they perceive that what they have to say isn't 'worthy' of being shared. This has often emerged where participants have not recognised or experienced discrimination in their lives. Reinforcing the right to for everyone to participate is important here and it can be helpful to be explicit in saying this. For example:

> Don't worry about whether what you're writing is 'right' or 'wrong' – there are no right answers here. If something comes to mind and feels important to you, then it matters. Your experiences are valid and valued.

At this point, we also feel it is important to acknowledge potential challenges in categorising certain characteristics. For example:

> If your role is that of a school headteacher, this is highly visible in school, but it may be invisible to school visitors and new people you meet in your personal life.

We also ask participants to consider their preferred way to be described. For example, when referring to race and ethnicity, a person may prefer to be described as 'a person of colour' or a member of the 'global majority'. Individuals cannot control how they are perceived but they can consider their preferred way of being described and use this in any interactions where certain traits are mentioned.

Modelling vulnerability

Next, we demonstrate vulnerability by sharing a partially completed awareness circle based on our identity. This supports participants with completing the awareness circle and demonstrates vulnerability as we are talking about characteristics that we may not necessarily draw attention to in the workplace. We also acknowledge where we need to raise awareness, reinforcing that such curiosity is required of everyone. Again, framing is important here and our rationale for doing this is not to spotlight our experience but to create a safer space by modelling vulnerability.

Acknowledging feelings

We know through our work that this may be the first time that people have engaged in such critical self-reflection in a professional environment. Consequently, there will be different responses to the activity – some may welcome it and feel empowered, while others may feel more uncomfortable and reluctant to complete it for varying different reasons. Chapter 6 contains more guidance about what measures are needed to ensure training remains a safer space for all.

Moreover, being aware of the challenges of committing to a characteristic is needed, especially if the characteristic is something which an individual is still questioning, such as gender identity, or coming to terms with, such as a recent diagnosis. We overcommunicate that participants can add any characteristics that they feel defines their experience e.g. physical size, introversion, accent etc. There are no right answers, only valued experiences.

Making links to threshold concepts

After participants have completed the awareness circles, we draw attention to the concept of intersectionality. We encourage participants to see past the visible to the invisible and understand that the unique combination of these characteristics will impact how an individual experiences the world and their experience of bias, prejudice and isolation. We share carefully crafted questions (see Tables 3.1, 3.2 and 3.3)

Table 3.1 Example questions for staff

Question	Key ED&I concept
1. Do you feel that your visible characteristics are the ones that have the most significant impact on your lived experience? Why? Why not?	Identity Intersectionality Lived experience
2. What assumptions might people make about you that they might not make about others? Examples? Feelings?	Intersectionality Lived experience Microaggressions Unconscious bias
3. Where do you feel your lived experience helps you to understand the complexities of another person's lived experience?	Identity Intersectionality Lived experience *Developing person-centred knowledge*
4. Where do you need to raise awareness? Feelings?	Identity Unconscious bias *Developing person-centred knowledge*

Table 3.2 Example questions for younger pupils

Questions for younger pupils	Key ED&I concept
1. What is important to you about yourself and your life?	Identity Lived experience
2. What might people not know about you?	Identity Intersectionality
3. What do you think people first notice about you when they meet you for the first time?	Identity Unconscious bias
4. What is different about how you speak or act at home compared to how you speak or act at school?	Identity
5. Think about someone who is very different to you. Do you think they get treated the same way as you wherever they go?	*Developing person-centred knowledge*

Table 3.3 Example questions for older pupils

Additional questions for older pupils	Key ED&I concept
1. What is important to you and those you live with that people wouldn't know unless you tell them?	Identity Lived experience Intersectionality

2. Think about a person who has different visible characteristics to you.
  Do you think they are treated differently to you?
  What might people think about them that they don't think about you?
  Do you feel you completely understand any challenges they might face?
	Developing person-centred knowledge

to enable critical self reflection. This is intentional so they have time to formulate their thoughts and self-regulate. Discussion in small groups could then take place. We recognise the challenges of this activity, and it relies on people entering a space they may feel unfamiliar and even uncomfortable. Learning within this space, especially learning about yourself, is not easy and part of the journey is pushing past this.

Examples of questions for pupils

While we have explained this activity with staff in mind, younger pupils can also engage in critical self-reflection or discussion. In fact, a focus on this is desperately needed if we consider that 'an infant is able to nonverbally categorise people by race and gender at six months of age' (Katz and Kofkin, 1997 cited in Agarwal, 2020b) and 'by the time children are six years old they already have well-formed attitudes that mainly stem from their environment and parents' (Agarwal, 2020b). Here, Natasha reflects on how she has managed a conversation about race with her three-year-old biracial daughter.

NATASHA'S DAUGHTER: *Mummy, I'm white.*

Natasha had the option to end the conversation by agreeing with her daughter but chose to continue the discussion to promote her daughter's pride in her identity and develop self-worth.

NATASHA: *You're white and brown. Mummy's brown and daddy's white. We all have different bodies and this is what makes you special.*

They have since had, albeit very short, conversations about race with Natasha telling her daughter about melanin. Even with very young children, though conversations may differ, we need to consider how we prepare them and empower them for life in wider society where they may experience prejudice and discrimination.

Providing a space for reflection and discussion of identity can prevent children from underrepresented groups from internalising stereotypes and experiencing negative self-worth, which commonly occur as a result of a lack of conversation and a lack of representation (Agarwal, 2020b). However, the way we navigate this must differ based on the age and individual needs of the child. For example, research has shown that children between 4 and 6 start to create assumptions based on lifestyle, religious belief and skin colour (Agarwal, 2020b). Therefore, it is more appropriate to talk about similarities and differences to promote respectful curiosity and self-worth, whereas older children benefit from being able to engage in more critical thinking e.g. 'Why do you feel this is unfair?' (Agarwal, 2020b). For brevity, we can only offer limited examples and so we direct you to Agarwal's must-read book, *Wish We Knew What To Say* (2020b).

Please be aware that the examples in Tables 3.2 and 3.3 may need further adaptation based on the age of the pupils you are working with. The associated threshold concept could also be shared, if appropriate.

Developing person-centred knowledge

While the primary aim of the awareness circles is to help participants develop self-awareness, it also serves as a powerful tool for encouraging them to reflect on the lives and experiences of others. We refer to this as developing person-centred knowledge. Schools and trusts are composed of diverse individuals, each with unique experiences and perspectives. By embracing a person-centred approach in strategic decision-making, educational institutions can better support the needs of their communities and create environments where everyone can thrive. To avoid reinforcing generalisations, this section will not present broad or assumed narratives. Instead, we encourage readers to reflect on the behaviours needed to raise their awareness of the lived experiences of those they frequently interact with at school. To develop person-centred knowledge, it is important to:

Be curious

Recognising the areas beyond our own lived experience helps us to reflect on the thoughts and assumptions we may unintentionally form about characteristics and identities that we are less familiar with. These thoughts or assumptions may be rooted in unconscious bias and stereotypes so it is important that we interrogate each thought to de-automatise our thinking. This needs to be hard and requires courage as in doing this we are challenging biases that we may not have ever been aware of. As ED&I educators we are trusted with information about people's lived experience. If we know the limits of our awareness, we can engage in active listening and seek to understand and learn more.

Show a commitment to learning and unlearning

Acknowledging a lack of understanding and potential bias is only the first step and we must next take responsibility for building our awareness. It is important to consider where we lack confidence when talking about certain characteristics (our 'unknown and unexperienced identities') and to engage in research from trusted sources to develop our knowledge base. Websites such as Diverse Educators can be a great starting point for those working in education. Caution is important when considering talk to staff or pupils about certain characteristics and this must not amount to an interrogation. Whilst some people may be comfortable in talking about their characteristics, others may not, and it is important to avoid pressuring anyone into doing so. Ultimately, individuals are not responsible for providing this education. Optional and broad invitations to speak are more appropriate than direct individual requests. In Chapter 2, we explore a range of mechanisms for developing knowledge of others.

Allow defences to fall

Recognising gaps in understanding and experience can bring to light past behaviours that may have been inappropriate or harmful. This increased awareness should be used to support reflection on any previous actions now understood as discriminatory. This process requires courage, as acknowledging being in the wrong can be difficult. Rather than feeling defensive, centring feelings of guilt, a proactive approach is to reflect on how our responses can be improved going forwards. Consider how a response such as, 'I'm sorry, I got that wrong and will do better moving forward' demonstrates accountability more effectively than responses like, 'I didn't mean it that way' or 'I'm sorry if I upset you, but…' which deflect responsibility.

Plan for future action

It is important to think practically about next steps and to reflect on the level of confidence in making meaningful change. This might include actions such as addressing lack of representation or challenging discrimination. Attention should be given to what is noticed and what goes unnoticed. It is also worth reflecting on moments where something is recognised but no action is taken – perhaps due to discomfort or fear of making a mistake. You may want to jump to Chapter 6 now where we share a framework for responding to bias.

Throughout the process of developing person-centred knowledge, it is important to remember that there are no easy answers, and no static person-centred knowledge base exists. ED&I educators must realise that constant learning – and unlearning – is needed.

Throughout the rest of this chapter, we will explore important concepts to consider throughout the learning process.

Understanding privilege

When raising self-awareness and developing person-centred knowledge, it is essential to understand the existence of privilege and the ways in which this can manifest.

Privilege is 'any and all unearned benefit, right or advantage an individual receives in society by nature of their identities…' (Malone, 2021, p.60). The words 'any' and 'all' are important here as anyone, no matter their characteristics, can carry privilege in some form. Privilege is a highly provocative concept and can make people feel defensive as they may perceive that the term implies they have had an easier life. However, understanding privilege is not about suggesting any individual's life is easy; it's about acknowledging the advantages we may have, even in the presence of other challenges.

The very existence of the Equality Act and its defined protected characteristics (as explored in Chapter 1) acknowledge the existence of privilege. The fact that a law is needed to prevent discrimination against certain groups suggests that these groups have historically faced higher levels of discrimination. That said, privilege expands beyond the protected characteristics and can manifest in many forms. For example, whilst social class is not a protected characteristic, there are many benefits and disadvantages experienced in relation to this. For some people, socio-economic privilege means being able to afford expensive items and holidays, whilst to others it means being able to afford a home, or to eat meals every day. In this sense, socio-economic advantage does not necessarily mean being incredibly rich; it can also refer to having the means resources to be able to survive comfortably. Privilege can also be contextual and ever-changing. For example, Funmi experienced poverty in her early childhood. However, she now works in a middle-class profession and experiences the advantages of this. Accepting her current privilege does not suggest that she has faced a life free from any struggle.

Due to the emotional responses that exploring privilege can bring, it is important not to frame discussions as an attack or an attempt to generate feelings of guilt. Tulshyan (2022), for example, states that a cisgender, heterosexual white man, who is 'overrepresented in the workplace', should not feel they have done something wrong in obtaining their role. She does state, however, that it is their responsibility to 'understand how those with marginalised identities are often held back at work because they face biases'. This is not about anyone's experience being easy, but it is about understanding how and why some people may have faced more challenges. Dr. Muna Abdi (2021) has moved away from the term 'privilege' to using 'structurally enabled' or 'embedded advantage'. Abdi argues that this ensures that people understand the concept as a manifestation of how a system operates, rather than it focusing solely on individuals. This is important learning because it highlights 'cooperation, compassion and care' and the idea that it is systems that require dismantling, not individuals.

The awareness circles can support colleagues to explore the concept of privilege. For example, the question 'What assumptions might people make about you that they might not make about others?' could be expanded in asking participants to consider 'Which other characteristics might lead people to make assumptions?' and 'How might this present barriers to others that you haven't yourself experienced?' We will now encourage readers to reflect on the case study of a teacher's experience navigating the education system as a gay man. Throughout the case study, we include reflection questions to prompt readers to consider the challenges this teacher has faced, thereby recognising privilege (or the absence of it) in their experience and that of others. As exploring privilege can often be met with resistance, it is worth investing time to raise awareness in this pivotal area. Examples more applicable from your context could then be used during ED&I training.

Case study

James – Head of Department in a secondary school

When I applied for my first job, I deliberately chose a school over an hour away from home. I told people it was because the school had a good reputation which is half true, but the full truth was, I wanted distance. I was terrified that if I taught closer to home, students might somehow discover personal details, or worse – make connections to my husband or family. I thought that by keeping my professional and personal life separate, I could protect myself and my family.

Reflection:

1. Have you ever had to take your safety into account when choosing where to work?

When I first started teaching, it felt like there was a clear line between who I could be around staff and how I could present myself in front of classes. I didn't see anyone else who was openly out as gay to the students which made it feel too risky.

Reflection:

2. Are you able to see yourself reflected amongst the staff body in your school?

In my first year, students would often ask questions like "What's your wife called, Sir?" and I panicked. I blurted out the name "Maria" and built a quick story – she was a nurse, I said. Ironically, my husband is a nurse, so I wasn't really lying about his job, just his gender. I felt a strange mix of guilt and self-protection. I thought I was keeping things simple, but really, I was creating a barrier between me and my students. For a long time, I justified it to myself – it wasn't relevant, it didn't affect my teaching, so why say anything? But that approach took a toll. Every time I said "Maria" or dodged a question, I felt like I was performing a version of myself that wasn't real. It made small moments – like casual chats with students or staff – feel loaded with pressure. I was constantly on edge, afraid I'd slip up and be found out.

Reflection:

3. Have you ever felt pressured to hide fundamental aspects of your identity due to fear of judgement from pupils?

In my second year of teaching, my husband and I got married. My social media accounts were all private, but I hadn't considered the visibility of posts from family and friends. One morning I arrived at school and immediately sensed something had happened. Students were whispering and giggling as I walked by. Then a student came to tell me that photos from our wedding had been seen. I tried to continue with my day but during my break duty a group of boys ran circles around me, mocking and blowing kisses to each other. I ended up having a panic attack.

Reflection:

4. Have you felt the emotional burden of hiding aspects of your identity on a daily basis?

A colleague supported me while I calmed down. It wasn't just about what was happening that day – it brought back all the trauma I had buried from high school. I was suddenly transported back to being a teenager, walking through corridors filled with whispers, judgement and fear. I remembered how I used to monitor every word and movement to avoid being found out. I'd worked hard to build confidence as an adult, but in that moment, all those feelings of shame, fear and helplessness came rushing back.

Reflection:

5. Have you ever found yourself unexpectedly reliving past trauma in the workplace?

Later that day, a member of leadership came to find me. She was incredible. She gave me space to talk, validated how I felt and then offered me two options. The first was to treat any talk about my sexuality as a behaviour issue, applying the policy strictly. The second was to acknowledge the truth and move forward, with the reassurance that it would likely blow over in a few days. After thinking, I chose the second option. I realised that trying to deny something students already knew would send the wrong message – especially to any young people in school who might be struggling with their own identity.

Reflection:

6. Have you ever had to choose between protecting yourself and advocating for others when it comes to revealing aspects of your identity?

Readers may or may not have experience of the feelings and situations outlined in the case study and reflection questions. Where this has not been experienced, this is an example of holding privilege. Other readers may relate to certain aspects of the experience, such as feeling they have to hide certain aspects of their identity e.g. a hidden disability. Even if you have faced challenges in other areas, such as racism or disability, you may still hold privilege in relation to sexuality and recognising the privileges we do hold does not remove the barriers that we face in other areas. Recognising privilege isn't about assigning blame or implying that you are responsible for others' experiences – it's about acknowledging the advantages that exist due to certain characteristics.

Recognising privilege is a positive step as it enables us to identify where we can use this to support others. Holding privilege can mean that we take for granted certain aspects of an organisation's culture and, where elements of our identity are reflected as the 'norm', we may not recognise where the identities of others are marginalised. This can result in some people being unaware of the challenges faced by others. Therefore, being intentional in raising our awareness is essential for working towards a more inclusive workplace for all (Beijbom, 2022).

Where we hold privilege, we hold power. Power comes with 'embedded advantage' and those with this power define what is 'normal' or 'acceptable' in society (CILIP, n.d.). Those of us with any element of power can use it to challenge archaic beliefs about what is 'normal' and 'acceptable', and this is a significant part of creating an equitable environment. In Chapter 4, we explore a range of examples of how this can be achieved. Personal power might be impacted if we come from a marginalised group or if we are excluded or underrepresented in society and the workplace; however, acknowledging our personal power can positively affect how we show up and the difference we can make. Through returning to James' story, we can see how he was able to manifest a sense of personal power and has used his experiences to support others:

> From then on, I decided to be open. If a student asked, "What's your wife called again, Sir?" I'd respond: "My husband is called David". Within a day or two, the fuss died down. Life returned to normal and in some ways, it was even better. I'd occasionally hear something homophobic, but the school were supportive in responding to those incidents.
>
> Even now, students will ask things like "What's your wife called?" I don't take offence – teenagers are naturally curious and sometimes these questions are a way of opening up a bigger conversation. I've come to see them as opportunities to connect, educate and normalise.
>
> Since coming out, I've found that my relationships in school have deepened. There's a level of trust and honesty that wasn't there before. It's not about my sexuality being a constant talking point – it's about being real, showing up as my full self and modelling that it's ok to be who you are. In communities where there aren't many openly LGBTQ+ people, they need to see someone living authentically, so they can ask questions and understand the world around them better.

James' story is a powerful example of how an individual's identity and interactions with others can deeply shape their lived experience. Remember, it is just one perspective. In every classroom, school, or trust, there are countless intersectional identities at play. It is our responsibility, as individuals, to develop knowledge of the people we interact with every day. ED&I educators and leaders have a key role in supporting and inspiring others to build this awareness (see Chapter 5 on planning powerful training).

Microaggressions

When raising our awareness of self and developing person-centred knowledge, it is not enough to *acknowledge* the lived experiences of others and to *identify* where we may lack understanding or hold bias; we also need to take practical steps to *change* our behaviours. A starting point is to consider the ways that bias can show up in our own interactions and within the interactions of those around us through microaggressions.

The term *microaggression* was coined by psychiatrist Dr. Chester M. Pierce in the 1970s to describe "subtle blows" experienced by Black people. Since then, however, the concept has evolved to encompass a broader range of marginalised identities and experiences (Freeman and Stewart, 2024). Derald Wing Sue (2021) defines microaggressions as:

> the everyday slights, insults, put-downs, invalidations and offensive [behaviours] that people of [marginalised] groups experience in daily interactions with generally well-intentioned people who may be unaware of their impact.

We have both experienced similar journeys with microaggression and our understanding became developed during the resurgence of the Black Lives Matter movement following the murder of George Floyd in 2020. It was during this time that we first became aware of the explicit terminology, and this was a strange feeling as, although the terminology was new, we suddenly had a name for the types of interactions that had long made us feel uncomfortable, unsafe, unseen and unheard in our authentic identities. These comments were often framed as 'banter' or said casually, without obvious malicious intent, yet their impact was deeply felt. Over time, we developed a heightened sensitivity to such seemingly harmless remarks, both in our own experiences and in observing the experiences of others.

Research suggests that, over the course of an entire career, microaggressions can have a significant impact with increased rates of depression, prolonged stress and trauma, physical concerns like headaches, high blood pressure, and difficulties sleeping. These experiences can have a significant impact on careers as they result in burnout, low job satisfaction and the process of recovering from them often requires significant cognitive and emotional resources (Washington, 2022). Sue et al. (2007) identify three prominent categories of microaggression: microassaults, microinsults, and microinvalidations.

Exploring this is useful in developing person-centred knowledge as it enables a deeper consideration of intent and impact from the perspectives of both the victim and the perpetrator. In Table 3.4 we provide some examples of how these may manifest in a school setting. Please bear in mind that this list is not exhaustive and the

Table 3.4 Forms of microaggression with definitions and examples

Microaggression	Definition	Examples
Microassault	An explicit derogation which could be a verbal or nonverbal attack that is intended to hurt the victim through name-calling, avoidant behaviour, or purposeful discriminatory actions (Sue et al., 2007).	Avoidant behaviour: A student says they don't want to work with a student that identifies as non-binary. A person telling a racist/sexist/homophobic joke and then saying, "I was just joking." A staff member rolls their eyes when a colleague speaks about their experience of prejudice.

(Continued)

Table 3.4 (Continued)

Microaggression	Definition	Examples
Microinsult	Communications that convey rudeness and insensitivity and undermine a person's visible or invisible characteristics. They represent subtle snubs, frequently unknown to the perpetrator, but clearly convey a hidden insulting message to the victim (Sue et al., 2007).	Instead of asking for the correct pronunciation in advance, a staff member repeatedly mispronounces/ asks to call a colleague or pupil by a different name, or nickname because it's more familiar to them. Making assumptions about someone's role of level of seniority based on their skin colour e.g. a person of colour attends PD for senior leaders and the person who greets them in the main reception says "Are you aware this is for the senior leaders?"
Microinvalidation	They are characterised by communications that exclude, negate or nullify the psychological thoughts, feelings or experiential reality of a person and again they may be unknown to the perpetrator (Sue et al. 2007).	A female staff member reports a misogynistic comment from a male staff member or student and receives the response 'Are you sure you aren't being a little sensitive?' During a conversation involving a pupil who uses a wheelchair, directing questions and comments to the accompanying staff member instead of speaking directly to the pupil. A mixed-race staff member speaks about their experience of racism and receives the response 'But you don't even look [insert race or ethnicity]' An assumption is made about someone having a 'husband' or 'wife (heteronormative language that fails to acknowledge the range of sexual orientations)
Non-verbal microaggression	Physical behaviours as opposed to verbal slights.	A man repeats an idea said by a woman in a meeting and receives a positive reaction, whereas the woman's contribution was not acknowledged. A person from an ethnic minority background feeling that their contributions are undervalued or overlooked by the wider team, especially in comparison to their white colleagues. Teachers can unconsciously act differently towards children from working-class backgrounds, exuding less warmth, giving less eye contact and providing lower-quality feedback (Olczyk et al., 2022).

examples we share reflect common experiences that have been raised across the various contexts we've worked in and the professional forums we've engaged with. We would like to provide a note on language here. We will describe the person on the receiving end of the microaggression as the 'victim' and the person responsible for the microaggression as the 'perpetrator'. We are aware that this language may be contentious, but we feel it is helpful in providing clarity and highlighting the deep harm that microaggressions can perpetuate.

Whilst reading, we encourage readers to reflect on their individual school contexts and consider the thought processes needed to change these behaviours where they emerge.

Reflection

1. What was your experience of engaging with the examples above?
2. Were you able to identify examples from within your context?

If the activity proved difficult, it is useful to consider the reasons why. It may be that you are not privy to this data and have not discussed the experiences of the school community in this way. It may be that you need to broaden your understanding, so you are vigilant to what discrimination looks like in your school. Admittedly, this is not easy because developing such vigilance requires you to know which behaviours are unacceptable and why, and this means coming to terms with any gaps in your person-centred knowledge base. This is something we must all do.

Responding to microaggressions

If, whilst reading, you identified with being a victim of microaggression, it may be helpful to think about possible responses moving forward. This is not to suggest that it is your responsibility to educate others about discrimination. However, understanding how to respond can help you regain a sense of personal power and reduce the feelings of helplessness that frequent exposure to microaggressions can often cause.

Challenging microaggression can feel daunting and it is common to be concerned about being labelled as hypersensitive. However, it can help to frame this as a learning experience for the perpetrator, who may not initially realise the impact of their words. Here, we will draw upon a range of sources to provide practical advice for responding to microaggression, which can be used by victims or witnesses.

Before engaging in the conversation consider

- Your frame of mind and feelings. Do you feel emotionally ready to have this conversation? Is the conversation likely to help or to cause you further harm in this moment.

- Your relationship with the person. How far do you know and trust one another? How might this impact your conversation? (National Equity Project, n.d.)

- The environment. Where is the best place for this conversation to take place? A public conversation may result in defensiveness, whereas a one-to-one conversation may leave you unprotected if your words are not received well. It may be useful to ask for an impartial witness to be present during the conversation to ensure that, if any further inappropriate languages or behaviours are demonstrated, someone is able to validate your account.

- How might you approach the conversation in a way that will actually get this person to open up to a new understanding and change their behaviour? (National Equity Project, n.d.)

- Your exit strategy. How will you end the conversation if it is not well-received? It is not your responsibility to engage in an argument if the perpetrator struggles to take accountability for your actions. A simple line such as *"I don't think it is appropriate or professional for us to continue this conversation at the moment"* can act as a reminder of the workplace environment and prevent any further negative developments.

Having the conversation

- Clarify your understanding of what was said: *"I think I heard you say, is that right?"* (National Equity Project, n.d.)

- Clarify the difference between intent and impact: *"While you didn't intend to convey... the words you used suggest that..."* (National Equity Project, n.d.)

- Consider connecting them to people and/or resources that may shift their perspective: *"Have you spoken to... about this? I think you might appreciate what they have to say."* Or *"This (video/podcast/article/book) had a big impact on me – I'd love to talk with you about it if you're open to that."* (National Equity Project, n.d.)

- Acknowledge potential feelings: *"I know this might be uncomfortable to hear, and it is also uncomfortable to raise, but I think it is important for both of us going forwards..."*

- Challenge stereotypes where applicable: *"I think that's a stereotype. I've learned that..."* or *"Another way to look at it is..."* (Goodman, 2011)

- When speaking with someone you know well, appeal to their values and principles: *"I know you really care about... but those comments/behaviours do not reflect that"* (Goodman, 2011).

Micro-inclusions

Another way to interrupt bias, and provide a counter to it, is through micro-inclusions. They are small acts that intentionally aim to include all team members and can promote belonging, self-confidence and commitment to an organisation (Muragishi et al., 2024).

Examples of micro-inclusions

- Provide a space for everyone to speak by sweeping around the group to ask for contributions. Allow "I have nothing else to add" as an acceptable response so people do not feel unnecessarily pressured to speak (Muragishi et al., 2024).

- Facilitate specific opportunities to support and acknowledge contributions. E.g. each member of the team comments on how 'invisible' work from another team member helped them (Muragishi et al., 2024).

- Evaluate team dynamics so you understand who might: dominate, get praised, receive high-profile work and be supported in their professional growth (Muragishi et al., 2024).

As a team member, amplification is a tool that can be used to respond to bias (Tulshyan, 2022). Examples of what amplification looks like in practice include:

- I'd love to hear more about the brilliant idea that (name of person) came up with.

- Can we just pause for a moment, I'd love to hear more about (name of person)'s suggestion.

- (Name of person) was talking. I'd love to hear what you were going to say. (This statement is particularly helpful if a person is interrupted.)

Reflecting on microaggression

You may have realised that you have committed a microaggression in the past. This is likely to generate feelings of guilt, as most of us do not wish to identify as holding prejudice. However, it is important to take this as a learning moment. Identifying our errors is a positive step as it means that we can actively seek to change our language and behaviours going forward. We acknowledge the feelings of discomfort that can arise when being challenged on our own behaviours. Here are some practical tips to support you in your response:

- Avoid reacting defensively – if a colleague or even a pupil has taken the time to speak with you about an incident, it is clearly important to them. Make a commitment to listening, rather than responding with denial or defence.

- Ask for clarification – if you are unsure what you did to offend your colleague, invite dialogue by asking for clarification: *"Could you say more about what you mean by that?"* (Washington, 2022) or *"Can I check I have understood correctly?"*

- Seek permission for further conversation: "Are you open to talking more about this?" (National Equity Project, n.d.). If they decline, remember this is their right and there are other ways to educate yourself going forwards.

- Acknowledge, apologise (Washington, 2022) and commit to changed behaviours: "I am so grateful that I now know that this was wrong. I will work to become more aware of…"

Remember, regardless of your engagement with the conversation, victims of microaggression may react in different ways. It may take time for them to rebuild trust, or they may not immediately believe in your intentions to change. Verbal reassurances alone may not be enough and consistent, thoughtful actions are likely to have a more positive impact. Over time, if your behaviour shows genuine growth and understanding, they may begin to feel more comfortable and confident in your presence.

Avoiding assumptions

Throughout this chapter, we have explored the benefits of raising awareness of both the self and others. This can help us understand what is required for the entire school community to feel a sense of belonging. While this knowledge is beneficial, it can also lead to unhelpful assumptions. Our own characteristics might lead us to assume that others with similar characteristics have had identical experiences. For example, when Funmi first engaged in anti-racism work, she was surprised to find that some ethnic-minority colleagues did not consider racism a significant factor in their lived experiences in the same way as her. We must reiterate the importance of person-centred knowledge in the sphere of ED&I. People are individuals with their own perceptions and experiences. While we can learn from those around us, we must not assume this makes us experts. Understanding that learning is never complete and will continue to evolve is crucial.

Questions

1. How has your lived experience impacted your identity?
2. Are you able to bring your whole authentic self to the workplace? What impacts this?
3. Which of your own behaviours may you change based on your learning in this chapter?

References

Abdi, M. (2021). Language Is Important: Why We Are Moving Away from the Terms 'Allyship' and 'Privilege' in Our Work. *MA Consultancy*. Available from: https://ma-consultancy.co.uk/blog/language-is-important-why-we-are-moving-away-from-the-terms-allyship-and-privilege-in-our-work [Accessed 20 March 2025].

Agarwal, P. (2020a). *Sway: Unravelling Unconscious Bias*. London: Bloomsbury Sigma.

Agarwal, P. (2020b). *Wish We Knew What to Say: Talking with Children About Race*. London: Dialogue Books.

Beijbom, U. (2022). *Striving for Equity, Inclusion, and Safer Spaces at Work*. Live Work Well Research Centre. Available from: https://liveworkwell.ca/sites/default/files/pageuploads/Striving%20for%20Equity%2C%20Inclusion%2C%20and%20Safer%20Spaces%20at%20Work_Beijbom2022_AODA.pdf [Accessed 10 March 2025].

CILIP (n.d.). *Leading for Inclusion 3.2a*. Available from: https://www.cilip.org.uk/page/Leading4Inclusion3_2a [Accessed 8 April 2025].

Diverse Educators (n.d.). *Unconscious Bias Toolkit*. Available from: https://www.diverseeducators.co.uk/unconscious-bias-toolkit/ [Accessed 20 March 2025].

Easy Sociology (2024). *The Social Constructionist View of Identity in Sociology*. Available from: https://easysociology.com/sociological-perspectives/social-constructionism/the-social-constructionist-view-of-identity-in-sociology/ [Accessed 8 April 2025].

Embark Behavioral Health (n.d.). *Intergenerational Trauma: What Is It and How to Heal*. Available from: https://www.embarkbh.com/blog/trauma/intergenerational-trauma/ [Accessed 13 April 2025].

Facing History & Ourselves (2021). *Exploring the Concept of Identity*. Available from: https://www.facinghistory.org/resource-library/exploring-concept-identity [Accessed 9 April 2025].

Freeman, L., Stewart, H. (2024) Microaggressions: A Brief History. In *Microaggressions in Medicine*. New York: Oxford Academic. Available from: https://academic.oup.com/book/55895/chapter/439274105 [Accessed: 30 March 2025].

Goodman, D.J. (2011). *Responding to Microaggressions and Bias*. American Academy of Child and Adolescent Psychiatry. Available from: https://www.aacap.org/App_Themes/AACAP/docs/resources_for_primary_care/cap_resources_for_medical_student_educators/responding-to-microaggressions-and-bias.pdf [Accessed 14 April 2025].

Kara, B. (2021). *A Little Guide for Teachers: Diversity in Schools*. London: SAGE.

Lee, A.T., Chin, P., Nambiar, A., Hill Haskins, N. (2023). Addressing Intergenerational Trauma in Black Families: Trauma-Informed Socioculturally Attuned Family Therapy. *Journal of Marital and Family Therapy*, 49, 447–462. Available from https://doi.org/10.1111/jmft.12632 [Accessed 12 April 2025].

Malone, T. (2021). *Equality, Diversity & Inclusion: The Practical Guide*. 2nd edn. Mendip Hills Studio Ltd.

Marschall, A. (2024). *Understanding Intergenerational Trauma and Its Effects on Mental Health*. Verywell Mind. Available from: https://www.verywellmind.com/what-is-integenerational-trauma-5211898 [Accessed 14 April 2025].

Muragishi, G., Aguilar, L., Carr, P., Walton, G. (2024). *The Power of Small Acts of Inclusion*. Available at: https://hbr.org/2024/12/the-power-of-small-acts-of-inclusion [Accessed 22 April 2025].

National Equity Project (n.d.). *Responding to Microaggressions and Unconscious Bias*. Available from: https://www.nationalequityproject.org/responding-to-microaggressions-and-unconscious-bias [Accessed 14 April 2025].

Olaniyi, N.E.E. (2020). Threshold Concepts: Designing a Format for the Flipped Classroom as an Active Learning Technique for Crossing the Threshold. *Research and Practice in Technology Enhanced Learning*, 15(2). Available from: https://doi.org/10.1186/s41039-020-0122-3 [Accessed 23 March 2025].

Olczyk, M., Kwon, S.J., Lorenz, G., Perinetti Casoni, V., Schneider, T., Volodina, A., Waldfogel, J., Washbrook, E. (2022). Teacher Judgements, Student Social Background, and Student Progress in Primary School: A Cross-Country Perspective. *Zeitschrift für Erziehungswissenschaft*, 26(2), 443–468. Available from: https://link.springer.com/article/10.1007/s11618-022-01119-7 [Accessed 2 April 2025].

Psychology Today. (n.d.-a). *Identity*. Available from: https://www.psychologytoday.com/gb/basics/identity [Accessed 9 April 2025].

Psychology Today. (n.d.-b). *Intergenerational Trauma*. Available from: https://www.psychologytoday.com/gb/basics/intergenerational-traum [Accessed 12 April 2025].

Steinmetz, K. (2020). She Coined the Term 'Intersectionality' over 30 Years Ago. Here's What It Means to Her Today. *Time*. Available from: https://time.com/5786710/kimberle-crenshaw-intersectionality/ [Accessed 30 March 2025].

Sue, D. W. (2021). Microaggressions: Death by a Thousand Cuts. *Scientific American*. Available from: https://www.scientificamerican.com/article/microaggressions-death-by-a-thousand-cuts/ [Accessed 10 April 2025].

Sue, D. W., Capodilupo, C. M., Torino, G. C., Bucceri, J. M., Holder, A. M., Nadal, K. L., Esquilin, M. (2007). Racial Microaggressions in Everyday Life: Implications for Clinical Practice. *American Psychologist*, 62(4), 271–286. Available from: https://doi.org/10.1037/0003-066X.62.4.271 [Accessed 10 April 2025].

Tulshyan, R. (2022). *Inclusion on Purpose: An Intersectional Approach to Creating a Culture of Belonging at Work*. Cambridge, MA: The MIT Press.

Washington, E. F. (2022). Recognizing and Responding to Microaggressions at Work. *Harvard Business Review*. Available from: https://hbr.org/2022/05/recognizing-and-responding-to-microaggressions-at-work [Accessed 10 April 2025].

Zheng, W., Kim, J., Kark, R., Mascolo, L. (2023). What Makes an Inclusive Leader? *Harvard Business Review*. Available from: https://hbr.org/2023/09/what-makes-an-inclusive-leader [Accessed 20 March 2025].

# Adopting an ED&I lens to create an inclusive school culture

Tulshyan (2022) signposts the idea of hiring for 'culture fit' as a significant example of exclusionary practice. She describes culture fit as 'an unspoken code that people have around what's acceptable and what's not within an organisation, or even in society' (p. 101). In this sense, hiring for culture fit leads to organisational leaders hiring people that mirror their existing team. This stems from a concept known as affinity bias, by which individuals are naturally drawn to others who share similar characteristics, experiences and interests to their own. Where a profession, like teaching, already lacks diversity, such practices compound the problem and prevent any significant increases in a diverse workforce population. Many researchers argue that instead of looking for 'culture fit', those seeking to develop inclusive and innovative workplaces should instead hire for 'culture add' which involves hiring people based on the new thinking and practice they can bring to an organisation (Tulshyan, 2022; Montgomery, 2022).

It is, however, necessary to understand that recruiting a more diverse workforce does not equate to achieving a sense of belonging. Macfarlane (2023) argues that 'the presence of racially minority staff in schools does not, of course, in and of itself indicate race equity' and this is true across the range of protected characteristics. Beyond simply adding numbers, equity and belonging can only truly be achieved through making the necessary changes to allow a diverse range of individuals to thrive in a range of areas. Throughout this chapter we will draw upon actions that we have identified (through feedback from a range of stakeholders) as contributing to a meaningful sense of belonging and adopting an ED&I lens is at the centre.

Adopting an ED&I lens

To adopt an ED&I lens is to be intentional in considering the lived experiences of those around us before making decisions, taking actions and going about our day-to-day practice. If we don't do this, it is highly likely that certain groups will be prevented from participating in the organisation to the best of their ability. Adopting an ED&I lens means that, rather than manifesting in occasional or one-off actions, ED&I becomes systemic and embedded in everything we do, right from the outset. If ED&I is treated as standalone, without being integrated into all policies, there is a risk that it may be perceived as something to opt in and out of, rather than understanding it as a fundamental expectation.

As an organisation, adopting an ED&I lens must apply to pre-existing as well as future policies. There would be no use in deciding to consider lived experience 'going forwards' if long-standing policies and practices continue to reinforce systemic barriers. This means that a good starting point is to review existing policies and consider which adaptations can be made to challenge any inequities that have become embedded over time. The following questions can be useful to ask when analysing organisational policies:

- Is this policy representative of our entire workforce and community? Who is included here? Who isn't?

- Have considerations been taken to meet the needs and entitlements of the full range of protected characteristics?

- Who benefits from this policy? Who does not?

- Would this policy support someone with *x characteristic*, should they work here in the future? Would it disadvantage them in any way?

This chapter will provide some examples of practices and policies that can be adapted through an ED&I lens. The examples included are not exhaustive, but the learning can be applied to a variety of contexts.

Establishing a prejudice-related incidents policy

All schools have behaviour policies that are designed to support staff in responding to behavioural incidents as well as encouraging students to understand the expectations surrounding behaviour within school. Whilst such policies are essential for the day-to-day running of a school, upon the application of an ED&I lens, they may not be comprehensive when responding to other common incidents that are likely to occur within schools.

A variety of terms are often used interchangeably when considering student behaviour. Terms such as 'bullying' are important for staff to know and understand, but are not always adequate in encompassing behaviours that may need a response in addition to the usual sanctions. This is particularly true of prejudicial incidents (incidents that are related to discrimination and bias). It is important to recognise that, in law, crimes that involve prejudicial behaviour are treated as distinguishable from others. The same must be the case within schools. The intention must not be to criminalise children but to ensure that students understand the seriousness of such behaviours. Whilst sanctions may punish students for their actions and act as a short-term preventative measure, they do not act to develop a student understanding of exactly *why* their prejudicial behaviour was wrong. If the same sanction is given to a student for shouting something silly in a lesson as for using racist or homophobic language – for example, a student may leave school with the misconception that prejudicial language equates to mere rudeness.

There are a multitude of reasons why a student may develop prejudicial and discriminatory attitudes. Students may be exposed to such attitudes via parents, families, on television and especially via social media. As educators, we have a responsibility to counter this with all pupils and an educational response for 'perpetrators' of prejudice is an essential aspect of any policy e.g. through having an age-appropriate conversation about intent and impact with a trained member of staff. This is with the aim of minimising the likelihood of a similar act of prejudice being intentionally committed in the future. Questions to consider when developing a prejudicial incidents policy include:

- How will the links to KCSIE be made clear to staff?
- How will incidents be identified?
- Is the perception of the 'victim' at the centre?
- How will 'victims' be supported?
- How will incidents be investigated?
- What is an appropriate sanction? How will sanctions vary for repeat incidents?
- Do school management systems need to be adapted?
- How far does the 'perpetrator' understand their actions? Which education will be put in place to support students in avoiding repeat incidents?
- Is any whole-school or whole-year group intervention needed?
- How will repeat incidents be monitored for both 'perpetrators' and 'victims'?
- Are sanctions and intervention age- and need-appropriate?
- Have any staff training needs emerged from the response to incidents?

Even though this policy focuses on prejudicial incidents in school, pupils can experience prejudice during extra-curricular activities, or school trips, and appropriate safeguarding measures are needed. There should be precise guidance in extra-curricular policies about what pupils should do if they experience prejudice and discrimination during school-related activities and this guidance should be overcommunicated to students before longer events take place e.g. work experience. It cannot be assumed that adults leading on external extra-curricular activities will notice or address prejudicial incidents and pupils need to know there is a trusted person they can talk to.

Inclusive uniform policies

School uniform policies represent a clear opportunity to embrace diversity and inclusion and, in fact, many of the rationales for having a uniform are centred around this. Schools have uniforms for a variety of reasons such as reducing the potential visible differences between students of differing socio-economic backgrounds, creating a shared sense of belonging amongst the school community, and preventing bullying linked to dress. Whilst the general intention of school uniforms may be to benefit students, if the uniform policy itself is not carefully considered it could potentially act as a barrier to true inclusion. Establishing a sense of belonging through the uniform policy should not equate to ignorance towards individual difference, particularly when considering the protected characteristics. Although this section is centred on the uniform for students, readers should consider how an ED&I lens can be applied to a staff dress code in a similar way.

Gender neutrality

There is a risk that uniform policies could reinforce gender norms. Prescribing certain uniform items to certain genders does not represent inclusive practice and may lead to feelings of extreme discomfort and alienation. The process to establishing a gender-neutral policy is simple – instead of differentiating between certain uniform options for 'boys' and 'girls', the term 'pupils' can be used instead. Alternatively, the uniform policy could be de-personalised and become more item-focused – for example, 'skirts should be black' rather than 'girls should wear black skirts'. Instating a gender-neutral policy does not take a significant amount of time but may represent an instrumental change for students. It means that students and families can look at the policy and prepare for attending school without the barrier of feeling any requirement to ask the school if they are able to wear certain items, which can be difficult for students from a diverse range of gender identities.

Acknowledging religious and cultural difference

The UK is incredibly diverse, and dress is used as an opportunity for the expression of a wide range of beliefs and cultures. A school uniform policy should not be used as a means to stifle this form of expression. Uniform policies should be considered carefully to ensure that they do not directly or indirectly discriminate against children from specific religious or ethnic groups. Whilst the PSED already requires schools to avoid discrimination against racial and religious groups and provides a wide range of case studies with explicit guidance surrounding hair discrimination, compulsory religious items, head coverings etc., there are many opportunities for schools to go beyond mere compliance. Rather than simply avoiding discriminatory language, schools that are truly committed to ED&I should actively celebrate and embrace diverse expressions of identity ensuring all students feel valued.

Afro hair

Discrimination linked to hair or hair style disproportionately impacts students with Afro hair and it has been formally acknowledged that some school uniform policies have the potential to embed this form of discrimination (EHRC, 2022b). However, avoiding discrimination does not equate to encouraging expression and schools can do significantly more than simply adhering to the law. In the case of Afro hair, even where a school policy is not discriminatory, where Black students are families are a minority within an area or school community and may have experienced hair discrimination in the past, they may have concerns and be reluctant to embrace certain styles without explicit recognition that they are able to do so. In 2020, the Halo Collective launched the 'Halo Code' – a guide for schools and workplaces to prevent discrimination around hairstyles or texture. The Halo Code provides a statement for schools to include within their uniform policy and this includes:

> We welcome Afro-textured hair worn in all styles including, but not limited to, afros, locs, twists, braids, cornrows, fades, hair straightened through the application of heat or chemicals, weaves, wigs, headscarves, and wraps.
>
> At this school, we recognise and celebrate our staff and students' identities. We are a community built on an ethos of equality and respect where hair texture and style have no bearing on anyone's ability to succeed.

As you can see, including the Halo Code in the school uniform policy goes beyond simply avoiding discrimination. Instead, it seeks to actively reassure families that their children's natural hair is fully accepted and celebrated. In doing so, it is likely to alleviate concerns without families having to go out of their way to ask for reassurance.

The PSED also requires schools that ban 'headgear' to make exceptions surrounding religion and belief, with Muslim students who cover their hair being named as an example (EHRC, 2022a). The following case study explores the journey of one school from complying with the PSED to truly embracing the feedback from its students.

Case study

Dixons Trinity Academy, Bradford

Dixons Trinity Academy had always adhered to legal requirements and had never discriminated against students wearing religious headwear, such as hijabs. However, when equalities surveys were conducted with students, they expressed a desire for more opportunities for self-expression and, following this, school leadership engaged in consultation with the student council to explore ways to make the uniform policy more inclusive.

> During these discussions, students highlighted their wish to wear hijabs in a wider range of colours beyond the previously permitted navy and black. In response, the school updated its uniform policy to allow hijabs in any colour, making it explicitly clear that students were able to express their individuality while maintaining a smart appearance. Additionally, whilst Year 10 and 11 students had traditionally been allowed to wear 'professional dress' instead of the lower school uniform, the existing guidelines only outlined requirements for shirts, jumpers, skirts and similar attire. Consultation revealed that some students were unsure whether religious dress, such as abayas and jubbahs, was permitted and considered 'professional'. To provide clarity and inclusivity, the policy was updated to explicitly allow these garments.
>
> These changes did not compromise the uniform policy, whereas dismissing students' requests could have negatively impacted their sense of belonging and inclusion.

The curriculum

The curriculum is an essential tool for developing belonging – it is accessed by all students within school and is the centre of their learning experience. For pupils to feel a sense of belonging in school, it is important that they should be able to see themselves within the curriculum. This is especially important given that many students are unable to see themselves reflected in the teacher workforce (see Chapter 1). As of 2025, the UK government are currently undertaking a review of the National Curriculum in England and the review panel's interim report revealed that young people had raised 'compelling arguments that the curriculum needs to do more in ensuring that all young people feel represented, and that it successfully delivers the equalities duties to support equality of opportunity and challenge discrimination' (DFE, 2025). The views of young people themselves demonstrate a significant need to diversify the curriculum and there is much research that demonstrates how curriculum leads may go about doing so.

In *The Diverse Curriculum (2025)*, Kara directs teachers to a range of practical strategies to decolonise and diversify the curricula and avoid tokenism e.g. through providing parallel stories and countering dominant narratives (Kara, 2025). By integrating ED&I within everyday learning experiences, pupils come to understand it as a natural and expected part of the world. This approach prevents misconceptions from taking root and helps them to develop a more inclusive mindset.

Macfarlane (2023) points out teachers' concerns about such curricula changes and provides lists of practical responses that are likely to be useful for ED&I leads. For example, if there are concerns about time constraints, Macfarlane points out that 'progress can be made by investing just a few minutes in a lesson to acknowledging and name-checking similar stories, achievements, inventions, and discoveries from other cultures'. In response to fears over political neutrality, she directs readers to Article 30 of the UN Convention on the Rights of the Child, which gives children 'the right to learn the language, customs, and religion of their family'.

Where teachers are struggling due to lack of direction, she explores how they could set up discussions with classes about *why* there is an absence of diversity in the maths textbooks.

We highly recommend both texts for those beginning their journey in curricula adaptation. Rather than simply restating their excellent ideas, we will shift focus in this section to highlight some significant learning points.

Case study

Catherine Sykes, Associate Assistant Principal, Chorus Education Trust

Our work on diversifying and decolonising the curriculum began with all staff training and then was followed up by work with middle leaders. There is so much guidance available to support with this and the work of Diverse Educators and Bennie Kara has been very influential. After attending various training courses, a starting point for us was to collate resources from different areas so departments had a toolkit they could use that allowed them to audit their current practice and gave them access to a variety of resources. The audits/checklists focused on representation, diversity, decolonising the curriculum and measuring impact. This allowed departments to reflect on their starting points and next steps. The impact of this so far is that only 14% of pupils feel that the curriculum doesn't reflect the diversity of our school. Whilst we cannot compare this to previous data, its impact for staff and pupils is reflected by the fact it is now part of the school improvement plan and a recent subject audit shows all departments are now moving forward with this essential work.

Table 4.1 Extract from the Diversifying checklist

Diversifying audit	Not yet started	Emerging	Embedded
We think about whose identities are represented in our curriculum and aim to widen the lens			
We avoid tokenism and single-story narratives			
We deliver sequenced lessons where EDI work is embedded, sequenced and purposeful			
We question our own subject knowledge and work to address any gaps. We don't just perpetuate what we were taught.			
We incorporate critical thinking into our classroom practice			

Prioritising learner safety in difficult topics

Limiting emotional harm is a significant aspect of creating safer spaces in the classroom, especially when discussing content with pupils that may be less familiar to staff. Ensuring this is achieved positively is not just through long-term curricula planning; short-term decisions also play a significant role. A fundamental part of this involves developing ED&I the knowledge, skills, awareness and confidence to talk about diversity, including things like protected characteristics. This doesn't come without being intentional in developing both subject and person-centred knowledge.

Conversations around diversity and protected characteristics can be challenging, particularly as not many of us have received long-term and explicit education in this area and these topics can be contentious. It can be even more challenging if what we teach does not at all align with our lived experience. Due to this, before teaching certain topics, time must be given to teachers to ensure they feel competent and confident in discussing less familiar content. It is not sufficient to talk only generically about ED&I.

Teachers must also gain confidence in navigating conversations and learning about race to ensure that they are developing anti-racist practice and to do this they need to keep it as an explicit focus, a parallel lens to broader inclusion and ED&I. Joseph-Salisbury (2020, p. 7) defines racial literacy as 'the capacity of teachers to understand the ways in which race and racism work in society' and to have the skills, knowledge and confidence to implement that understanding in teaching practice. We mention race specifically here as research shows an explicit lack of confidence from teachers in this area. After conducting a survey of over 1000 teachers in the UK, Show Racism the Red Card (2024) found that 56% had not received any anti-racism-focused CPD in the past two years, or were unsure if they had (4%). Additionally, only 25% responded to say they were 'extremely confident' in tackling racist behaviour.

Due to the absence of the intentional teaching of racial literacy, many people are likely to have internalised and often-unconscious stereotypes. Some may also have a lack of awareness as to which terminology is appropriate, or which language may be harmful. For example, Natasha is an English teacher and, when she taught *Of Mice and Men*, there was never any discussion of the impact of the racial slurs on individuals or any guidance around how such racial slurs should be sensitively managed in racially diverse classrooms. A lack of training can cause significant difficulties for all, and the process of 'unlearning' harmful ideas is much more difficult than learning beneficial ideas in the first instance. If teachers haven't developed their own racial and ED&I literacy, there is a risk that they may transfer any deficits to students or harm students. To encourage students to appreciate diversity, teachers need to be supported to upskill themselves in these areas so they can, in turn, develop these skills amongst young people.

It can be easy to fall into the trap of thinking that because teachers are delivering a topic linked to themes of equality and justice, we are naturally educating students in the best ways possible. However, having positive intentions does not naturally result in a positive impact and a gap can easily manifest between the two. The intent–impact gap is the space between what we *mean* by our words and actions and what others *feel* from those words and actions (Bravely, 2021). This means that, whilst we may have positive tensions in delivering something to students, without thorough planning we may unintentionally communicate something in an inappropriate way. We will now explore a scenario that a teacher shared with us:

> A staff member is teaching a lesson on life on the plantations for enslaved people. To inform students about the punishments inflicted, an image of an enslaved man being whipped is displayed on the board. A Black pupil puts their head on the desk. The teacher challenges this and asks the student to focus, but the student does not respond. The teacher proceeds to follow the behaviour system and logs a detention.

How does the intent–impact gap manifest in this scenario?

The teacher's *intent* was to educate students on harrowing realities of slavery. However, the *impact* was distressing for the pupil. The teacher had not considered how such graphic imagery and discussions of oppression may impact the students in front of them, particularly those with direct connections to Black history. As a result, instead of being able to engage with the lesson content, the student experienced emotional distress, which was subsequently met with disciplinary action rather than support.

What could the teacher have done differently in this scenario?

- **Frontloading**

Had the teacher developed their ED&I and racial literacy, they may have foreseen the likelihood of discussions surrounding slavery being difficult for students. They could have taken the time to frontload the emergence of the topic earlier in the year, and again prior to the lesson. They could have provided opportunities for students, and even families, to raise questions and concerns about the topic prior to the lesson.

- **Using appropriate resources**

The teacher should have taken the need to consider the necessity of including graphic images in the lesson. In this case, the teacher had opted for the 'shock factor' as a form of hook to engage students. However, as teachers, our role is to limit the risk of harm to students and there is no reason for any student, especially those from marginalised groups, to see harmful imagery.

- **Support over sanction**

Instead of immediately assuming the worst of the student, the teacher should have spoken to them privately rather than immediately enforcing discipline. The student clearly needed time to process their emotions because of the teacher's chosen content. The teacher should have taken the time to speak with the student to discuss how the lesson made them feel. In this case, the use of such imagery did result in a breakdown in trust. Where this happens, it is the teacher's responsibility to ensure that the student is able to speak with a trusted staff member.

- **Owning errors and apologising where necessary**

It was important for the teacher not to see this as a mistake that can simply be put behind them. Following the event, the teacher needed to demonstrate awareness that their actions may have altered the pupil's perception of them, potentially leading to a breakdown in trust. Given the power imbalance between teachers and pupils, it was not the student's responsibility to seek out the teacher and explain their distress. Instead, the teacher needed to take ownership of their decision-making, acknowledge the harm caused, and offer a genuine apology, as well as reassuring them of the changes that would be made to prevent similar situations from arising in future.

- **Demonstrating awareness of the rest of the class**

Additionally, the teacher needed to extend their apology and explanation to the whole class. Although only one student visibly reacted, this does not mean that others were not impacted. Some students may have internalised their discomfort for fear of sanction. Addressing the entire class would have allowed the teacher to acknowledge the potential harm caused and to reinforce their commitment to handling such topics with greater sensitivity in the future. Coming back to this after the lesson would have made clear that the teacher had not simply brushed off the event. It would also have modelled accountability, respect, and appropriate behaviours to students.

Our intention in sharing this scenario is to demonstrate that even unintentional errors can cause upset or harm. Similar experiences could occur where a teacher is asked by the head of department to deliver lesson content that they are uncomfortable with. Such experiences could also be linked to the range of protected characteristics, as well as other aspects of identity. The intent–impact gap may also manifest in our daily interactions with staff, students and families. We hope that the learning from the above scenario can transcend beyond just classroom practice and into readers' wider communications with those around them. Teachers should be supported in developing their knowledge in this area. Leaders should use opportunities such as this to embed training across the school – this can help to support the development of all teachers.

Avoiding harmful narratives

Pupils have also expressed the harm caused by encountering only negative portrayals of people they identify with in the curriculum (DFE, 2025). The scenario above may be useful to consider here. Some schools may fall into the trap of operating a tick-list approach to diversification, in which they focus mainly on ensuring that all protected characteristics feature at least once within the curriculum. Whilst this may ensure some diversity in the curriculum, this can cause more harm than good.

Take, for example, the scenario above. The teacher in question may feel that they had included representation for Black students in the curriculum through addressing the topic of slavery. However, it is important to reflect on the potential repercussions of this. If the *only* topic that Black students can see themselves in is a lesson that centres brutality and a lack of agency, this representation does not encourage students to thrive. This is by no means to suggest that historical marginalisation should not be taught in schools – it is important for young people to understand the struggles that people have overcome. However, it is important to ask which messages are being delivered through the content that is chosen. Teaching students about the power demonstrated by enslaved people fighting against slavery addresses the necessary themes, whilst also depicting the sense of agency that was very much in existence. Teaching students about the magnificence of African kingdoms such as Mali and Benin first deconstructs the narrative that Black history has always been negative.

This is true, also, of lessons surrounding sexuality in schools. If students only ever learn about the LGBTQ+ community through lessons centring on challenging homophobia in PSHE, they may inadvertently begin to associate different sexualities with negative experience. Of course, it is important for students to learn how to challenge discrimination, but they should be provided with opportunities to see a range of different families, LGBTQ+ role models and people with different gender identities and the ways in which they are able to thrive. This may be through texts and poems written by LGBTQ+ authors or through exploring the significant contributions of LGBTQ+ individuals throughout history. However, being exposed to people from a range of backgrounds does not always have to occur through the explicit teaching of certain characteristics. For example, Stonewall (2019) advocate for the inclusion of LGBTQ+ families in lesson examples across the range of subjects. In maths, for example, they suggest 'Mark's dads increase his pocket money by 10%. If Mark had £2 before the increase, how much pocket money does he have now?'. These changes are not time-consuming but are wholly significant in weaving diversity across the curriculum.

Acknowledging and appreciating difference

Although changes to policy and curricula are incredibly important, there is potential for the impact of these to be limited if offset by negative communication and daily interactions. Adapting policy through an ED&I lens is essential but we can also strive for belonging through our daily practices (see Chapter 3) and being intentional in creating safer spaces through our language and behaviour (see Chapter 6). One clear way to do this is to either establish and/or refine common school practices so they demonstrate that difference is truly valued, and we share some examples here.

Reasonable adjustments

In Chapter 6, we explore strategies for establishing safer spaces in ED&I training, many of which can be applied to the classroom. However, it is necessary to ensure that school is safe for all members of the school community all year round. We are going to consider this with a focus on staff experience rather than pupils as, even though there is always more that we can do for pupils, current provision through, for example, adaptive teaching, and consistent routines for learning, ensures classrooms are theoretically safer for pupils. This, however, may not be the case for staff.

We outline the legal obligations surrounding reasonable adjustments in Chapter 1. Ensuring reasonable adjustments meet the needs of the individual is complex. Individuals cannot be expected to have complete awareness of how a disability and/or health condition can impact them in the long term because symptoms change, affecting how a person can respond to their planned and unplanned roles and responsibilities in a school setting. For example, a person who is in the early stages of their pregnancy might not realise that they could discuss safety during lesson transition times in narrow school corridors. Consequently, they might not raise this unless the person leading the conversation explicitly raises this as an area to discuss. If HR and line managers have more focused questions linked to school experience, e.g. transitions, assembles, evacuation, how to request help when teaching, room requirements etc., the conversation is more holistic, ensuring more considered reasonable adjustments. This is especially necessary for those new to teaching who may not have the knowledge needed of the workplace that can inform effective reasonable adjustments.

It is important that line managers and HR teams do not assume their expertise extends to complete awareness of which reasonable adjustments would be helpful for every condition, as experiences are not monolithic and are often deeply dependent on the individual. Developing person-centred knowledge here is essential so the person discussing reasonable adjustments with the individual has a more informed stance, but questions should not presume a lived experience. To avoid this, employers should follow an individual's lead and allow them to use their own terms for identification (Cochran, 2024). More open-ended questions are helpful to elicit a response. For example, 'What can we do to ensure you feel supported in...?' or 'Is there anything you would like to share to ensure we can facilitate...?'

Additionally, assumptions should also not be made as to what individuals can and cannot do. For example, assuming that a staff member cannot complete certain tasks may hinder their professional growth opportunities. The very nature of reasonable adjustments means reducing the barriers faced by individuals to ensure they can access the same opportunities as the rest of the school community. Conversations about reasonable adjustments are not isolated conversations. They should be revisited so that adjustments are appropriate, responsive and specific rather than vague.

For reasonable adjustments to be co-constructed, the person seeking the reasonable adjustment needs to engage in self-advocacy. This is challenging, however; if an equitable culture is not yet developed in the school, school systems may be biased towards those who have the confidence and knowledge to ask, rather than being open to all. Moreover, it cannot be assumed that everyone is willing or able to advocate for themselves and engage in help-seeking behaviour (see Chapter 8 for more on self-advocacy). For example, a person is less likely to ask for the help they need if: they have not received it in the past; they have been a victim of gaslighting in the workplace; or if they have internalised prejudice and feel that they are a burden to their peers. Therefore, it cannot be assumed that silence is acceptance, but neither can an adjustment be thrust upon someone.

To begin to cultivate a school culture where those who need reasonable adjustments feel able to honestly talk about their needs, school leaders should make their commitment clear, modelling what it means to show solidarity to staff. It is important that meeting staff and pupils' legal rights – because it is a right, not a privilege – to reasonable adjustments does not later result in bias and all pupils should see such adjustments being made and valued. Being inclusive must involve breaking down barriers that may limit people's confidence in raising awareness to their needs and openness and understanding is essential to this.

School spaces

An ED&I lens can also be applied to the spaces within the school building. It is important to pause and think who can and cannot access the space as their authentic selves. Having an awareness of the protected characteristics helps to ensure we are *responsive* to the needs of all individuals, but we should also be *proactive* in dismantling the barriers that individuals may face. We cannot discuss all areas but here are some examples of how more inclusive school spaces can be created.

Prayer spaces

We know the teacher workforce and student populations are incredibly diverse, and it is likely that school communities will encompass a variety of faiths. With this in mind, it is important to make sure that everyone has a space to pray, should they want to. If the school does not have an extra room that is available immediately, consider which classrooms or offices could be closed off at certain points in the day to allow for prayer. New staff, students and families may not feel comfortable in asking for such provisions and being upfront in outlining these can remove the need for them to do so. However, it is important to avoid making assumption about what people's religions might be and offering them a space that they do not need. By outlining this information to *all* staff, it affords clarity to anyone that may need it.

Women's health

It is important to consider how the environment can be made wholly accessible for teachers and students who menstruate with appreciation of how conditions such as endometriosis can affect menstruation. Teachers, who often have busy schedules with back-to-back classes, need clear mechanisms to leave the classroom if they need to. Ensure there's a straightforward process for them to contact someone and step out if needed. There should also be a clear, confidential system in place for students to access sanitary products without the need to speak to someone they might not feel comfortable approaching. Make sure these provisions are well signposted to ensure students feel supported and respected. Adequate provision should also be in place for breastfeeding mothers so they can breastfeed in a suitable private space rather than a makeshift cupboard.

Creation of safer spaces for specific groups

Here we refer to the provision of safer spaces for LGBTQ+ people through Pride Groups because 'schools still remain spaces of entrenched heteronormativity', leaving many LGBT+ young people vulnerable to increased chances of poor mental health (Bradlow et al., 2017; Just Like Us, 2021; Kosciw et al., 2022 cited in Brett, 2025). These groups tend to run during lunchtimes or after school and they are a safer space for 'LGBT+ students and allies to socialise, learn and access support' (Brett, 2025). We'd urge you to read Brett's article if you are interested in implementing this.

Case Study

Saima Akhtar, Inclusion and **Diversity** Co-ordinator, Cabot Learning Federation

We have established an inclusion group for students, encompassing safer spaces for LGBTQ+ youth and for Black and Brown children, alongside equality councils and social action groups. For our staff, we are developing safer spaces, exemplified by the Global Majority Staff Forum at Bristol Metropolitan Academy. This approach will be expanded throughout the trust to develop additional safer spaces for LGBTQ+ colleagues. We recognised that creating spaces that are for "everyone" does not automatically ensure a sense of belonging or that these communities feel safe and comfortable within them. Therefore, the need for fairness and equity guided this work. Furthermore, we will soon launch a racial literacy reading group online, which will be accessible to all staff across the trust.

Colleagues have reported that access to these spaces and forums has contributed to improved wellbeing, enhanced mental health, and reduced feelings of isolation. In many ways, these spaces serve a similar purpose to supervision in counselling, providing essential support. Students have also shared that these environments help them feel acknowledged and seen and assist them in exploring their own cultural identities and heritage, including gender identity.

Specialist spaces

Based on contextual needs, schools may create specialist spaces to promote belonging for pupils who may feel like they are on the fringes of the school community.

Case Study

Cath Rowell, Director of Inclusion, Archway Learning Trust

We have focused on helping pupils to feel like they are part of the school community by having a real emphasis on culture and belonging. Some specific strategies are to consider how pupils are reintegrated back into the classroom, especially those pupils who have low attendance and behavioural or SEND needs. In some academies we have implemented Triage, which is a space that students are directed to, if they are removed from the classroom, so they can talk to a trusted adult and feel listened to. It is not a punishment, and in this safer space, students have the opportunity to self-regulate and then return to class or a further intervention may be required. Having the right people in this space is essential as is training. In some academies a physical room isn't required for this; however, allowing staff to implement the 'Art of Triage' ensures that there isn't an unnecessary accelerated escalation of sanctions.

We have also worked around the language we use with students, ensuring positivity prevails and in some cases this has seen the introduction of scripts. One example of this is with students who have been absent or who are late to increase feelings of belonging. Hearing "Good morning, it's great to see you. I missed you" rather than "Where have you been?" or "Why are you late?" enables students to feel seen and valued. We will continue to review our approach and adapt it as necessary. At the moment, we are noticing that scripting allows positive language to be the first point of call which students appreciate and respond better too, thus seeing a de-escalation in the allocation of sanctions.

Meaningful celebration of cultural events in school

Stand-alone school-wide celebration events can be subject to criticism. Throughout our experience of working in the ED&I space, we have heard a variety of different opinions as to the impact that such days can have. Some critics believe that limiting cultural celebrations to one specific day or month of the year is tokenistic. In contrast, some proponents see such events as important and necessary acknowledgements of marginalised groups that have been historically overlooked (Stewart, 2021). In reality, understanding the broader school context is crucial before making such judgements.

In schools that have fully embraced an ED&I approach – embedding representation, inclusivity and diversity throughout the curriculum and school culture – cultural events serve as a meaningful enhancement. After all, can there ever be too much celebration of diversity? Even in schools that have yet to implement long-term change, these events can signal a genuine willingness to evolve over time. However, the issue arises when schools limit their commitment to one-off celebrations without any intention of making meaningful structural changes. In such cases, these events risk being perceived as tokenistic; if staff and students do not feel a true sense of belonging, a single day of recognition may do little to create lasting impact.

It is important to avoid being encouraged of dissuaded by the opinions of external audiences here, and listening to the school community is likely to support schools in understanding the best steps forward. Funmi has conducted student voice across a range of schools in different contexts over the past few years. Lots of schools began to arrange 'culture days' on which staff and students have been able to wear outfits or items of clothing that represent their culture. Initially, Funmi was concerned about these events may come across as tokenistic. However, in focus groups that have taken place across an academy trust with 17 different schools, students have almost unanimously named 'culture day' as the most joyous way in which diversity is celebrated.

It is important to take the time to map out a range of celebrations across the year, to ensure a rage of characteristics are represented (consider the questions referenced at the beginning of this chapter – who is included here? Who isn't? And so on). In addition to this, it is important that staff are equipped with the necessary ED&I and racial literacy to deliver content across a range of areas, as well as ensuring that they are aware of the policy or process for responding to prejudicial incidents, should there be a spike during the time at which events are taking place. Here, we will provide some examples of considerations that should be taken into account when celebration days are planned:

- On days that involve pupils being given the option to wear cultural dress, no assumptions should be made about what they might wear. Remember, unconscious biases can lead us to make assumptions based on visible characteristics unless we are intentional in challenging these.

- Staff should be reminded of what microaggressions might look like during events so they are more conscious of the language they use and any prejudicial behaviour they should be more aware of.

- Schools should also consider that, like on other non-uniform days, pupils may not have the means to wear a brand-new outfit to school. Pupils' circumstances should be considered so that no child is excluded.

- Pupils should be made aware of where to report any prejudicial incidents that arise during cultural celebrations. Staff should also be vigilant surrounding these. For example, challenging misogynistic comments during International Women's Day celebrations, or racist comments during South Asian Heritage Month.

- Pupils and staff should be given the option to support in the planning and delivery of celebrations. Those with lived experience may wish to support or may have concerns about hypervisibility. Rather making assumptions, outline options such as: "If you feel passionate about supporting with the event, please let us know" or "If you have any concerns about the day, please do not hesitate to raise them."

Ultimately, there is no fixed interpretation of school-wide celebration events and, as is usually the case, listening to your school community can support in broadening your understanding to plan for success.

Connecting with families

The Education Endowment Foundation (EEF) estimates that parental engagement helps young people make an average of four months' additional progress in education, with higher impact for students with lower prior attainment and younger students. The Institute for Fiscal Studies (IFS) has shown that parents and carers account for almost 50% of the factors that influence the socio-economic gap in education at age 11. Parent Power empowers parents/carers to secure opportunities for their children and support them to achieve their academic potential' (Brilliant Club, 2023).

Many of the practices we have referred to so far are centred on building inclusion for staff and pupils. However, we must also consider inclusion for parents and families with the headteacher acting as a 'community connector' who has "frontline' knowledge' of individual pupils, parents/carers and other community residents (Sim and Major, 2025). If parents and families do not feel as though they have a positive relationship with the school, a huge range of problems could follow. For example, if a pupil witnesses negative interactions between their family members and the school, they may begin to develop a negative perception of their own teachers. Additionally, if a family member feels as though the school is uncommunicative,

Table 4.2 Examples of potential barriers to belonging for parents and families with potential solutions

Potential Barrier	Potential Solution/ Pre-emptive measure
Some parents/families may not be able to read English and may struggle to read school letters that are sent home.	Provide translated copies of school letters in multiple languages. Offer verbal communication through phone calls or voice messages in the family's preferred language.
Single parents may have difficulties in attending parents evening due to working hours or difficulties with childcare. Some parents may need to attend with young children.	Flexibility – proactively arrange telephone or video appointments in place of face to face. Ask if any families need to access a space for breastfeeding or nursing a baby and provide a suitable and accessible space for this.
Families with limited or negative prior experiences of the education system.	Develop opportunities for families to connect with the school – this may be with an academic focus e.g. GCSE information evenings through which the exams and mechanisms for supporting students are explained.

they may be deterred from coming forward for support with issues like prejudicial behaviour experienced by their child, or even safeguarding issues that the school may have been able to support with. Like with all other aspects of ED&I, building a safe space for families requires being intentional in understanding diversity.

Here is an example of community support which builds 'relationships between the school and parents and helps parents to develop peer support networks and opportunities to find out about wider support that's available' (Sim and Major, 2025).

Case Study

Cath Rowell, Director of Inclusion, Archway Learning Trust

Within one of our schools, we have a large Roma population, and we want our Roma families to feel like they are part of the school community, something that they may not have felt before. Through listening to our Roma families, we learnt that they feel the educational environment is daunting and education is not representative of their culture and traditions. To enable our Roma families to understand that we value them as members of our school community, we have put in place several interventions and this work is very much in its infancy. We have held coffee mornings, both in the community and in school, with the aim of seeing more families crossing the school threshold, feeling welcomed and part of the family. The impact so far has been an increase in attendance, increased level of engagements from families, as well as increased engagement from students within the school.

Additionally, having spoken to a wide range of families about the cost-of-living crisis, we have shared a Winter Welfare Checklist and this provides information about the location of foodbanks and how to get financial support. It is available in school receptions so it is accessible to all. We all want to know that we belong and therefore we need to ensure that all of our families feel this way too.

Questions

1. Which policies and practices may need to be adapted with an ED&I lens?
2. How might you begin to break down any barriers that are faced by parents and families?

References

Bravely (2021). *Intent vs. Impact: Closing the Gap*. Available from: https://workbravely.com/blog/diversity-equity-inclusion/closing-the-intent-impact-gap/ [Accessed 9 March 2025].

Brilliant Club (2023). *Parent Power at the Brilliant Club*. Available from: https://thebrilliantclub.org/wp-content/uploads/2023/05/Parent-Power-brochure.pdf [Accessed 9 March 2025].

Brett, A. (2025). Safe Spaces and Beyond: Examining the Role of LGBT+ Pride Groups in Fostering Ontological Security and Allyship within UK Schools. *Bera* [Online]. Available from: https://doi.org/10.1002/berj.4141 [Accessed 19 April 2025].

Cochran, J. (2024). *How to Be More Inclusive of Disabilities in the Workplace*. Available from: https://www.idiversityconsulting.co.uk/2502-2/ [Accessed 8 March 2025].

Department for Education (2025). *Curriculum and Assessment Review: Interim Report*. Available from: https://assets.publishing.service.gov.uk/media/67e6b43596745eff958ca022/Curriculum_and_Assessment_Review_interim_report.pdf [Accessed 19 March 2025].

Equality and Human Rights Commission (2022a). *The Public Sector Equality Duty (PSED) | EHRC*. [Online] Available from: https://www.equalityhumanrights.com/guidance/public-sector-equality-duty-psed [Accessed 8 March 2025].

Equality and Human Rights Commission (2022b). *Preventing Hair Discrimination in Schools*. [Online]. Available from: https://www.equalityhumanrights.com/guidance/public-sector-equality-duty/preventing-hair-discrimination-schools-decision-making-tool [Accessed 8 March 2025].

Joseph-Salisbury, R. (2020). *The Runnymede Trust | Race and Racism in Secondary Schools*. [Online]. Available from: https://www.runnymedetrust.org/publications/race-and-racism-in-secondary-schools [Accessed 21 January 2024].

Kara, B. (2025) *The Diverse Curriculum*. London: Corwin.

Macfarlane, R. (2023). *Unity in Diversity: Achieving Structural Race Equity in Schools*. London: Routledge.

Montgomery, L. (2022). Culture Fit versus Culture Add: Hiring for Growth. *Forbes* [Online]. Available from: https://www.forbes.com/councils/forbeshumanresources council/2022/06/08/culture-fit-versus-culture-add-hiring-for-growth/ [Accessed 8 March 2025].

Show Racism the Red Card (2024). *Education Survey Reveals Alarming Disparity: Incidents of Racism Prevail in Schools while Anti-Racism Training for Educators Lags*. Available from: https://www.theredcard.org/news/education-survey-reveals-alarming-disparity-incidents-of-racism-prevail-in-schools-while-anti-racism-training-for-educators-lags/ [Accessed 8 March 2025].

Sim, A.M. and Major, L.E. (2025). *Heart of the Community: A study of the Reach Foundation's Cradle to Career Partnership*. Available from: https://static1.squarespace.com/static/6633596cd8ba466019733efa/t/6793273e5279b176c53bac69/1737697100459/Heart+of+the+Community+%7C+South-West+Social+Mobility+Commission+%282024%29.pdf [Accessed 19 April 2025].

Stewart, F. (2021). Is Black History Month Enough? *Bett.* [Online]. Available from: https://www.bettshow.com/bett-articles/is-black-history-month-enough [Accessed 8 March 2025].

Stonewall (2019). Creating an LGBTQ+ Inclusive Primary Curriculum. Available from: https://files.stonewall.org.uk/production/files/stw_pearson_creating_an_inclusive_primary_curriculum_2022_1_-_march.pdf?dm=1724230520 [Accessed 8 March 2025].

Tulshyan, R. (2022). *Inclusion on Purpose An Intersectional Approach to Creating a Culture of Belonging at Work*. Cambridge, MA: MIT Press.

Creating an ED&I training curriculum for staff and pupils

What is ED&I training?

ED&I training enables participants to raise awareness of self, develop person-centred knowledge and feel equipped to promote feelings of belonging in both themselves and others. The most impactful ED&I training is context-specific and aligned with ED&I strategic priorities; it responds to the ever-changing current contexts and cohorts of the school and allows pupils to navigate the world beyond the school gates. This may be even more necessary in contexts where there is limited representation of certain characteristics or dominant groups are prevalent e.g. single-sex schools. Such training is less likely to be part of current provision for varying reasons (see Chapters 1 and 2). Although this chapter is focused on designing a specific ED&I curriculum, we know that not all contexts have a specific ED&I lead or dedicated time for ED&I staff training. This chapter can also support readers who hope to apply an ED&I lens to adapt professional development and/or lessons as long as they are aware of the risks of doing this in isolation.

Through diversifying and decolonising the curriculum, and through access to any enrichment or extracurricular activities linked to ED&I, pupils' person-centred knowledge can be developed. Another opportunity is provided through personal development, or equivalent curricula, where pupils can focus in depth on aspects of ED&I. Such training could be part of character education where pupils get the opportunity to 'express their character and build the skills they need for resilience, empathy and employability' (Department for Education, 2019). Research suggests that enabling character traits, such as high self-belief, are 'associated with better performance, more persistence and greater interest in work' (DfE, 2019). Access to such opportunities leads to 'pupils that take part to be highly motivated (OECD Skills Studies, 2015 cited in Department for Education, 2019), report fewer absences (Bavarian et al., 2013 cited in Department for Education, 2019) and have lower levels of emotional distress' (Taylor, Oberle, Durlak, Weissberg, 2017 cited in DfE, 2019).

In England, Personal, Social, Health and Economic (PSHE) education provides an opportunity to educate pupils on ED&I. Most of this content, namely Relationships Education (primary) and Relationships and Sex Education (secondary) was made compulsory in 2020. This content 'must be taught sensitively and inclusively, with respect to the backgrounds and beliefs of pupils and parents' (DfE, 2019). Ofsted have called for all schools to have a 'carefully sequenced RSHE curriculum' (Ofsted, 2012) and a more in-depth focus on ED&I concepts can be provided through any time available for non-statutory PSHE or when PSHE statutory content[1] is taught with a more refined ED&I lens. For example, in PSHE, when instructing pupils about strategies for building resilience (Department for Education, 2021), the teacher could sensitively show an appreciation of the additional layers of resilience a person may need, if they are from a historically marginalised group, due to the increased risk of discrimination either now or later in their lives.

To ensure ED&I training has a positive impact on pupils and safer spaces are created within schools, staff require access to high-quality ED&I training that is a fixed feature of school professional development programmes. This allows ED&I knowledge to be revisited and expanded upon based on changing school contexts. There is perhaps more scope for ED&I staff training as there is less statutory training for teachers; with competing priorities in schools, however, such training can fall to the wayside unless it is incorporated into school self-evaluation or long-term strategic plans (see Chapter 2). Without this, any ED&I training runs the risk of being performative because, without robust organisational support at all levels, it is less likely that any new learning or practices that emerge from training will be embedded.

The amount of time dedicated to ED&I training will vary based on the school's context. Examples of ED&I training for all staff working in schools include:

- A series of shorter training sessions dedicated to developing person-centred knowledge based on characteristics of particular interest to the school due to either their perceived presence or absence in the school and/or local community e.g. certain protected characteristics, socio-economic background, accent etc.

- An external provider delivering a whole staff training on creating safer spaces in school with a focus on effectively managing microaggressions and other prejudicial incidents.

- Compulsory training at the start of the academic year on working in a diverse community with a focus on the characteristics most relevant to the school's specific context.

Examples of ED&I training for pupils include:

- Responsive ED&I education, through a series of assemblies, based on significant events in the world or media that can impact pupils e.g. Trump's stance on ED&I.
- An external provider delivering training on a context-specific ED&I concern e.g. challenging a heteronormative school culture.
- Class teachers adopting an ED&I lens when planning individual lessons as part of a creating a diverse curriculum. For example, a secondary school English teacher sharing inclusive modes of address when teaching letter writing (e.g. Mx) and explaining the importance of this to pupils.

Topics within ED&I training tend to contain more sensitive content so they might provoke a strong emotional response linked to an individual's lived experience, the response of key stakeholders, or contentious local and global figures and events. Staff may have already formed ideas about what ED&I training is, some of which may be based on unconscious and established biases. This means that training often involves a process of unlearning, through which misconceptions are addressed, and systemic issues are explored.

In contrast, pupils are often encountering ED&I concepts for the first time so teachers are presented with a valuable opportunity to introduce inclusive ideas before misconceptions begin to manifest or become embedded. Within the ED&I space, it cannot be assumed that the teacher is the expert and pupils are novices; our lived experiences will affect how much knowledge we have of discrimination. Listening to and learning from pupils is essential to bridge the gap between what is taught and their reality. It requires careful teaching to ensure that biases are not unintentionally transferred to participants. This is all the more significant with children as they inherit biases from the word around them, including from the adults in their lives (Agarwal, 2020). For this reason, any adult delivering learning on such themes must be well-trained.

Who should be trained?

All staff should receive, or be aware of the key messages of, ED&I training so they can reinforce key messages. School-based training often targets pupils first but unless staff feel confident and competent in supporting pupils to talk about ED&I, the impact on pupils is questionable. We recommend referring to the ED&I training cascade model in Chapter 2.

When should training take place?

ED&I training involves a commitment to ongoing and revisiting learning (Baum, 2021; Cumberland et al., 2021 cited in Beijbom, 2022) and it should be built into curriculum plans and professional development programmes to ensure time is protected. Holding spaces minimises the risk of time being taken away. This enables the construction of a realistic ED&I curriculum that supports the school's ED&I strategic outcomes.

For this commitment to be maintained, it must be supported and endorsed by school leadership who should aim to remove or minimise barriers to attendance e.g. offer catch-up training to part-time staff who may miss training if it's their non-working day. Moreover, senior leadership need to go beyond ED&I advocacy and commit to the resources needed for buy-in to be fostered (CIPD, 2019). In schools, this is most often demonstrated by providing realistic gauges of the time needed to embed new practice.

Even if there is dedicated time, the reality is it could be taken away as schools respond to changing contextual priorities. Consequently, continued advocacy and creative thinking is needed so ED&I staff training remains ongoing, albeit in different forms. This could be achieved through the adoption of a more refined ED&I lens with existing training. For example, every year in England, all staff have statutory training on Keeping Children Safe in Education (KCSIE), and specific examples of what prejudice-based and discriminatory bullying look like in the school setting could be shared during this time. This minimises the risk of child-on-child abuse being downplayed by staff or dismissed as 'just banter' (DfE, 2024). Another example includes adopting an ED&I lens with professional development for high-quality teaching. If the training is based on questioning, staff could be asked to reflect on how bias may affect which voices are heard and the helpfulness of psychological safety in a classroom context.

Other alternatives to whole-staff in-person training include:

- Sharing case studies to spotlight common experiences of those from underrepresented groups and explicitly warning staff against assuming homogeneity.
- Responses to FAQs based on a protected characteristic being shared in the staff bulletin.
- Examples of context-specific microaggressions with guidance outlining how teachers could tackle this with pupils (this should be age appropriate).
- Relevant evidence informed literature, videos or podcasts shared with staff.
- The offer of additional training for staff to opt into.

These options won't be accessed by everyone but serve as a reminder that ED&I is still on the agenda and remains, even in a more diluted form, a leadership commitment.

Where should ED&I training take place?

Ideally, ED&I training should take place in person for both staff and pupils, rather than relying on asynchronous training, videos or online training. ED&I is about relationships so social support matters in this space. For larger groups (pupils in assemblies or whole staff training), it is worth thinking about the layout of the room and whether participants need to break out into smaller groups. Discussion is a key part of ED&I training so avoiding participants being seated in rows is advisable. With staff, there is perhaps more scope with different delivery models to make training more accessible. While remote delivery may not lend itself to authentic discussion, it does enable staff to access training who might otherwise not be able to. If remote delivery is the most feasible and accessible option, it's essential to establish strong contracting. It is worth addressing the limitations of the time and location of training to maximise staff attendance: if ED&I training excludes groups, due to time and location, it already undermines the ED&I agenda.

Who should be involved in planning and facilitation?

Here, we assume that there is an ED&I lead within the school who is remunerated accordingly or a member of senior leadership who has ED&I as part of their remit. Whilst the ED&I lead has overall strategic oversight of the ED&I training curriculum, it does not mean that they alone should plan and facilitate training. When ED&I training is developed in consultation with others (e.g. headteachers, those responsible for quality of education, behaviour and attitudes and recruitment etc.) it enables more meaningful and data-led sessions to be developed. Involving others in the process reduces the risk of unconscious bias or self-fulfilling prophecies, where a single perspective shapes policies without sufficient challenge or reflection. The more people engaged in ED&I work, the more likely it is that diverse viewpoints and lived experiences will be considered. To minimise strong challenge and/or reputational risk, key stakeholders should be made aware of any particularly sensitive contents so a pre-emptive, rather than reactive approach, can be engendered.

Effective co-planning and facilitation

When we refer to co-planning, we mean at least two people meeting to plan a training session. Co-planning does not necessarily mean planning a session during an allocated meeting time. It could refer to:

1. Deciding on, and carefully crafting, the aims of the session, including the key concepts to focus on.
2. Dividing the planning based on the aims of the session.
3. One person adding examples to be used as part of the practice part of the session. A diversity of thinking is helpful here so even if you're unable to co-plan, ask trusted colleagues or even student leaders for their feedback.

4. One person acting as a critical friend after the session has been planned and providing feedback and/or making amendments.

5. Reviewing the content and what may be seen as highly provocative and/or divisive (see Chapter 3). This discussion isn't necessarily about removing content. In ED&I training, there will be a level of challenge and discomfort and that is part of the learning, but it is helpful to discuss the rationale for this to decide together on any additional framing or activities that are needed to support sensitive delivery.

There can be real power in the co-planning relationship as it means the ED&I educator is not alone (see Chapter 10). This power comes through dedicating time to understanding one another and this is more important in the ED&I space than in others. Both in the planning and the delivery of ED&I training, there is potential that those involved will reveal aspects of their identity without even intending to. We have already explored, in Chapter 3, how modelling vulnerability can support participants in being open within sessions. It is equally vital in the co-planning process. For example, it might be that one educator holds a characteristic that links to negative historic experiences. If the second educator has an awareness of this, they can take responsibility for conducting the research, and later facilitation, on this specific topic. It is additionally essential that co-planners are receptive to each other's feedback and critique. All of this can be established through the process of contracting (see Chapter 6).

Questions to discuss at the start of the co-planning process might include:

1. How should we work together?

2. Is there anything you need from me so we can work together effectively?

3. What would you like the opportunity to be involved in?

4. What are you worried about with this work?

Considering who will be involved in facilitation is another part of the planning process. When launching an ED&I strategy with staff, trust leaders or headteachers should make explicit their commitment to ED&I through being part of the facilitation team. This makes visible the support from school leadership so participants understand that ED&I is an integral part of school improvement. When deciding on facilitators for future staff training, a diversity of voices promotes the school's ED&I agenda as inclusive of everyone, not certain groups. It is particularly powerful if there are facilitators from 'traditionally dominant organisational groups. For example, senior male managers were viewed as important agents for change in furthering gender equality' (CIPD, 2019). It cannot be denied that there is risk involved with facilitating ED&I training because of the facilitator's visible and/or invisible characteristics and Chapter 10 contains more information about how to protect yourself as an ED&I educator. Teachers will most often facilitate ED&I training for pupils and, to do this effectively, they need to have access to high-quality training where they can raise any concerns, ask questions and be listened to.

Designing the ED&I curriculum

When creating an ED&I training curriculum, we have been influenced by a variety of credible sources, including: texts such as *Inclusion on Purpose* and *Wish We Knew What to Say: Talking with Children About Race*; networks such as Diverse Educators and LinkedIn; and online articles accessed through the Harvard Business Review. Furthermore, we have drawn on our lived experience as people from underrepresented groups, based on intersecting protected characteristics, and learning from our networks to consider what concepts need to be understood for belonging to occur. This has enabled us to identify threshold concepts (see Chapter 3) to allow all participants to be provided with foundational understanding before moving on to strategies for change.

Given the wealth of powerful concepts in the ED&I space and time constraints in schools, context-specific prioritisation is needed. This should be based on: the school's context, vision and values; learning from the school community; the school improvement plan; and the time and resources available. It should also allow for responsive content based on the ever-evolving ED&I space. While we cannot provide readers with a set ED&I curriculum (because it would lack context-specificity), we are firm believers that any ED&I training should begin with raising self-awareness (see Chapter 3).

The way in which ED&I training is advertised could influence how much people are invested in it before it even begins. The titles of the training we will share are suggestions, and we recommend adapting them to meet the needs of those within your school community.

Table 5.1 Examples of ED&I training content for all staff

Training	Concepts
Raising self-awareness	Lived experience, identity and intersectionality
Understanding the lived experience of those from underrepresented groups	Bias and discrimination, identity, lived experience
Understanding intent and impact – managing microaggressions and other forms of discrimination	Unconscious bias, microaggressions, lived experience
Developing ED&I literacy	Person-centred knowledge
Confronting your own privilege to create a more equitable culture	Privilege, equity

(Continued)

Table 5.1 (Continued)

Training	Concepts
Creating psychological safety in the classroom*	Psychological safety
Creating safer spaces in schools	Lived experience, microaggressions
Responsive training based on the school context e.g. tackling misogyny/homophobia/ableism	Lived experience, microaggressions, discrimination
Creating a diverse curriculum (with a focus on one characteristic initially)[a]	Diversity, identity, stereotypes
Understanding and demonstrating solidarity[b]	Bias, solidarity
Developing self-advocacy in pupils.	Bias, advocacy

a Denotes the sessions not applicable for non-teaching staff.
b Dr Muna Abdi provides a compelling argument to promote the use of 'solidarity' over 'allyship' (Abdi, n.d.).

Table 5.2 Examples of ED&I training content for pupils

Training	Concepts
Who am I? Understanding my identity	Identity, protected characteristics, lived experience, intersectionality
Understanding different experiences within our school community	Person-centred knowledge
Understanding bias, where it comes from and its impact on ourselves and others	Unconscious bias, microaggressions
How to be an upstander and show solidarity	Intent, impact, solidarity
The importance of self-advocacy	Unconscious bias, advocacy
Responsive training based on the school context e.g. tackling misogyny/homophobia/ableism	Lived experience, identity, person-centred knowledge

Please note that the ED&I curriculum for pupils must be age-appropriate and sensitive to individual needs as well as any feedback from families. This content is likely to be part of the PSHE curriculum so the ED&I educator must discuss where there will be more central input with senior leadership. For example, those with expertise in ED&I might support the PSHE lead or class teacher when reviewing a lesson focusing on stereotypes so there is consideration of: reducing the risk of hypervisibility; the inclusion of a perspective-taking approach relevant for the school community; examples that take into account common experiences those from historically represented groups might encounter (e.g. based on someone's skin colour, there might be assumptions of someone's country of origin); and tangible ways to show respectful curiosity.

Example ED&I training curriculum during an academic year

In Chapter 2, we shared an implementation plan with the outcome of ensuring:

> pupils feel safe in school and feel able to speak-out about prejudicial incidents because they know it will be 'dealt with quickly, consistently and effectively whenever they occur.'
>
> (Ofsted, 2024)

We will now share an example ED&I training curriculum linked to this which has been crafted based on a school's context-specific priorities. In this example, training will take place over two academic years as time has been set aside for this in the professional development calendar and during PSHE and RSHE. It is supported through intersession work and school leadership are committed to revisiting the training in subsequent years, in a condensed form, once it is embedded. Undoubtedly, this plan is based on strong leadership commitment to ED&I and we are aware that such a plan cannot be replicated in its entirety in all contexts. We hope it will demonstrate the ED&I cascade model and how content could be sequenced so readers can consider the extent to which such an approach can be used in their specific school context.

Table 5.3 An example of an ED&I training curriculum linked to the implementation plan in Chapter 2

Aims	Brief outline of training	Time needed for training	Participants	When?
To support participants to raise awareness of self and others.	Participants reflect on their visible and invisible characteristics and the impact of this on their lived experience. Time is provided to centre the voices and experiences of those impacted by inequality within the school community with a focus on prejudicial incidents. It acts as a call to action so participants recognise the significance of ED&I beyond abstract principles.	2 hours	All staff	September

(Continued)

Table 5.3 (Continued)

Aims	Brief outline of training	Time needed for training	Participants	When?
To support participants to understand: • What unconscious bias is and how it manifests itself in the school setting. • Understand how to tackle prejudicial incidents (policy and practice).	Participants develop a shared understanding of unconscious bias, microaggressions, overt discrimination and hate crime using any context-specific examples available. The prejudicial incidents draft policy is shared with the opportunity for reflection and discussion. This training acts as a rehearsal for training for all staff where these participants will co-facilitate and work with specific groups.	2 hours	Senior leaders and pastoral leads	December
To support participants to understand: • What unconscious bias is and how it manifests itself in the school setting. • Understand how to tackle prejudicial incidents (policy and practice).	Participants receive the same training as senior leadership with the final prejudicial incidents policy being shared. See a more detailed outline using the IDEALS framework at the end of this chapter.	2 hours	Train all staff	Training day in January
To support participants to: • Understand what an ED&I lens is. • Review and make changes to existing PSHE long term plans with an ED&I lens.	Participants understand how to review the PSHE and RSHE curriculum with an ED&I lens to look for opportunities to raise awareness of prejudice and discrimination. Staff should understand what the school deems as age-appropriate and how more contentious content can be addressed as well as avoiding assumptions of homogeneity i.e. not all people who share a characteristic will experience discrimination.	1 hour, 30 minutes	Personal development leads and any other staff involved in planning PSHE and RSHE.	January to July with the new content to be taught from the summer term (subject to change if time cannot be provided for curricula changes).

(Continued)

Table 5.3 (Continued)

Aims	Brief outline of training	Time needed for training	Participants	When?
To support participants to: • Understand what an ED&I lens is. • Use an ED&I lens to review and make changes to existing curricula long term plans.	Curricula plans are reviewed to explore opportunities to explicitly discuss prejudice and discrimination linked to the subject and how such prejudice and discrimination was addressed (negative and positive experiences)	1 hour	All teaching staff and learning support assistants	Training day in September the following academic year with adapted curricula plans to be taught from January (subject to change if time cannot be provided for curricula changes).
To support pupils to: • Understand the difference between 'banter' and discrimination. • To understand the impact of discrimination on those involved.	This raises awareness of self and develops person-centred knowledge with a focus on understanding bias, where it comes from and its impact on ourselves and others. It needs to be age appropriate and take into account any individual needs. See the more detailed outline using the IDEALS framework at the end of this chapter.		All pupils	September
To support pupils to: • Understand the importance of connection. • Know who they can talk to if they need help. • Know how to ask for help from a trusted adult.	Pupils understand the importance of speaking up, seeking help and self-advocacy. The prejudicial incidents policy is shared as well as information about how to access safer spaces. The content and concepts covered need to be age appropriate and take into account any individual needs.	1 hour	All pupils	January

(Continued)

Table 5.3 (Continued)

Aims	Brief outline of training	Time needed for training	Participants	When?
To support pupils to: • Understand the importance of solidarity • Understand how to show solidarity to those in our school community.	Revisit learning from the previous session and pupils are given specific tools to show them how to be an upstander and show solidarity to those from underrepresented groups.		All pupils	September next academic year

A note on responsive training

Time should be made available for any responsive training for staff and/or pupils e.g. a specific focus on a characteristic may be needed if there are growing concerns about this in the school. Additionally, ED&I educators need to respond to any national or global events or media stories which will have particular significance for the school community and plan a response. Indifference or lack of acknowledgment belie a true commitment to ED&I. This does not necessarily mean in-person training. It could be through:

- Sharing Frequently Asked Questions so staff feel comfortable with knowing what to say and what not to say.
- Sharing global scripting so staff know how to talk about an event with sensitivity.
- Sending an email to staff or sharing messages with pupils in assemblies that show compassion, and address misinformation and misconceptions, whilst maintaining political neutrality.

ED&I and effective professional development

Admittedly, when we first began planning ED&I training for staff, we grappled with knowing what ED&I concepts to include and how to sequence training. Our choices were based on trial and error and intuition rather than evidence. To help us to share the essential components of ED&I training, we have drawn on the Effective Professional Development Guidance Report as a steer (Collin and Smith, 2021). The Effective Professional Development Guidance Report discusses mechanisms (evidence-informed 'core building blocks' of the type of professional development in place) and there are 14 mechanisms that belong to 4 groups: building knowledge; motivating teachers; developing teaching techniques; and embedding practice (Collin and Smith, 2021). We will focus primarily on the first three groups and explain what these mechanisms look like within ED&I training. Chapter 9 discusses the final group of mechanisms. This is in a separate chapter because ensuring practice is embedded can be the most challenging part of ED&I training. If you require more information about each mechanism, please refer to the Effective Professional Development Guidance Report (Collin and Smith, 2021).

This section is most appropriate for professional development for staff, but many of these mechanisms are very much relevant for pupils.

Building knowledge

The first group of mechanisms contribute to building knowledge and this refers to how the knowledge is structured and built across training (Collin and Smith, 2021).

Managing cognitive load

To achieve the necessary balance between instruction, reflection and discussion in the ED&I space, it is important to ask, "What must first be taught in order for X to be wholly understood?" This then allows the ED&I educator to prioritise concepts so training is not overburdened with jargon. By centring training on one or two concepts, cognitive overload can be reduced or it might be that, for younger pupils, concepts are not shared. It is impossible to address all protected characteristics meaningfully within training or explore associated concepts in relation to protected characteristics e.g. colourism and race. Transparency is needed to avoid participants wondering why certain content is omitted. We have already stressed the importance of context-specific prioritisation based on the ED&I concepts selected; this not only minimises cognitive load, but also ensures there is time to meaningfully engage in reflection and discussion.

ED&I jargon can be daunting and highly provocative (see Chapter 3 where we explore the concept and framing of privilege). Consequently, there is more of an emotional load attached to ED&I training and this can then impact working memory performance. Knowing that emotional response needs to be managed enables cognitive load to then be managed more effectively (see Chapter 6).

Other ways to manage cognitive overload include:

- Focusing on one key concept or topic in a session and briefly touching on another concept but not foregrounding it.

- Using a similar structure of reflection, discussion and practice (see the IDEALS framework towards the end of the chapter) because if participants know what is expected of them during training, working memory is not overburdened.

- Creating an ED&I glossary and asking participants to read selected definitions with context specific examples.

Revisiting learning

Revisiting learning can be difficult due to time constraints. Different forms of retrieval are already known to teachers so we are going to focus more on how learning can be revisited outside of ED&I training so that learning is reinforced rather than lost.

> **Case study**
>
> Catherine Sykes and Rooda Hassan, Associate Assistant Principals, Chorus Education Trust, share how they have encouraged staff to revisit learning.
>
> Our ED&I training began with a focus on anti-racism during whole-staff training at the beginning of the academic year and this focus is reflective of our school context and the national educational landscape in relation to race. In the training, we defined anti-racism, provided examples of what it looks like in practice and shared strategies to equip teachers with the tools to tackle this.
>
> It was particularly powerful to hear from a former pupil who shared how some of the things that had been done (with the best of intentions) may not always have had the intended impact and how we can start to change this. The learning from this two-hour session was then reinforced and developed in weekly shorter training sessions as part of professional learning briefings.
>
> Training to staff was delivered alongside assemblies to pupils on topics such as: race, microaggressions (and how to deal with them), Ramadan, and diversity through storytelling. ED&I training is also part of new staff induction, with training included for trainee teachers. It's had significant impact with staff commenting on the commitment of the school to ED&I as well as how much they have valued learning about the lived experience of pupils. It's strengthening relationships between staff and pupils from the global majority. For example, a pupil was made to feel he didn't have to change his name to make it easier for others to pronounce. His teacher, by having a conversation about this, showed they valued him being his authentic self and that they needed to learn the pronunciation rather than a pupil change who they are. By creating space for these conversations in training, it's making a difference to teacher confidence with having these necessary conversations.

Other ways to revisit learning include

- Sharing linked materials with participants e.g. a podcast or a short article to develop person-centred knowledge. For example, if training focuses on race, videos inspired by Kenneth and Mamie Clark's 'Doll Test' will allow participants to understand the effects of racism, or a video, such as Pantene's 'Sorry, Not Sorry' advert, allows participants to reflect on gendered use of language and understand the need for self-advocacy. Similarly, Norwich City's Football Club's powerful video 'Check in on those around you' raises awareness of the importance of speaking out and mental health. This could be enhanced with a short reflection task that will then be revisited during training.

- Completing a questionnaire to engage in self-reflection e.g. Harvard's Implicit Association Test, privilege tests. Please be aware that such tools have benefits as well as limitations and the facilitator should be transparent about this with participants.

- Ensuring the ED&I curriculum is a spiral curriculum so key concepts are revisited and, for pupils, understanding is developed in an age-appropriate way.

Motivating teachers

Once teachers and pupils have gained the required knowledge and understanding of the threshold concept, they need to be sufficiently 'motivated so they act upon that knowledge' (Collin and Smith, 2021). Maximising motivation during ED&I training is essential as not everyone within the school community will welcome such training. Research indicates that mandatory training can have the opposite of the intended effect by provoking resistance and frustration in employees (Chow et al., 2021 cited in Beijbom, 2022) or by being seen as overly didactic (Dobbin and Kalev, 2016 cited in CIPD, 2019). In schools, this training has to be compulsory as, without consistency across the school, the impact will be limited. Therefore, consideration of motivation is essential so all stakeholders buy in to ED&I.

Presenting information from a credible source

The Education Endowment Foundation (EEF) guidance report states that, to develop motivation, content should be provided from 'trusted sources (such as EEF guidance reports, published trials of interventions, or other evidence brokers)' (Collin and Smith, 2021). Quantitative datasets can provide the necessary sway for some participants who respond to this more than qualitative data. The National Foundation for Educational Research (NFER) Racial Equality in the Teacher Workforce (2022) research report has been an influential source of evidence for us during training as it provides comprehensive data on career progression in England based on race. Nonetheless, the availability of such data is limited and does not exist for certain protected characteristics e.g. disability. During training, it is helpful for the facilitator to be honest and open about any data gaps so participants are aware that there has not been a deliberate omission.

If the required quantitative data is not available, an evidence-informed response can still be provided through referring to literature reviews, articles, blogs and books outside of education. Whilst we appreciate the merits of these forms of evidence, acknowledgement is needed of the gaps existing in 'research opportunities, publishing, academic promotions, and speakers at conferences' with Boghdady asserting that this is due to systemic bias as a result of: 'lack of role models, cultural and structural barriers, as well as the lack of support systems' (Boghdady, 2025). In consequence, academically recognised sources may not always be representative and such omissions again should be recognised.

Even if representative research is used, we would strongly recommend that ED&I educators draw on the lived experience of those from the school community as there is no source more credible than this. Through our experience, we have found that sharing real-life experiences deeply resonates with participants. This approach humanises the sessions, making them more impactful than simply presenting national statistics. Examples drawn from the school or trust community could be used to inform a 'perspective-taking' approach, which is based on the idea that through 'walking in someone else's shoes' enables individuals to understand different viewpoints and lessen bias through contact between groups (Dobbin and Kalev, 2016 cited in CIPD, 2019). This can generate more buy-in and have a greater impact on behavioural change (CIPD, 2019). ED&I educators may wonder how they can collate relevant examples if the school or trust they work in is not diverse. Here, consideration of visible and invisible characteristics is needed and a shared understanding of diversity: it's not just about race and gender. As discussed in Chapter 2, the beginning of any ED&I intervention begins with listening and learning from the school community and, if this data provides limited representation, draw on wider contexts and literature.

To share the lived experience of the school community, the ED&I educator could: quote someone (with permission or by providing anonymity); produce a graph or chart sharing context-specific data; or include a speaker or panel of speakers from the school community who feel comfortable sharing their lived experiences. These examples could form the basis of an activity to develop understanding of a topic or threshold concept, like the privilege case study in Chapter 3, which could also be described as having a perspective-taking approach. Anecdotal evidence (again, with permission and/or anonymity) has its place in the ED&I space as, when you are leading on this, people see you as a trusted person and share their experiences. By being privy to this, you can then see patterns in the content of what is disclosed and draw on this during the planning process. Finally, when drawing on lived experience, an intersectional framework minimises the effect of facilitator bias and this is why co-planning is desirable.

External speakers may be brought in where there is an absence of the expertise or lived experience to talk about a specific characteristic. This may be more relevant if there are fears over assumptions being made about the facilitator's credibility due to their visible characteristics. Those within our networks, who are leading on ED&I, have shared that, when collaborating with others, they have actively sought out a diversity of voices to counter accusations of affinity bias, especially if they are a woman or a person of colour (as so many ED&I leads are). Understandably, there may not be the required resource or diversity within a school for this to occur so admitting where the facilitator may lack credibility is key, as is considering how other voices can be incorporated into training.

By providing context-specific examples or drawing on wider research, the training becomes less abstract. Participants cannot dismiss the experiences of those from underrepresented groups in the school community or deny the prejudice or discrimination some will face beyond the parameters of the school. Such data centres this work in reality and acts as a call to action.

Providing affirmation and reinforcement after progress

Within the ED&I space, affirmation is essential as there can be a real fear with engaging with new ED&I practices and "getting it wrong". Buy-in may be strengthened through affirmation, particularly for stakeholders who feel there are other more pressing priorities, with research suggesting this is more likely to be middle managers (CIPD, 2019). ED&I leads should think about what is worthy of affirmation as there is a spectrum of behaviours that show progress in this field, especially if we consider the lived experiences of discrimination of those within the school community. A further risk of affirmation in ED&I training is that only dominant groups receive such praise because they are seen as having to change the most. However, no one is immune to unconscious bias: all our interactions benefit from adopting an ED&I lens and for those observing to notice that we are actively cultivating a culture of belonging.

There may be risks involved with progress being highlighted. For example, a senior leader may praise pupils on the 'speak up' culture that is starting to be established but some dominant voices could describe those who do this as 'snitches'. If senior leaders are to support with providing affirmation, they need to be able to notice and name what they are looking for as well as understand potential counter narratives to affirmation and how these can be pre-empted and addressed.

Some examples of affirmation and reinforcement after progress include:

- Spotlighting great practice in a whole-staff meeting, including sharing the impact of this.
- Ensuring any ED&I interventions, following training, are high-profile e.g. the creation of an LGBTQ+ safer space group.
- Noticing when training is being applied, whether that be in or outside the classroom, and praising the member of staff or pupil in private.

- Thanking pupils for demonstrating certain behaviours and sharing the impact so far e.g. the number of pupils who feel they have a trusted member of staff to talk to.

Progress in ED&I can fluctuate and facilitators should be honest about this. ED&I strategies are complex and challenging; therefore, showing appreciation and acknowledgement of such challenge makes a difference both during and after training.

Setting and agreeing on goals

To increase the likelihood of behavioural change, the setting of 'sufficiently difficult goals' makes it more likely that performance will improve (Sims et al., cited in Collin and Smith, 2021). Some examples include:

- At the end of a training session for school leaders on psychological safety, the facilitator could ask participants to plan how they will create psychological safety in their next meeting and then complete a short evaluation after they have conducted the meeting.
- Staff could create their own ED&I coaching goal to bring to their next coaching meeting if a facilitative coaching model is used in the school.
- Pupils could create an ED&I pledge or promise, based on their learning, that they revisit every half term and reflect on any progress made.

Table 5.4 Some examples of techniques to share in training

Training focus	Participants	Technique
Raising self-awareness	Staff and/or pupils	Understand how to talk about visible and invisible characteristics with peers with respectful curiosity
Understanding what the protected characteristics mean in practice	Staff and/or pupils	Notice and name discriminatory behaviour to develop an ED&I lens
Understanding intent and impact – managing microaggressions and other forms of discrimination	All staff	Use of a framework so participants understand how to address prejudicial incidents in school
Creating a safer space during structured discussion	Teachers	Using a Philosophy for Children approach during PSHE and RSHE.

Developing techniques

A criticism of ED&I training can be that it only provides a strong theoretical understanding; therefore, belonging should be codified so it is clear what these practices look like. The techniques shared should equip teachers and pupils with what is needed to change practice and, with staff, develop confidence to address sensitive and complex topics with pupils.

Instruction on how to perform a technique

It can be challenging to provide participants with clear instruction on how to perform techniques to create a culture of belonging. Even if those planning training draw on evidence, there may not always be consensus around the language, framework or approaches used and context further affects what works. For example, if you are talking to a pupil in year 2 about an ableist comment, this conversation will be different to a pupil in year 6 or in secondary school. Whilst training can touch on this, it is not possible to provide a comprehensive list of all possible scenarios and some approaches and frameworks may not apply. This is why planning for ED&I training must be in collaboration with others, so there is a shared agreement of what works in the specific school setting.

Arranging practical social support

'In various contexts, both within and beyond teaching, peer support may support development' (Collin and Smith, 2021) and peers 'are often able to provide emotional or informational assistance' (Sims et al. 2021 cited in Collin and Smith, 2021). We see practical social support in the ED&I space being largely provided by the opportunity to engage in planned discussion, whether that is whole-group discussion or discussion in smaller groups. However, ED&I educators could allow time for spontaneous discussion as this can provide opportunities for participants to show solidarity.

Creating a space for participants to reflect, discuss and learn from each other deepens person-centred knowledge of peers and provides participants with the opportunity to, 'address their biases and prejudice-related attitudes, to work together towards inclusive engagement and sustained respect (Lingras et al., 2021; Sekerka & Yacobian, 2018 cited in Beijbom, 2022). This provides a forum for thoughts to be shared and questions to be asked and answered so sensitive topics are spoken about, not internalised or pushed to the side. If this isn't present, participants may feel pressured to conform to views which may greatly differ to their own, affecting behavioural change, and perhaps reinforcing opinion as fact.

Planned points for reflection and/or discussion work well after the introduction of a threshold concept or contentious content. Discussion, based on a question and answer format, can address misinformation and develop critical thinking which 'involves assessing the validity of arguments, discerning biases, and considering alternative perspectives' (Jones, 2024). Connection is strengthened and this then moves participants out of echo chambers or the realm of their own lived experience. Planning has to make explicit the protocols for any discussion, so that it is managed with sensitivity. For example, during small-group discussion, participants could sweep around the group so everyone has a chance to contribute or individual reflection may be more appropriate, based on class dynamics, with the facilitator responding to what they see in a way that maintains anonymity. Discussion will not provide practical social support if participants interrupt their peers or disparage what they say.

Another approach to structuring discussion for pupils is through a Philosophy for Children (P4C) approach and this allows teachers and pupils to 'think in a caring, collaborative, creative and critical way through philosophical enquiry' (Education Endowment Foundation, 2021). Discussion stems from questions and, for the purpose of ED&I training, could be linked to key ED&I topics. For example, pupils could be presented with the question 'What is belonging?' accompanied by a picture of an all-white male boardroom. Research by the EEF shows that this approach 'encouraged pupils to share opinions in a non-judgmental way, finding it particularly beneficial for EAL pupils, those who lacked confidence or SEN pupils' (Education Endowment Foundation, 2021). This approach emphasises the group working together and supporting each other towards a common goal – listening and learning as a reciprocal process. In order for a facilitator to be able to do this, training around managing discussion in the ED&I space is needed.

Group size and dynamics will affect whether participants feel they are able to ask honest questions in person, or whether other mechanisms need to be used. The balance between knowing what question are appropriate to ask in public (to address misinformation and misconceptions) and how to maintain participant safety and safeguarding must be a vital area of consideration during planning. We would recommend sharing examples and non-examples of appropriate questions with pupils. The ED&I educator should provide opportunities for participants to ask questions at key points during the session. With smaller groups e.g. less than 35, this might be through providing time for questions or leaving post-its on tables for participants to write questions on. With larger groups, it might be more feasible for participants to write questions at the end of the session and for these questions to then be answered in future training.

Modelling the technique

Worked examples are a form of modelling and they provide a step-by-step demonstration of a given task, reducing the burden on working memory (Pritchard, 2022). As some ED&I techniques may be around interrupting unconscious bias and/or developing person-centred knowledge, a 'think aloud' process is helpful. A 'think aloud' is when the thought process is narrated as a particular task is undertaken (Mulholland, 2022); this process makes the ED&I lens visible and tangible. For example, a context-specific example might be shared on religious discrimination, the facilitator could use the "think-aloud" process to explain how they notice the problem, the intent and the impact. Research indicates that children and young people may have normalised certain harmful behaviours e.g. sexual harassment (Ofsted, 2012) so context-specific examples allow participants to 'see' acceptable and unacceptable behaviour, widening their ED&I lens beyond their own lived experience and that of loved ones. It is recommended that worked examples are used two or three times if the technique is new to participants (Kalyuga, Chandler, Tuovinen, Sweller, 2001 cited in Pritchard, 2022). The repeated exemplification not only develops understanding of the technique but also reinforces the behaviours needed to promote belonging.

In ED&I training, models provide participants with something observable which is often not seen or spoken about on a day-to-day basis (see several examples of this in Chapter 3). Nevertheless, there are risks with providing models because they could trigger trauma or cause a strong emotional response. For example, if someone models how to address a microaggression, someone who has been the victim of many microaggressions may experience distress as the realistic model reflects their lived experience. For those who may be perpetrators (and no one is immune from being a perpetrator of a microaggression), there may be resistance and denial that such conversations are even required so the model is then rejected. Therefore, models should not only be there to be imitated but also be used as a focus of discussion so participants can discuss any concerns (linked to their intersectional identities and lived experience), potentially improving the model. Multiple models may need to be shared, depending on the technique, to demonstrate respect for individual experiences.

Providing feedback

Within the ED&I space, monitoring may not always occur so feedback may be more likely to be through structured critical self-reflection, essentially feedback to self (see Chapter 3). To raise an individual's awareness of how they respond to prejudicial incidents, researchers have suggested that reflective questions have an emotional base, e.g. how did this experience make you feel (Beijbom, 2022)? Consequently, questions need to be carefully crafted and thoughtfully sequenced. For critical reflection to be meaningful, planned reflection points, e.g. preceding discussion, enable participants to grapple with how the content makes them feel before they hear the responses of their peers.

Rehearsing the technique

This mechanism refers to 'prompt practice and rehearsal of a technique, at least once in a context outside of the classroom, may support teachers in enhancing their skills and embedding habits' (Sims et al., cited in Collin and Smith, 2021). Rehearsal of techniques within the ED&I space may feel daunting due to worries around being perceived negatively. To minimise risk, rehearsal could take the form of scripting. For example, participants write down what they would say and do to act as an upstander and show solidarity if someone is the victim of discrimination in school. Alternatively, participants could respond to hypothetical scenarios e.g. 'What would you do if…?' or deconstruct examples to demonstrate, for example, an understanding of key ED&I threshold concepts or intention and impact. If live rehearsal would be beneficial, consider how feelings of safety could be engendered through providing different options. Options include: watching a rehearsal and providing feedback or rehearsal in a different room.

Embed practice

To effectively embed new ED&I practice, participants must be supported to 'change their behaviour' (Collin and Smith, 2021). Four mechanisms can be used to enable this. We will only focus on one of the mechanisms here and the remaining mechanisms will be explored in Chapter 9 *Actions to take after ED&I training to enable lasting change*.

Prompting action planning

This is where the participant 'plans how they will perform a technique, and their plan includes at least one of the context, frequency, duration, and intensity of the technique'. This makes it more likely that the technique will be used (Collin and Smith, 2021). There should be dedicated time for this within training, but the scope of the action plan will vary based on any monitoring of progress needed after training. Among the examples of action planning for staff are:

- Reviewing a lesson plan with an ED&I lens and adapting content and/or framing so it is more representative.
- Deciding on what aspect of person-centred knowledge requires development and how they plan to build this knowledge.
- Reflecting on prejudicial incidents in a class or interactions in another school space and planning how they will address similar incidents in the future.

Some examples of action planning for pupils include:

- Creating an ED&I promise at the end of training to show a commitment to learning about the experience of others with respectful curiosity.
- Planning what they will say or do to show solidarity if a peer is experiencing discrimination.
- Planning what they will say or do if they experience discrimination.

Planning training

By discussing each mechanism individually and then considering each in relation to ED&I, we are aware that it might be challenging to imagine what an individual ED&I training session could look like. To provide cohesion, we have provided examples of training using the IDEALS framework (which allows at least one mechanism from each group to be addressed allowing for a 'balanced design' and more impact (Collin and Smith, 2021). To create impactful training, the ED&I educator should engage in backwards planning by taking into account the final outcomes for pupils and staff and any associated monitoring. The IDEALS framework could be applied to longer training sessions (1 hour or more). Alternatively, aspects of the IDEALS framework could be applied: in shorter training sessions; across a series of shorter sessions; or through opportunities that arise by adopting an ED&I lens. Bear in mind that more time will be needed if reflection and discussion are key components of the training.

IDEALS framework

Introduce

Data landscape

Explain, include worked examples here

Ask – reflection and discussion

Learn through practice (rehearsal, deconstruction, co-planning, scripting)

Summarise with action planning

A training session for staff

The example in Table 5.5 is based on the ED&I curriculum shared in this chapter and links to the implementation plan in Chapter 2.

Table 5.5 An example of how the IDEALS framework can be used to train staff on unconscious bias and tackling instances of bias

IDEALS	Mechanism	Content
Introduce	Building knowledge	Introduce the concept of microaggressions and explain it in relation to overt discrimination and hate crime.
Data landscape	Motivating participants	Provide context specific examples of microaggressions. Share research to show the impact of microaggressions.
Explain, include examples here		Provide worked examples to allow participants to name the behaviour they are seeing in class and the action required (based on school policy)
		Teachers are provided with a framework to address microaggressions with pupils
Ask – reflection and discussion		In smaller groups, discuss the benefits and limitations of the framework. How could the limitations be minimised? Participants can raise any concerns here.
Learn through practice (rehearsal, deconstruction, co-planning, scripting)	Developing techniques Embedding practice	Independently, teachers script their response based on a hypothetical but common scenario in the school. They then work in smaller groups to share their scripts and make amendments based on peer feedback linked to the framework.
Summarise with action planning	Embedding practice	Teachers reflect on which stage of the process they need to further develop and will share this with their line manager so appropriate support can be given.

Training aims

To support participants to understand:

- What unconscious bias is and how it manifests itself in the school setting.
- How to tackle prejudicial incident (policy and practice).

A training session for pupils

This is based on the ED&I curriculum shared in this chapter and links to the implementation plan in Chapter 2.

Training aims

To support participants to understand:

- The difference between 'banter' and discrimination.
- The impact of discrimination on those involved.

Table 5.6 An example of how the IDEALS framework can be used to train pupils on different forms of discrimination and its impact

IDEALS	Mechanism	Content
Introduce	Building knowledge	Introduce the concept of discrimination and how this can manifest as 'banter'
Data landscape	Motivating participants	Share pastoral data on the number of pupils who have reported a prejudicial incident and any associated national data
Explain, include examples here		Provide context-specific and age-appropriate scenarios that take into account any individual needs. If harmful language is shared, be aware that it may be misused or misunderstood so it is essential to plan and prepare for this.
		Use 'think alouds' to explain how they are forms of discrimination.
		Explain the long-term impact of the behaviour on the individual, the perpetrator and school culture.
Ask – reflection and discussion		Pupils engage in critical self-reflection and answer this question: Did any of the examples stand out more than others? Why?
Learn through practice (rehearsal, deconstruction, co-planning, scripting)	Developing techniques Embedding practice	Pupils are given two more examples and they need to deconstruct them to identify the type of discrimination and explain the impact on the individuals. This is in small groups.
Summarise with action planning	Embedding practice	Pupils are given time to reflect and make a promise to their peers.

Examples of training for staff to support with work on diversifying and decolonising the curriculum

We know a starting point for ED&I work is diversifying and decolonising the curriculum. After the necessary training on developing subject knowledge, staff require training on ensuring participant safety so such work has real resonance with pupils. Indeed, this could be part of a wider strand of ED&I work on creating an inclusive school culture.

Table 5.7 An example of how the IDEALS framework can be used to train staff on diversifying the curriculum

IDEALS	Mechanism	Content
Introduce	Building knowledge	Introduce the concepts of safer spaces and hypervisibility.
		Explain that work on diversifying and decolonising the curriculum requires classrooms to be safer spaces for pupils and staff so hypervisibility is avoided as well performative teaching of ED&I.
Data landscape	Motivating participants	Provide context-specific examples of behavioural and attitudinal challenges when teachers have tried to present content diversifying the curriculum e.g. some pupils making dismissive comments, some pupils pointing to a member of the class who shares the spotlighted protected characteristic.
Explain, include examples here		Explain the importance of pre-empting challenges and how you plan to address this. Provide three worked examples to showcase this.
Ask – reflection and discussion		In small groups, teachers discuss any limitations and ways to minimise the limitations.
Learn through practice (rehearsal, deconstruction, co-planning, scripting)	Developing techniques Embedding practice	Teachers review a lesson plan to think about where there might be challenge from pupils. They plan how they will pre-empt challenges and address them and make the necessary changes to their lesson. They discuss their plans with their group and get practical social support.
Summarise with action planning	Embedding practice	Participants share what further actions and support are needed so they are able to enhance participant safety and share their learning in the next ED&I training session.

What to consider when working with external organisations?

There are many excellent consultants and organisations leading on ED&I work and, understandably, many schools draw on this expertise. For expert help to have lasting impact, training should align with the school's overall strategic ED&I priority. Here are some recommendations to strengthen the collaboration:

- Share your ED&I strategy and where you hope their training will fit into this.
- Discuss the ED&I starting point of the school to enable the facilitator to pitch the training appropriately and address any misconceptions.
- Share the relevant learning from the school community and find out if any further information is needed.
- Ask them how they intend to incorporate any learning from the school community into their training.
- Know which mechanisms you'd like to prioritise during training.
- Ask the facilitator about how they are aiming to create a safer space within training and what data about participants would be helpful. Ask them to confirm their preferred layout for the training room.
- Ask about representation and positive and negative stories to provide balance.

Questions

1. Reflect on any ED&I training you have attended. How have the mechanisms of effective professional development been applied?
2. What do you feel is essential ED&I content for your setting? What data leads you to this conclusion?
3. Which mechanism(s) do you want to build in more effectively into your training? What are you hoping to achieve with this?

Note

1 Most PSHE education became statutory in September 2020 under the Children and Social Work Act. Relationships Education is compulsory in all primary schools and Relationships and Sex Education is compulsory in all secondary schools in England. Health Education (both mental and physical) became statutory from key stages 1 to 4 (PSHE Association, n.d.). At the time of writing, this is subject to change under the Labour government.

References

Abdi, M. (n.d.) *Language Is Important: Why We Are Moving Away from the Terms 'Allyship' and 'Privilege' in Our Work.* Available at: https://ma-consultancy.co.uk/blog/language-is-important-why-we-will-no-longer-use-allyship-and-privilege-in-our-work [Accessed 3 April 2025].

Agarwal, P. (2020). *Sway: Unravelling Unconscious Bias.* London: Bloomsbury Sigma.

Beijbom, M. (2022). *Striving for Equity, Inclusion, and Safer Spaces at Work: A Review of the Literature.* Guelph, ON: Live Work Well Research Centre, University of Guelph.

Boghdady, M. E. (2025). *Equality and diversity in research: building an inclusive future.* Available at: https://bmcresnotes.biomedcentral.com/articles/10.1186/s13104-025-07096-4. [Accessed 22 April 2025].

CIPD (2019). *Diversity Management that Works an Evidence-Based View.* Available at: https://www.cipd.org/globalassets/media/knowledge/knowledge-hub/reports/7926-diversity-and-inclusion-report-revised_tcm18-65334.pdf [Accessed 22 April 2025].

Collin, J., Smith, E. (Education Endowment Foundation) (2021). *Effective Professional Development Guidance Report.* Available at: https://educationendowmentfoundation.org.uk/education-evidence/guidance-reports/effective-professional-development [Accessed 28 March 2025].

Department for Education (2019). *Character Education Framework Guidance.* Available at: https://assets.publishing.service.gov.uk/media/5f20087fe90e07456b18abfc/Character_Education_Framework_Guidance.pdf [Accessed 20 April 2025].

Department for Education (2021). *Relationships Education, Relationships and Sex Education (RSE) and Health Education Statutory Guidance for Governing Bodies, Proprietors, Head Teachers, Principals, Senior Leadership Teams, Teachers.* Available at: https://assets.publishing.service.gov.uk/media/62cea352e90e071e789ea9bf/Relationships_Education_RSE_and_Health_Education.pdf [Accessed 3 April 2025].

Department for Education (2024). *Keeping children safe in education 2024 Statutory Guidance for schools and colleges.* Available at: https://www.gov.uk/government/publications/keeping-children-safe-in-education--2#full-publication-update-history [Accessed 3 April 2025].

Education Endowment Foundation (2021). *Philosophy for Children – Second Trial.* Available at: https://educationendowmentfoundation.org.uk/projects-and-evaluation/projects/philosophy-for-children-effectiveness-trial [Accessed 21 March 2025].

Jones, A. (2024). *Critical Thinking in Schools: Can It Be Taught – And How?* Available at: https://www.sec-ed.co.uk/content/best-practice/critical-thinking-in-schools-can-it-be-taught-and-how [Accessed 6 April 2025].

Mulholland, K. (2022). *EEF Blog: Thinking Aloud to Support Mathematical Problem-Solving.* Available at: https://educationendowmentfoundation.org.uk/news/eef-blog-thinking-aloud-to-support-mathematical-problem-solving [Accessed 7 April 2026].

Ofsted (2012). *Research and Analysis Review of Sexual Abuse in Schools and Colleges.* Available at: https://www.gov.uk/government/publications/review-of-sexual-abuse-in-schools-and-colleges/review-of-sexual-abuse-in-schools-and-colleges [Accessed 6 April 2025].

Ofsted (2024). *School Inspection Handbook.* Available at: https://www.gov.uk/government/publications/school-inspection-handbook-eif/school-inspection-handbook-for-september-2023#evaluating-behaviour-and-attitudes [Accessed 6 April 2025].

Pritchard, B. (2022). *The EEF's Bob Pritchard Introduces the 'FAME' Approach to Maximising the Effectiveness of Worked Examples in Teaching.* Available at: https://educationendowmentfoundation.org.uk/news/eef-blog-working-with-worked-examples-simple-techniques-to-enhance-their-effectiveness [Accessed 7 April 2025].

PSHE Association (n.d.) *What Is PSHE Education?* Available at: https://pshe-association.org.uk/what-is-pshe-education#:~:text=Do%20schools%20have%20to%20teach,Education%20in%20all%20secondary%20schools [Accessed 2 April 2025].

Creating a safer space during ED&I training

What is a safer space?

The concept of safe spaces originates from 'the LGBTQ+ community's efforts to establish separate spaces in society in which members could be free to be themselves without judgement' (Bairstow, 2007 cited in Beijbom, 2022) and this has since been expanded and adopted by different groups and organisations (Beijbom, 2022). In these spaces, those from historically marginalised groups feel more able to be their whole self because they are at less risk of emotional or physical harm or discrimination. At this point, we feel it would be helpful to provide an example of what an unsafe space might look like because it is not only marked by verbal abuse or the threat of or acts of violence. Natasha has attended training with several organisations within the education sector where she has been the only person of colour in the room. For Natasha, like many from historically marginalised groups, this hypervisibility (see Chapter 10) can cause unease, thereby affecting personal and professional behaviours e.g. a person may be in a state of hypervigilance or it might hinder a person from fully participating.

Rather than 'safe spaces', we have decided to refer to 'safer spaces' as a result of Beijbom's comprehensive literature review (Beijbom, 2022). If a space is labelled as safe, it can give participants a false sense of security (Wallian-Ruschman and Patka, 2016 cited in Beijbom, 2022) and leaders cannot assume what 'safe' looks like for all participants (Page et al., 2021 cited in Beijbom, 2022). Beijbom (2022) points out that:

> For those who hold historically privileged identities, professional contexts – often marked by norms associated with White heterosexual masculinity – have likely been experienced as safe spaces all along.

The strategies shared in this chapter seek to create a psychologically safer training space for all participants. Some of the strategies might be more suitable for staff or for pupils so please consider the audience you have in mind when reading the chapter. For strategies on prioritising learner safety through planning, refer to Chapter 4.

Why is it important to create a safer space during ED&I training?

Striving to create a safer space, whether the training is aimed at pupils or staff, is essential because it:

- Demonstrates that lived experience is valued, through a consideration of intersectional identities, the specific school setting and the wider community.
- Promotes a speak-up culture where participants feel able to be vulnerable, ask questions and seek help, if needed.
- Shows a commitment to seeing and hearing all individuals and respecting different lived experiences.
- Allows the facilitator to sensitively balance representation and hypervisibility so attempts to be more inclusive do not unintentionally place some participants under the spotlight.
- Normalises vulnerability, empathy and compassion rather than other more toxic traits.
- Ensures there is a space where people are given the time to reflect and discuss and so avoid echo chambers.

We recognise that this is ambitious, perhaps seemingly impossible, as feelings of safety within school and society are not always the reality, especially for those from underrepresented groups. For this to occur, it requires conscious and consistent cultivation as participants need to feel a safer space exists not only in one room but in the rest of the school. It is worth mentioning that this 'does not necessarily refer to an environment without discomfort, struggle, or pain, and confronting issues that make one uncomfortable can be essential for learning and growth' (Holley & Steiner, 2015 cited in Beijbom, 2022).

Psychological safety and avoiding a dangerous culture of silence

When considering how to create safer spaces, psychological safety is a key threshold concept. The construct of psychological safety was first introduced in 1965 by Edgar Schein and Warren Bennis (Wietrak and Gifford, 2024). Professor Amy Edmondson (cited in Sutherland, 2025) coined the phrase 'team psychological safety' in the 1990s and it is a belief shared by all members of a team that:

> It's okay to take risks, to express their ideas and concerns, to speak up with questions, and to admit mistakes – all without fear of negative consequences. As Edmondson puts it 'it's felt permission for candour.'

There can be the misconception that psychological safety allows individuals to share whatever they are thinking but this is not the case as true psychological safety 'thrives in an environment of mutual respect' (Edmondson, 2019). Moreover, psychological safety is not synonymous with being nice; it is about 'productive conflict so as to learn from different points of view' (Edmondson, 2019).

In our imagining of the safer space in ED&I training (whether it is a dedicated ED&I training session or an opportunity to adopt an ED&I lens), we want participants to be able to share their thoughts and lived experience in a way they feel most comfortable with because, for those from underrepresented groups, 'to be seen and heard is transformational and healing' (Shah, 2022). We want participants to feel they will be given the benefit of the doubt when they ask questions or express their viewpoint, whether that is in private or public. We want to welcome a diversity of voices to ensure ED&I interventions are relevant for the school community. Ultimately, we want to avoid a culture of silence which is a 'dangerous culture' (Edmondson, 2019).

In a group setting, silence might be used as a response so people avoid: being seen in a bad light; embarrassing or upsetting someone; feeling that their response will be dismissed; being labelled negatively and to avoid the fear of damaging working relationships (Milliken et al., 2003 cited in Edmondson, 2019). Edmondson further comments that many have simply inherited beliefs from their earliest years of schooling or training so keep quiet as a safety mechanism which is 'instinctive' and offers 'self-protection benefits' which are 'immediate and certain' (Edmondson, 2019). This is more likely to be the case for those from historically marginalised groups who have experienced frequent prejudice and discrimination; it may be safer to avoid being in the spotlight to minimise any unwanted scrutiny.

In addition, there may be the need to manage the risk of speaking out because of how those from underrepresented groups are perceived and they then have to navigate these preconceived stereotypes (Tulshyan, 2022). For example, women may fear being seen as aggressive or unlikeable if they talk too much (Agarwal, 2020). Speaking out, especially for pupils, may pose real risks, which is why training must be part of a wider strategy and not stand alone. As an ED&I educator, understanding why participants may not want to contribute means that, when planning, thought can be given to how to alleviate fears.

What barriers might participants encounter during training?

Being aware of different responses to ED&I training is helpful as it ensures, within your context, you consider possible challenges to participant safety and how safer spaces can be created with intention and sensitivity. As well as silence, here are more examples of barriers to learning and unlearning:

- The participant experiences strong emotions, such as shock, guilt, sadness, or shame, and this stems from raising awareness of the lived experience of those from underrepresented groups and their role in relation to this.

- The participant is emotionally drained after training as they are not used to hearing people talk about their lived experience with such honesty in a school environment.
- The participant is not comfortable with revealing aspects of their whole self and may feel such disclosure is not suitable in a professional environment.
- Participants may see it as part of a 'woke' agenda, driven by 'snowflakes', and not buy into training.
- Participants may feel that their view is correct and refuse to engage in alternative ways of thinking.
- Participants may feel that they already have developed awareness of the concepts being discussed and may tune out of the training as result.

How can you create a safer space in training?

Respond to the needs of participants from the outset

Literature about safer spaces highlights that all equity efforts are most effective when they start by responding to the experiences of the most marginalised (Wong, 2019 cited in Beijbom, 2022). As an ED&I educator, you act as an advocate for those from historically marginalised groups and this is not only based on the content of your training but how individuals from these groups feel in your training session. If there isn't intentional consideration of the needs of underrepresented groups, the comfort of dominant groups is prioritised when, the reality is, those from historically marginalised groups may be more at risk.

Even with the best intentions, the facilitator may not be able to support those from historically marginalised groups if their lived experience means they lack awareness of certain experiences or they are influenced by unconscious bias. They should be mindful of who they might interact with the most; how they respond to different individuals; whose experiences they might show the most empathy for; who they may be more likely to interrupt and unplanned examples they might share with the group. For example, Natasha is a Brown woman and during training aimed at the global majority, she intentionally included examples linked to colourism and the challenges faced by individuals who are white passing, even though she does not have direct experience of this. Through reading and listening to participants, Natasha realised where she needed to raise awareness. The intention here was not to spotlight participants (and facilitators should actively avoid doing this unless the individual comes forward) but to demonstrate awareness of intersectionality and deliberately avoid assumptions of homogeneity so people felt seen and heard as their unique selves. An ongoing commitment to raising awareness is needed by all ED&I educators.

Where there are those from historically marginalised groups in ED&I training, and especially training where the protected characteristic they possess is the focus, the ED&I educator needs to consider the concept of hypervisibility and how this might affect personal and professional behaviours. For example, during Black History Month, the only two Black pupils in a class might smirk at each other when an inspirational Black figure is shared. In this instance, an ED&I educator would not draw attention to this; rather, they may discuss this with the pupils in private afterwards so they can learn why this behaviour has been demonstrated and consider what needs to change to prevent this in the future. The ED&I educator also needs to be aware of tokenising those from underrepresented groups and seeing these participants as subject matter experts. During her time at school, Funmi was pinpointed by teachers to provide examples and experiences linked to what was described as 'African culture'. Being unable to answer these questions led to feelings of discomfort and added to Funmi's struggles with her identity. Due to intersectionality and the context people find themselves in, the lived experience of those who share an underrepresented characteristic greatly differs, as does their response to ED&I work.

Ensuring participants are correctly named is another area that requires ED&I educators to act with intention so they reduce the margin of error when pronouncing names or distributing personalised materials. With personalised materials, where possible, ensure names are exported from school management systems and ask someone to double check the spelling of names. Be aware that school management systems may not include a person's preferred name or all the information you need, e.g. preferred pronouns, so alternative ways to gather this information will need to be considered. It is also necessary to cast a critical eye over such data as it may contain omissions (if people do not feel comfortable disclosing aspects of their identity) or it may not reflect the person's identity e.g. if they are questioning their gender identity. If a register needs to be taken, participants should be given explicit permission to correct any mispronunciation of their name or share their preferred name. By doing this, the ED&I educator is showing that this matters and that it is their role to get it right so the person feels seen through their lens, not whatever makes it easier for the facilitator.

The ED&I educator should use participant data to decide whether group composition is conducive to feelings of safety or whether new groups could be formed based on available resources and the feasibility of making changes. Seating plans could be a helpful tool for enabling a safer space and promoting a diversity of voices. However, seating plans require the facilitator, or the person creating the seating plan, to know participants well and understand group dynamics. Creating a seating plan can be like solving a Rubix cube and, within the ED&I space, there is an additional layer of complexity. Some characteristics are hidden or still being questioned, and you may not be privy to this information, so seating plans could hinder safety despite the facilitator's best intentions. There is no easy solution to remedy this other than the facilitator knowing to be vigilant to, and responsive to, the social and emotional needs of participants during training. If participants are known to the facilitator, they should think about group dynamics, especially dominant voices and potentially whose comfort is prioritised, knowingly or unknowingly. As a result of this, the facilitator can intentionally put in place inclusive practices to manage group interactions e.g. clear protocols for asking and answering questions; for smaller groups, participants sweep around the group so everyone is heard or more frequent revisiting of contracting.

For some ED&I training, it might be helpful to separate groups based on specific characteristics e.g. a women's network in a school. This enables participants to feel more comfortable with sharing their experiences and asking questions. However, such demarcation may cause division within the school community or put individuals with invisible characteristics at risk. For example, when making decisions based on perceived gender, there is a strong risk of alienating individuals that identify as non-binary. To overcome this, it is essential to provide opportunities for individuals to provide their own necessary context. This might involve one-to-one conversations if the person is known or, alternatively, giving advance notice of training so there is an opportunity for concerns to be raised and solutions discussed.

Pinkett mentions how prejudice and discrimination may be seen as a social bonding tool in all male environments e.g. stag dos. Whilst an individual may not engage in such behaviour when alone, in a group, they may be more likely to as there may be more risks involved in calling out such behaviour (Pinkett, 2024). Therefore, in single-sex groups, there needs to be consideration of what dominant behaviours might be demonstrated, even if contracting is in place, and how to ensure there is participant and facilitator safety. This may be through ensuring there are two facilitators (including one with a more senior role), having smaller groups and/or a seating plan. We recognise that time and resource, as always, is the challenge but ED&I training cannot promote belonging if some individuals feel threatened or intimidated.

Providing for different access needs shows a visible commitment to belonging. This might be easier to do with pupils than with staff who may not disclose their access needs for fear of the stigma attached to it, hypervisibility or being perceived as a burden to others. Some examples of how accessibility could be provided in training are:

- Ensuring modes of delivery are accessible e.g. font size and colour, subtitles on videos.
- Providing a quiet space for participants to go to if needed.
- Thinking about whether videos or images are really needed and whether the learning benefits are worth any harm they could cause.
- Ensuring historical or cultural references, business jargon, concepts, etc. are appropriately explained rather than assuming all participants have a shared understanding.
- Recognising that some techniques might not work for some individuals and adapting how you introduce strategies to take this into account.

- Ensuring an individual is seated in a place in the room where they feel most comfortable e.g. if content could be triggering, they may prefer to be sat closer to the exit so they can leave the room discretely.

Providing staff with the opportunity to share any access needs and saying in person why accessibility disclosure needs matter will demonstrate an authentic commitment to ED&I; it is being practised rather than just being words on a PowerPoint slide.

Engage in contracting

One person alone cannot decide on what a safer space looks and/or feels like for others so training needs to facilitate the means through which participants can share what a safer space looks and feels like for them (Bairstow, 2007; Linder and Rodriguez, 2012; Page et al., 2021 cited in Beijbom, 2022). In order to do this, contracting is needed. Contracting is a coaching tool and can be defined as 'an explicit agreement of what the consultant and client expect from each other and how they are going to work together.' (Block, 2000 cited in Bennett, 2008). Within the ED&I training space, this means dedicating time at the beginning of training to contract (initially 5 to 10 minutes) so participants:

- Have a brief overview of the content of the session as well as how it links to the wider strategy or school policy.
- Know what to expect in training (e.g. a strong emotional response, reflection, discussion and deliberate practice).
- Understand the expectations of language and behaviours needed from the facilitator and the participants to engender psychological safety e.g. a commitment to respectful curiosity.

To enable this, contracting could stem from a discussion of participants' fears in this space, what they feel could challenge them and consideration of the behaviours needed that would facilitate learning and mitigate risk. How a group engages in contracting will vary based on group size. Smaller groups could contract together while larger groups may work from a suggested list of contracting ideas and amend it based on their needs. Some may argue that contracting silences participants who may not share the same views as the facilitator but, if done effectively, it is inviting everyone to have a voice as long as comments and/or questions are aligned with the co-constructed contracting behaviours, safeguarding and school policies. Contracting is not an isolated activity, it is a 'complex human interactive process requiring sensitivity, skill and flexibility' (Rothwell and Sullivan, 2005 cited in Bennett, 2008). Therefore, contracting should be revisited (e.g. for two minutes at the beginning of ED&I training), or even renegotiated, to make visible the commitment from the facilitator(s) to creating a safer space in all ED&I training.

Example of contracting framing (more suitable for pupils)

We are going to begin by spending some time contracting and this is when we agree on the behaviours needed from you and from me so we create a safer space during our time together. Today, you will have the opportunity to ask questions and engage in discussion about ... This training might make you have more of a strong emotional response so it's important you feel you can be honest and participate in a way that's comfortable for you. In a moment, we will decide on how we should speak and act together so that we have a shared agreement of what is expected from all of us today.

Examples of contracting behaviours

- Demonstrate curiosity by being open to learning, discussion and overriding strong negative emotions.
- Demonstrate vulnerability (if you feel able to at this time).
- Listen to understand, not judge.
- Act with courage by asking questions with kindness either in the session or after the session (especially if you're not sure if the question is appropriate).
- Embrace discomfort; it is part of the learning process in this space.
- Be committed to continuous learning, relearning and unlearning.
- Show that all voices matter by being conscious of the language you use and your non-verbal communication.
- Seek support outside of this session if needed (state the name of the trusted person they can talk to or the relevant professional body that can be contacted).

With pupils, contracting is enhanced if the facilitator shares specific examples and non-examples of desirable behaviours based on hypothetical scenarios so pupils are clear about what is expected of them, especially in relation to safeguarding responsibilities being adhered to.

The concept of social norms is also helpful when we consider contracting for pupils. Some contracting behaviours may be more difficult for pupils to observe and it may be more difficult for a facilitator to hold pupils to account, especially in larger groups. Social norms can be defined as:

> rules and standards that are understood by members of a group, and that guide and/or constrain social behaviour without the force of laws. These norms emerge out of interaction with others; they may or may not be stated explicitly, and any sanctions for deviating from them come from social networks
> (Ciadldini and Trost, 1998 cited in Rauch, 2022)

Mccrea further states that social norms can be 'so powerful that they often override more formal policies and rules' (Mccrea, 2025a). For example, in a training session for secondary pupils focusing on understanding masculinity, a male pupil may want to engage in whole-class discussion but may fear doing this in case he is seen as 'weak' by his peers. If pupils are strongly influenced by their peers, facilitators must consider how they can promote desired behaviours. One way to do this is to draw on existing networks (Rauch, 2022) so a facilitator could speak to influential pupils before training to understand their viewpoint (including counter arguments) and, consequently, bridge the gap between pupil and teacher person-centred knowledge or ask them to take on specific roles during training.

Another strategy is to encourage commitment (Rauch, 2022) and a facilitator could ask pupils to make a promise to themselves and their peers that they will act with kindness and respect during training. ED&I educators should deliberately 'raise the visibility of those behaviours and attitudes that we want others to emulate' (Mccrea, 2025b). For example, if a pupil demonstrates vulnerability, the facilitator should thank the pupil, name the trait and briefly explain why it is important and valued. There is no denying that this requires time but with particularly sensitive topics, it is worth the investment.

Act with courage and demonstrate vulnerability

Courage is needed from the outset when facilitating training because, undoubtedly, an ED&I educator will be judged based on their visible characteristics or presumed characteristics. Research suggests that when you meet someone for the first time, the first characteristics you notice are age, race and gender unless there is another characteristic that makes the person stand apart from the dominant majority e.g. a person with a distinctive birthmark (Agarwal, 2020). These facial cues are 'the primary motivators for a stereotype' (Agarwal, 2020). As ED&I works seems to 'fall disproportionately on women and minorities' (Mackenzie, 2023), assumptions are inevitable.

As an ED&I educator, courage arises from intentionally drawing attention to these characteristics, or absence of visible characteristics, and embracing hypervisibility to minimise assumptions being made about your motivations and priorities. When facilitating ED&I training, we have been intentional in stating that we are women of colour. Admittedly, the first time we said it, it felt strange because neither of us had articulated this before, but it was also empowering. We were owning our gender and race and reminding participants that we had a commitment to other characteristics, overriding assumptions from the outset. We know this can take people by surprise as it is not spoken about but it is what is first noticed. This may not seem to create a safer space as it addresses unconscious bias from the outset but, ultimately, it highlights the importance of courage and vulnerability. If participants see it modelled, they are more likely to demonstrate it.

Furthermore, facilitators may engage in self-disclosure practices by sharing aspects of their lived experience and this sets the tone for ED&I training. In education, Sorenson (cited in Henry and Thorsen, 2018) defines self-disclosure as:

> statements in the classroom about the self that may or may not be related to the subject content but reveal information about the teacher that students are unlikely to learn from other sources.

Research indicates that when teachers self-disclose, pupils:

- Feel more willing to participate in activities (Zhang et al., 2008 cited in Henry and Thorsen, 2018)
- Have increased levels of participation (Goldstein and Benassi, 1994 cited in Henry and Thorsen, 2018)
- Have greater engagement (Cayanus 2004 cited in Henry and Thorsen, 2018)
- Have greater interest in the subjects they are learning (Cayanus, Martin, and Weber 2003 cited in Henry and Thorsen, 2018)

Pupils see the sharing of these personal stories as attempts 'to create an open and positive learning environment' (Cayanus, Martin, and Goodboy 2009 cited in Henry and Thorsen, 2018). Self-disclosure could be planned or more spontaneous if it arises from discussion. The aim of this is not to foreground the ED&I educator's experience but to indicate that, within a school setting, it is acceptable to share such experiences and speak about what is so often unspoken. It is also helpful for the ED&I educator to draw on research and/or learning from the school community to highlight that some experiences are not singular. This can have an immediate impact on feelings of safety as some participants realise they are not alone in thinking or feeling a certain way, reducing feelings of isolation. For staff, it reimagines the concept of professionalism in the workplace.

Kara states that 'teachers fear to disclose parts of themselves because there is a perceived lack of professionalism in doing so' (Kara, 2021). Choosing what to disclose is deeply personal and undoubtedly involves risk-taking (see James' case study in Chapter 3). Within the ED&I space, experiences may be articulated for the first time or a participant, who may usually prefer to stay silent, may feel more able to speak out. To minimise the risk, especially in relation to safeguarding, ED&I educators should ensure that there is a shared agreement of what appropriate self-disclosure looks like in their setting and understand how they will be supported by school leadership if participants respond in a way that is harmful to either themselves or others. Some examples of appropriate self-disclosure (and this needs to be age-appropriate and sensitive to individual needs) include: experiences of discrimination; experiences of not feeling safe; experiences of feeling like you are not part of the community; experiences of not feeling listened to, valued or understood or experiences of privilege.

There also needs to be the recognition that not everyone is willing to disclose personal information about themselves and this must be respected e.g. if a person is new to a school or new to role. When Natasha first disclosed her experience of having epilepsy as a teacher to trainee teachers, to reiterate the importance of engaging in help-seeking behaviour and obtaining reasonable adjustments, she was apprehensive about doing so. She was worried about how she would be perceived and, afterwards, felt exposed and emotionally drained. Now, the demonstration of vulnerability does not feel as risky because she feels more confident with how to manage this. In Natasha's case, it is through carefully considering the limitations and benefits of the disclosure, based on the intended audience, with a critical friend and through scripting to help her feel more able to articulate more difficult experiences. To be an effective ED&I educator does not mean you need to have had experiences of discrimination. In this case, vulnerability could be shown through talking about your privilege and your learning when other facilitators and/or participants share their lived experience.

Another way the ED&I educator can show an appreciation of vulnerability is through how they respond to participants sharing their lived experience. Gaslighting is when 'someone is intentionally distorting reality to make you feel like what you're seeing or feeling isn't real' and 'it hinges on self-doubt' (Conrad and Spann, 2024). Consequently, a person may feel their experiences are dismissed or diminished through seemingly innocuous comments such as: "It was just a joke"; "I didn't mean it like that" or "You're being over-sensitive" which trivialises what the victim is disclosing, especially because it tends to come from a trusted person. Gaslighting can be hard to identify as 'it's confusing at its core' (Conrad and Spann, 2024), but signs of it taking place include: feelings of confusion and powerlessness after an interaction; feelings being dismissed or trivialised or a person being told that they are exaggerating (Conrad and Spann, 2024).

Those from underrepresented groups are more at risk of being victims of gaslighting. For example, due to societal structure and social inequalities, women are more likely to experience gaslighting and racial gaslighting can be described as a way to maintain 'a pro-white/anti-black balance in society by labelling those that challenge acts of racism as psychologically abnormal' (Wolstenholme, 2021). ED&I educators need to consider the language they use when responding to participants who have shared their lived experience. For example, a statement such as: "That must have been a challenging time. Thank you for sharing this with us and trusting us with your experience" shows the participant that you hear what they are saying and value their contribution. Vulnerability is an important trait in shaping school culture because it encourages people to reach out and seek support because they may feel they are more likely to be listened to and believed.

Acting with courage is demonstrated by being vigilant to acts of prejudice and discrimination during training, ranging from subtle acts of microaggression to overt abuse or intimidation. The ED&I educator should be confident that they can notice prejudicial incidents, feel equipped to intervene and know they will be supported by school leadership. If prejudicial incidents are not addressed, the space will not feel safer and this then undermines the whole purpose of ED&I work. Undoubtedly, this is challenging because it requires awareness of what discrimination looks like so you may have the best intentions but fail to notice prejudicial incidents. The only way to develop this radar is to engage in active listening (see Chapter 7) and be intentional in developing your person-centred knowledge based on your specific school setting. Challenging prejudicial incidents should not be a solitary endeavour; it requires training to raise awareness, foster responsibility and provide 'the needed behavioural skills for addressing a prejudice-related incident' (Chen, Carboni, Tutwiler, 2023).

Once you have noticed discriminatory behaviour, one approach might be to return to contracting e.g. "We all agreed to … during contracting. As we continue, let's ensure that we do this so… (explain the impact)." If you feel the discriminatory behaviour could be addressed in public, because you feel confident there is no malicious intent and it will help to develop person-centred knowledge, there needs to be consideration of the risk to others to avoid making those from underrepresented groups hypervisible. Another approach might be to discuss the incident with the individual(s) in private, especially if you suspect there is more harmful intent. However, rushing to punishment should not be the immediate response; if a person does not feel heard, they are more likely to resent such training as they see it as a way to silence some, rather than hear all. Discussion should come from a place of curiosity rather than judgement with the ED&I educator listening to understand, providing a space for the person to speak and then deciding on the most appropriate next step based on the relevant policy or procedure. With some pupils or members of staff, it might not be appropriate for the ED&I educator to have the conversation or to have it alone so it may require a referral to the safeguarding team or, with staff, contact with HR or a more senior member of staff.

We have provided a framework to share an example of how to respond to prejudicial incidents during training. This could also be used outside of the training space if the individual feels confident to address prejudicial incidents with peers. The script is influenced by Latanè and Darley's model where those who intervene must: 'notice the event; define the event as warranting action/intervention; take responsibility for acting; decide how to act and actually act' (Latanè and Darley, 1970 cited in Chen, Carboni, Tutwiler, 2023). To enhance this model, we have also drawn on the National Equity Project's guidance on how to respond to microaggressions and unconscious bias (see Chapter 3). We would recommend adapting the script so it captures your voice and making the necessary changes if this conversation is taking place with an adult.

Consider this scenario: a pupil says about the title Mx, "There's no such thing as that. You're making it up."

During training

1. Notice and decide – is action needed? If no, continue to be vigilant. If yes, continue with the following steps.

2. Address (consider whether in public or private would be best and when during training). E.g. "I heard your comment and we'll talk about this afterwards."

After training

When talking to the individual, in this case the pupil:

3. Clarify what was said to check your own assumptions: "I think I heard you say… is that right?" or "Can we just talk about something I heard during training?"

4. Be curious: "Can you tell me more about what you mean by…?" or "What led you to say /believe…?"

5. Clarify the difference between intent versus impact: "I know you didn't mean to convey …but the words you used can send a message that…'"

6. Appeal to the person's empathy: "How do you think a non-binary person may feel if they are regularly hearing things like…?" or "How do you think you'd feel if you or someone close to you were regularly experiencing…?" (National Equity Project, n.d.)

7. Invite more questions: "What other questions do you have?"

Such conversations are not easy, especially if the conversation is with a member of staff. For those from historically marginalised groups, there can be real fear with having such conversations. You may: fear being accused of being aggressive; be anxious that you will not be supported by leadership or you may doubt what you hear and prefer to assume the best. There could be real fatigue with having such conversations because, the reality is, for those from underrepresented groups, there is a risk of you experiencing discriminatory behaviour as soon as you step out of the training space. This can be even more difficult to manage if the comment or question feels personal due to either your lived experience or the lived experience of loved ones. Courage is required here because if such behaviour isn't noticed and addressed, there is no guarantee it ever will be. Courage can be cultivated by knowing you have leadership support (you will be believed) and working with the ED&I planning team to pre-empt prejudicial behaviour linked to the training and script responses and/or ensure the provision of additional support.

Vulnerability is further demonstrated when the ED&I educator makes a mistake. Even if you are leading on this work, it does not mean you will always get it right e.g. you might clumsily express an idea, commit a microaggression or not use inclusive language. If this is pointed out, listen to learn and apologise. This in itself is an act of solidarity. For example, "I'm sorry and I appreciate you flagging this. I'll ensure it won't happen again." We are all human and will make mistakes. When such incidents occur, feelings, such as shame and embarrassment, might instinctively make us respond with silence, change the topic, or deny or dismiss what was said. By owning the discomfort, being vulnerable and admitting that you have made a mistake, you model the desirable behaviours needed.

Undoubtedly, there are risks with demonstrating these traits and see Chapter 10 for more guidance about how to protect yourself as an ED&I educator.

Demonstrate compassion

ED&I educators have the opportunity to demonstrate compassion through how they respond to participants who share aspects of their lived experience that force them to either reencounter trauma or experience distress. Trauma can be defined as:

> Any disturbing experience that results in significant fear, helplessness, dissociation, confusion, or other disruptive feelings intense enough to have a long-lasting negative effect on a person's attitudes, behaviour, and other aspects of functioning.
> (The American Psychological Association cited in Drevitch, 2023)

Research suggests that certain groups are more likely to experience trauma than others and experience it more often e.g. people of colour, refugees and asylum seekers, LGBTQ+ people and people experiencing poverty (Mind, n.d.). Some people with mental health problems may also find the ED&I space challenging. An ED&I educator needs to listen, show empathy and support those who have strong emotional responses. The difficulty with showing compassion is that people respond to such feelings differently e.g. they may prefer to leave the room or they may prefer to stay in the room and to be given time to self-regulate. Sensitivity from the ED&I educator is needed here so they gauge when they are able to have a discreet discussion with the participant or whether it is best to check in with them again after training.

Another strategy that shows compassion is, before training takes place, to share a brief overview of the training and to ask participants to contact the ED&I educator should they have any questions or concerns. This will help the facilitator to anticipate what could cause a strong emotional response but they still need to be aware that this will not provide all the answers. A person's response to sensitive content is shaped by their intersectional identity and contextual factors. Careful framing of such communication is needed so it sets the tone for the training rather than causing fear or disengagement. This then allows the ED&I educator to put in place the necessary support e.g. ensuring there is another facilitator who can provide support and act as a trusted person.

Compassion is shown through active listening (see Chapter 7) and how the ED&I educator reaffirms a person's experience or encourages them to engage in more balanced thinking about themselves. Consider this scenario: a participant shares a microaggression that they experienced and their account concludes with "It's just a little thing. It doesn't matter." In this example, the ED&I educator can gently challenge by responding with: "Thank you for sharing this. I noticed that you said 'little' and I feel that it's not a 'little thing' because xxx." By explaining why their experience should be recognised, it develops person-centred knowledge for all participants and allows the participant to know that microaggressions are not micro, they have a lasting impact and their feelings count. A risk of ED&I training is that it can perpetuate the idea that those from historically marginalised groups have only negative experiences. By asking questions and inviting participants to counter this, it shows compassion because you are seeing the whole person, not the 'protected characteristic'.

Encourage safer reflection and discussion

To model vulnerability and the desired behaviours during reflection and discussion, ED&I educators could model their responses and articulate the challenges that participants might face to provide reassurance. To do this effectively, the ED&I educator should plan their responses beforehand. This serves two purposes as, firstly, it allows the ED&I educator to experience training as a participant and adjust tasks accordingly. Secondly, it ensures that the ED&I educator can plan their response and share it with brevity. Such modelling is not to spotlight the ED&I educator unless this is the intention e.g. there is an external speaker or a panel. If the facilitator feels more comfortable using a script to share their example, they should explain why and this again demonstrates vulnerability.

For reflection and discussion to feel safer for participants, spontaneous questions, asked by the facilitator, need to be carefully considered. One option is for questions to have a wide and open steer such as, "What are your thoughts and/or feelings based on this?" This allows participants to share their responses without the fear of getting it wrong; you cannot argue with how someone feels, but you can seek to understand more. If more specific questions are needed, there needs to be thoughtful consideration of language. For example, if you feel it would be helpful for participants to reflect on where they need to develop person-centred knowledge, a question such as "Where do you need to raise awareness?" might cause less resistance than "What are your gaps?" This might seem like we are treading softly but it is about picking battles and deciding on where the strongest challenge needs to come from in an already challenging space.

Discussion is a necessary part of the ED&I space so silence can be damaging. It can cause division, resentment and misunderstanding with some groups feeling that they are not valued rather than being part of a community supporting each other to belong. Before discussion points, contracting needs to be revisited with the facilitator stressing the importance of hearing all voices and providing participants with permission not to share, if they don't feel comfortable. It is helpful to state how you will ask questions e.g. avoid cold call, and explain that there might be awkward silences but this is to be expected. This may seem like the ED&I educator is encouraging opting out but, as ED&I content can be so personal, it is more important to safeguard the individual.

Participants may be more likely to engage in discussion based on the facilitator's response to participants whose views are incorrect, potentially as a result of misinformation spread online. The facilitator should not shame the person but respond in a more neutral way if thinking is to be influenced e.g. "That's actually something that a lot of people believe; however,..." Tone and non-verbal behaviours matter when gently challenging so the participant does not feel undermined or patronised.

See Chapter 5 for more guidance around effective planning for reflection and discussion.

Signpost the help available to participants after training

For the space to feel safer, the ED&I educator needs to be explicit about how this training connects to wider ED&I activity and signpost the wider in school and/or external support available. Research indicates that children and young people might not report an experience, in this case sexual abuse, because they did not know what would happen next (Ofsted, 2021). If pupils and staff feel there is an organisational commitment to address prejudice and discrimination, they may feel more able to speak up. This could include reminding participants of the relevant school policies and procedures or providing an anonymous question box so participants can get their questions answered in a way that maintains their safety.

Another way to support participants after training is by providing the option of additional time to talk afterwards. For staff, this could be knowing who to go to should support be needed or working with a peer, their mentor or coach to get further guidance and support with embedding new practice. For pupils, it might be being made aware of: an in-school designated safer space; a peer network aimed at those who share a protected characteristic; knowing which adults they can talk to e.g. through a drop-in session and/or directing participants to wider local, national or international networks.

The ED&I educator, due to the nature of their role, will be seen as a trusted person to talk to so creating spaces for listening, whether that is in person or through other mechanisms, shows a commitment to compassion. The ED&I educator should also remember that they are not solely responsible for listening and ensure any necessary boundaries are in place.

Demonstrate a commitment to consistent 'reflection, feedback and re-negotiation' (Beijbom, 2022)

To create a safer space, an ED&I educator cannot adopt a fixed stance and assume, because participant feedback about safety has been positive, that these feelings of safety will naturally occur in future training. Psychological safety has to be carefully cultivated as participants may be influenced by the content of training and/or external factors linked to the content of training. For example, at the time of writing, *Adolescence*, a series on Netflix, has sparked much debate about the 'corrosive impact of social media' and incel culture. (Hamilton, 2025) and there have been calls to show it in schools. If ED&I training is in response to something in the public domain, teachers need training on how to address the issues raised sensitively and with confidence and strong contracting is needed. This is because the ED&I space may be immersed in strong feelings and misinformation with some participants feeling empowered and others silenced. There is also the risk of normalising certain behaviours or reinforcing perceptions e.g. in this case, young men feeling they are a problem group. Here, the facilitator needs to be vigilant, neutral and show a commitment to listening to all, whether that be in public or private based on the nature of the comments or questions. Without reflection on the needs of participants in advance, a safer space cannot be created and ED&I training could do more harm than good.

One of the most important ways to show a commitment to feedback is through sharing important learning with school leadership and explicitly stating that you will do so. This requires courage as you may need to share messages that are hard to hear but are essential to create a culture of belonging. By doing this, it shows participants that leadership teams are committed to developing their person-centred knowledge and launching or enhancing ED&I interventions to meet the needs of the community they serve. ED&I learning is a joint endeavour and organisational change is less likely to occur if participants feel only they should change, not the educational environment.

Questions

1. Have you ever felt unsafe during staff training? What caused this? What could have been put in place to prevent this?
2. What traits or skills do you feel you need to develop and nurture? Why?
3. Consider the section on challenging prejudicial incidents during training. How would you feel using such a script and what changes are needed so it is more authentic for you and more applicable for your specific school setting?

References

Agarwal, P. (2020). *Unravelling Unconscious Bias Sway*. United Kingdom: Bloomsbury Sigma.

Bennett, J. L. (2008). Contracting for Success. *The International Journal of Coaching in Organisations* 4. Available at: https://researchportal.coachingfederation.org/Document/Pdf/2955.pdf. [Accessed 20 February 2025].

Beijbom, M. (2022). *Striving for Equity, Inclusion, and Safer Spaces at Work: A Review of the Literature*. Guelph, ON: Live Work Well Research Centre, University of Guelph.

Chen, J.A., Carboni, I., Tutwiler, M. S. (2023). EDI Skill-Building Tools: Preparing Learners to Effectively Intervene in Bias Incidents. *American Psychological Association*, 9(4), 419–434.

Conrad, M, Spann, R. T. (2024). *What Is Gaslighting? Examples And How To Deal With It*. Available at: https://www.forbes.com/health/mind/what-is-gaslighting/ [Accessed 18 February 2025].

Drevitch, G. (2023). *Are You Misusing the Term "Trauma"? 6 Questions to Determine If You're Using the Term Correctly*. Available at: https://www.psychologytoday.com/gb/blog/simplifying-complex-trauma/202301/are-you-misusing-the-term-trauma [Accessed 20 February 2025].

Edmondson, A. (2019). *The Fearless Organisation Creating Psychological Safety in the Workplace for Learning, Innovation and Growth*. United States of America: Wiley.

Hamilton, C. (2025). *Drama Shines Light on 'Growing Problem' – PM*. Available at: https://www.bbc.co.uk/news/articles/cd7ew52d2y3o [Accessed 28 March 2025].

Henry, A., Thorsen, C. (2018). *Teachers' Self-Disclosures and Influences on Students' Motivation: A Relational Perspective*. Available at: https://www.tandfonline.com/doi/full/10.1080/13670050.2018.1441261 [Accessed 1 March 2025].

Kara, B. (2021). *A Little Guide for Teachers Diversity in Schools*. London: Sage Publications Ltd.

Pinkett, M. (2024). *Combatting Misogyny in Schools*. Chartered College of Teaching – Bristol Network. Available at: https://my.chartered.college/event/matt-pinkett-combatting-misogyny-in-schools/ [Accessed 11 November 2024].

Mackenzie, K. (2023). *DEI Leadership – And Who's Actually Doing the Work?* Available at: https://resources.workable.com/stories-and-insights/dei-leadership-and-whos-actually-doing-the-work-dei-survey-report [Accessed 1 March 2025].

Mccrea, P. (2025a). *Norms Override Rules the (Under-Appreciated) Power of Norms*. Available at: https://snacks.pepsmccrea.com/p/norms-override-rules (Accessed 15 March 2025).

Mccrea, P. (2025b). *Amplify Desirable Behaviour How to Influence Norms in the Classroom*. Available at: https://snacks.pepsmccrea.com/p/amplify-desirable-behaviour [Accessed 1 March 2025].

Mind (n.d.). *Trauma*. Available at: https://www.mind.org.uk/information-support/types-of-mental-health-problems/trauma/about-trauma/ [Accessed 18 February 2025].

National Equity Project (n.d.). *Responding to Microaggressions and Unconscious Bias*. Available at: https://www.nationalequityproject.org/responding-to-microaggressions-and-unconscious-bias#:~:text=Acknowledge%20the%20feelings%20the%20person,if%20you%20felt%20disrespected%20when%20.%E2%80%9D [Accessed 30 March].

Ofsted (2021). *Research and Analysis Review of Sexual Abuse in Schools and Colleges*. Available at: https://www.gov.uk/government/publications/review-of-sexual-abuse-in-schools-and-colleges/review-of-sexual-abuse-in-schools-and-colleges#how-does-the-current-system-of-safeguarding-listen-to-the-voices-of-children-and-young-people [Accessed 5 March 2025].

Rauch, C. J. (2022). *Social Norms: At the Intersection between Psychology and Behaviour.* Available at: https://evidencebased.education/social-norms-at-the-intersection-between-psychology-and-behaviour/ [Accessed 18 February 2025].

Shah, S. (2022). *Diversity, Inclusion and Belonging in Coaching.* Great Britain and United States: Kogan Page Limited.

Sutherland, L. (2025). *Part 1: Creating the Conditions for Innovation – Psychological Safety and Some Pointers from Behavioural Science.* Available at: https://gcs.civilservice.gov.uk/blog/creating-the-conditions-for-innovation-psychological-safety-and-some-pointers-from-behavioural-science/ [Accessed 28 March].

Tulshyan, R. (2022). *Inclusion on Purpose An Intersectional Approach to Creating a Culture of Belonging at Work.* Cambridge, MA: The MIT Press.

Wietrak, E. and Gifford, J. (2024). *Trust and psychological safety: An evidence review. Practice summary and recommendations.* London: Chartered Institute of Personnel and Development.

Wolstenholme, R. (2021). *The Hidden Victims of Gaslighting.* Available at: https://www.bbc.co.uk/future/article/20201123-what-is-racial-gaslighting [Accessed 29 March 2025].

Coaching and mentoring with an ED&I lens

What do coaches and mentors do?

Coaching and mentoring are personalised forms of professional development that can be defined as 'facilitative or helping relationships intended to achieve some type of change, learning and/or enhanced individual and/or organisational effectiveness' (Maxwell, Hobson, Manning, 2022). They can have a powerful impact for the participant in terms of their professional understanding and practice, job satisfaction and retention (Goldhaber et al, 2020; Hobson et al, 2009a cited in Maxwell, Hobson, Manning, 2022). Both approaches require a close working relationship. If the participant feels they cannot share challenges linked to certain aspects of their identity, feelings of belonging and safety within the school community could be affected as well as professional growth.

There are many overlaps between coaching and mentoring as practitioners use the same process skills to meet the needs of their participant e.g. clarifying and summarising (Stokes et al., 2020). While this chapter focuses on coaching and mentoring, we are not using these terms interchangeably. They are distinct approaches but the distinction can be blurred based on the extent to which a directive approach is used. We recognise that a formal coaching model may not be offered in all schools but the strategies shared here are of relevance if a coaching approach is adopted in line management meetings.

Although mentoring forms part of every teacher's experience, especially early in their career, there is not always a shared understanding of what mentoring is and the different roles of a mentor. Without this, the mentor may not realise the different layers of support that should be provided. Mentoring is a:

> one to one relationship between a relatively inexperienced teacher (the mentee) and a relatively experienced one (the mentor) which aims to support the mentee's learning and development as a teacher, and their integration into and acceptance by the culture of the school and profession.
>
> (Hobson and Malderez, 2012)

For trainees and early career teachers, mentoring can lead to improved confidence and self-belief, 'enhanced teacher-student interactions and an improved classroom environment' (National Institute for Teaching, 2023a). For mentors, it can improve 'self-reflection and problem-solving capacities' (McIntyre and Hagger, 1996 cited in Hobson and Malderez, 2012) and increase 'confidence, self-efficacy and job satisfaction' (Johnson et al., 2005; Marable and Raimondi, 2007 cited in Hobson and Malderez, 2012).

An effective mentor may adopt several roles:

- Educator – listening, coaching and creating appropriate opportunities for the mentee's professional learning (Hobson and Malderez, 2012).

- Model – inspiring, demonstrating and making aspects of being a teacher visible (Hobson and Malderez, 2012).

- Acculturator – helping the mentee into full membership of the particular professional culture (Hobson and Malderez, 2012).

- Sponsor – 'opening doors' and introducing the mentee to the 'right people' (Hobson and Malderez, 2012).

- Provider of psychological support – providing the mentee with a safe place to release emotions or 'let off steam' (Malderez and Bodoczky, 1999; Malderez and Wedell, 2007 cited in Hobson and Malderez, 2012).

A more negative stance is that of the 'judgementor', where a mentor shares their judgements of the trainee or early career teacher's practice too readily and this overly-critical stance reflects the mentor's apparent belief that their approach is right, minimising the agency of the mentee and their ability to forge an authentic professional identity (Hobson and Malderez, 2012). In order for mentoring to have positive outcomes for both mentors and mentees, effective mentors are able to establish positive and purposeful relationships and create a safe and supportive environment where the mentee feels able to be open and honest (National Institute of Teaching, 2023a). This is particularly necessary for those from underrepresented groups who may face additional challenges, as the research indicates, in a school setting.

Informal mentoring and reverse mentoring are other types of mentoring within the ED&I space. Staff may seek an unofficial mentor and this relationship often develops organically. This research provides some rationale as to why this may be the case. Aspiring leaders from diverse ethnic backgrounds do not always have access to mentors who have an understanding of their cultural contexts (Bush et al., 2006; Miller, 2019 cited in Worth, McLean, Sharp, 2022) and peer support is particularly important for trainees from ethnic minority backgrounds (Wilkins, 2011 cited in Worth, McLean, Sharp, 2022). Members of historically marginalised groups within our networks have shared the importance of having an informal mentor and the lasting impact it has had on their feelings of self-worth and their ability to progress in their career. Perhaps, this is because some people from historically marginalised groups might not have an informal network which can provide insider information (knowledge about systems that enable an individual to be more successful e.g. having a family member who is a teacher) and such guidance and support can affect performance. For example, Natasha is the first person in her family to go to university and become a teacher. When she applied for her first teaching job, she did not have any insider networks to draw on impacting her self-efficacy.

Another form of mentoring is reverse mentoring. This provides senior leaders with the opportunity to learn about the experience of those with underrepresented characteristics within the school community. Here, the emphasis is more on organisational growth than that of the individual. This chapter will focus more on the role of a formal mentor of trainee and early career teachers but many of the strategies will be applicable for informal mentors and mentors of members of staff at different stages of their career.

Coaching is increasingly being used in schools as a form of professional development and, typically it is a 'structured process focused on improving specific skills or achieving particular goals' (Amos, n.d.). Instructional coaching (a more directive form of coaching) can be used to support early career teachers and, in some contexts, is a key component of the professional development model for all staff. Frameworks, such as Bambrick-Santoyo's Six Step Model, can be used to structure the coaching interaction and research suggests that instructional coaching is 'the best-evidenced form of professional development' (Sims, 2019). Even though this is a more directive approach, there is still space for discussion and collaboration through the 'agreeing the next best step' and 'plan and rehearse' stages (Goodrich, Mccrea, Sims, 2024). The latter stage can be described as deliberate practice, which is where the coachee participates in intentional practice of a narrow and clearly-defined skill area they want to develop (Chartered College of Teaching, n.d.). With the introduction of Intensive Training and Practice, as part of the new Initial Teacher Training (ITT) statutory requirements in England, deliberate practice is now part of the ITT experience. In fact, with some ITT providers, for example Ambition Institute, instructional coaching is an integral part of their ITT programme.

Another coaching model is facilitative coaching, where there is a more non-directive approach, and the coachee is empowered to find solutions and lead the direction of the coaching conversation and their professional growth (Goodrich, 2024). A facilitative coaching model can be used in a one-to-one relationship or adapted to be used with groups (see Chapter 8). Where coaching is embedded in the school's professional development model, there may be one preferred model or a more responsive approach with the coach selecting the model best suited to the needs of the coachee they are working with. In this chapter, we will assume that coaches are school staff rather that external coaches as this model is more prevalent in schools.

Why is it important to coach and mentor with an ED&I lens?

We'll begin by referring to the NFER Racial Equality in the Teacher Workforce research report. This research shares some stark findings based on teacher retention and progression and tracks this from applicants to ITT to executive headteachers. It shows there is an overrepresentation of people from Asian, Black and other ethnic backgrounds among applicants to postgraduate ITT and underrepresentation of these groups entering the teaching profession, showing a lack of progress in the application stage and the number of people within these groups achieving Qualified Teacher Status (Worth, McLean, Sharp, 2022). Moreover, 'teachers from ethnic minority backgrounds are also less likely to stay in the profession or progress to leadership than their white counterparts' (Worth, McLean, Sharp, 2022). Consequently, the teacher workforce is not representative of society and racial equality needs to be prioritised (Worth, McLean, Sharp, 2022).

Existing research provides some possible reasons for these differences with key barriers arising from:

- Government policy (Miller, 2019 cited in Worth, McLean, Sharp, 2022).
- Racism/race discrimination (Hargreaves, 2011; Haque and Eliott, 2016; Lander and Zaheerali, 2016; Haque, 2017; Miller, 2019, Tereshchenko et al., 2020 cited in Worth, McLean, Sharp, 2022).
- Dealing with microaggressions that are 'such a burden that it amounted to an additional workload' (Lander and Zaheerali, 2016; Tereshchenko *et al.*, 2020 cited in Worth, McLean, Sharp, 2022).
- Institutional practices (Miller, 2019 cited in Worth, McLean, Sharp, 2022).
- Affiliation/group membership (Miller, 2019 cited in Worth, McLean, Sharp, 2022).
- Religion (Miller, 2019 cited in Worth, McLean, Sharp, 2022).
- Lack of opportunities for progression (Hargreaves, 2011; Haque and Eliott, 2016; Lander and Zaheerali, 2016; Haque, 2017; Tereshchenko et al., 2020 cited in Worth, McLean, Sharp, 2022), including 'being encouraged or self-selecting into middle leadership roles (such as pastoral responsibility) that have limited opportunities for further progression' (Lander and Zaheerali, 2016; Tereshchenko et al., 2020 cited in Worth, McLean, Sharp, 2022).
- Teachers from ethnic minority backgrounds being made to feel that they did not belong in teaching (Tereshchenko et al. 2020 cited in Worth, McLean, Sharp, 2022) and that they are not perceived as professionals and their views are not valued by school leadership (Haque, 2017 cited in Worth, McLean, Sharp, 2022).

While we are not able to access similar datasets for other characteristics, we know some of these challenges will be familiar to those from other historically marginalised groups. For example, a person with a disability may experience 'additional workload' due to ableism and some LGBTQ+ people may feel their appearance might be perceived as 'too visibly LGBTQ+, or not professional enough' and feel they are not 'seen as a valid member of the workplace community' (Stonewall, 2025). Oberholzer points out that 'colleagues from diverse backgrounds often have signs of low self-efficacy' so, despite having the necessary skillset, they may not feel they 'meet the requirements for their next role or next step' (Oberholzer, 2019 cited in Oberholzer and Boyle, 2024). Such barriers can affect an individual's personal and professional behaviours and influence whether they cope or thrive in a school environment.

Shah's excellent book *Diversity, Inclusion and Belonging in Coaching* offers insights on common strategies that coachees might use to cope with feelings of not belonging. For example, a participant might: be too agreeable; avoid challenging; avoid the limelight; and/or let others take the credit for their work (Shah, 2022). Feeling excluded can lead to alienation or feelings of helplessness and this contributes to the development of coping skills which don't always 'move people forward' (Shah, 2025). For example, resilience is often seen as a desirable trait in the workplace but research shows that 'resilience can, in some situations, cause a person to become stuck in an undesirable state' (Shah, 2025). Thus, educators need to think carefully about which traits are vaunted in the workplace and whether they enable all to thrive or merely those from more dominant groups who, historically, have shaped workplace practices.

Case study

Louise Ishani of Integrity First Training provides further insights into the behaviours that those from historically marginalised groups might demonstrate.

I have worked with many people from underrepresented groups and there tends to be some reoccurring behaviours. Some clients choose to take a more difficult route to achieve their career goal, such as taking on more work, often without remuneration, and this can work against them in terms of career progression. Clients have spoken of others promoted before them as they feel too overburdened to seek promotion. In essence, leadership have got used to them doing the heavy lifting. However, when leadership changes, there are real risks with work not being formally recognised, valued and appreciated. Engaging in self-advocacy is another area that tends to be explored. Some clients bring themselves down and, whilst I don't want to devalue what they say, I do endeavour to challenge their thinking so they think about how they might be perceived outside of their organisation. At times, I have found it is helpful to give factual information because if a person doesn't fully understand how an organisation works, they are less likely to be able to navigate it successfully. Finally, those from underrepresented groups may be strongly influenced by family or their community and may have even internalised discrimination, sensitive questioning allows the client to reflect on options they may not have thought of so they do not cap their aspirations or engage in self-limiting beliefs.

The practitioner must not assume that an individual coping equates to them experiencing personal and professional fulfilment. Such assumptions will affect the development of a relationship based on trust which 'is necessary at both personal and professional levels for fostering innovation and growth of expertise' (Chambers, Warnes, Adams, 2025). Trust takes time to develop and understanding the impact of discrimination on a person is helpful as long as the practitioner bears in mind that the impact may not be known and their role is not to diagnose. For example, Natasha's experience of discrimination means she can be hypervigilant. A positive of this is that she notices when people experience discomfort and seeks to help, but it also means that it takes time for Natasha to feel safe (Shah, 2022). Furthermore, if the coachee or mentee has not been able to trust people in positions of power before, they may not benefit from such a close working relationship. Even though we have emphasised more negative strategies in this section, the practitioner should demonstrate respectful curiosity and empathy to cultivate a relationship built on trust and better understand the unique needs of the participant.

How to coach and mentor with an ED&I lens

Coaching or mentoring with an ED&I lens means searching for evidence that allows the practitioner to really see and hear the person they are working with, not the person they are choosing to see which is shaped by bias. To do this, the practitioner should:

1. Demonstrate curiosity.
2. Be intentional in creating a safer space.
3. Adjust support and guidance whilst maintaining high expectations.

We recognise that there are different levels of motivation with these roles and that time constraints may impact how far these responsibilities are fulfilled. It is not always feasible with changing staff bodies to match coaches and mentors based on coachee and mentee characteristics and/or preferences. Even if this were the case, it may not benefit the specific needs of the individual; our fluid, sometimes hidden, identities and changing contexts mean that we cannot always anticipate who can make the biggest difference for us.

In recent years, in England, there has been more of an investment in training for mentors at ITT and ECT level, but knowing how to effectively mentor those from underrepresented groups is not an area of explicit focus. Training for mentors must make clear what the roles and responsibilities involve and go beyond procedure and paperwork. Part of being an effective mentor means adopting different stances and realising, as an 'educator', that the ITT or ECF framework is limited and teachers may need support with personal skills or self-advocacy if they are to thrive. Mentors have to receive high quality training as there cannot be the assumption that everyone is skilled in this.

Similarly, coaching training may focus on different models or different stages in a process rather than delve into how the coach can encourage self-advocacy in their coachee. By sharing videos of examples and non-examples of what adopting an ED&I lens looks like in practice, practitioner competency and confidence can develop as it minimises the fear of "getting it wrong", a fear often shared with us. This is enhanced if practitioners have the opportunity to engage in practice by either rehearsing or co-planning possible responses. When adopting an ED&I lens, language matters so practice and practical social support can further alleviate any fears. These relationships deserve this investment if mentoring and coaching are to have the desired positive outcomes.

Demonstrate curiosity

People are more likely to trust you when they believe they are interacting with the real you (authenticity) and when they feel cared for (empathy) (Frei and Morriss, 2020). In order to establish trust and allow the participant to bring their whole self to coaching, it is essential that the practitioner demonstrates curiosity to raise awareness of themselves (see Chapter 3) and the person they are working with.

Be prepared to see the whole person

McClelland's Iceberg Model is a useful tool to raise the practitioner's awareness so they are more able to provide personalised support and guidance. The tip of the iceberg shows everything that is visible or observable (e.g. teaching practice) and, typically, guidance and support is given for this. However, what lies beneath 'fuels the visible layer and can be either limiting or empowering' (Coaching the Shift, 2024). A coachee or mentee's beliefs, norms and values, self-image, drives and motives and personality all affect the visible layer, their behaviour, competencies and knowledge (Coaching the Shift, 2024). The practitioner should understand the whole person they are working with so they can best effect behavioural change that meets the needs of the individual.

To do this, the practitioner should ask questions that allow the participant to know the value they bring as their authentic self to the school community. A broad question such as "Is there anything that I need to know about you that would enable me to coach or mentor more effectively?" provides a starting point for the development of respectful curiosity.

Table 7.1 Example questions that could be asked during coaching and mentoring

Aspect of identity	Question
Beliefs	What makes you think this?
Norms and values	'What are your ideals? How would you like to see change?' (Coaching the Shift, 2024).
Self-image	How do you think others see you?
Drives and motives	What is important to you right now?
Personality	'What is important for you to think about? How do you view…? What is your opinion on…?' (Coaching the Shift, 2024).

An individual's intrinsic motivation and professional fulfilment may be affected by their identity, personal circumstances and the school's specific context. For example, knowing that a trainee or early career teacher has not previously had a paid job would allow a coaching approach to be used if personal and professional conduct (PPC) is a concern, rather than engaging in judgementoring and assuming that they should know how to be professional. A further example links to socio-economic background as 'teachers usually identify themselves as middle-class' (Dunne and Gazeley, 2008 cited in Major and Briant, 2023). This assumption is dangerous as it may affect an individual's ability to navigate an organisation's language and systems or their ability to remain within the profession if they are required to work alongside training to teach. With both examples, without appropriate support being provided (e.g. coaching with PPC, flexibility with assignment deadlines, support with managing time), there is an increased chance that trainees might have to withdraw.

Those leading on training for coaches and mentors could share examples of common experiences, either representative of their cohort (size-dependent) or wider research, to develop person-centred knowledge. For example, a career changer's self-image may be challenged due to their new status as a novice. Research shows that 'older mentees, particularly career changers, reported less positive experiences, suggesting mentoring approaches may need to be adapted to better meet their needs' (National Institute of Teaching, 2023b). By intentionally creating a space to find out about the participant (and this will take place throughout multiple interactions), the practitioner demonstrates that they value the individual as well as what they bring to the school community.

Avoid confirmation bias

Confirmation bias is the tendency to 'look for information that supports, rather than rejects, one's preconceptions, typically by interpreting evidence to confirm existing beliefs while rejecting or ignoring any conflicting data' (Simkus, 2023). If the practitioner exhibits curiosity, they realise that, rather than relying on assumptions, they need to search for evidence. Thinking about your initial responses to these statements, based on the coachee or mentee you are working with can help to raise awareness of confirmation bias. The statements are linked to professional growth and are influenced by the research cited in the *NFER Racial Equality in the Teacher Workforce*:

- They know the value they bring to the school.
- They know they are appreciated.
- They feel listened to.
- They are interested in a pastoral route.
- They are interested in career progression.
- They are interested in obtaining wider experience.
- They have the confidence to apply for a role.
- They don't need any help with applying for jobs.
- They are considering working in all schools in the local area.

If a practitioner is not informed by evidence when responding to these statements, and they do not critique the evidence they have, confirmation bias will affect the questions they ask, the language they use and, ultimately, their ability to establish a relationship based on trust. Without true curiosity, a coach or mentor cannot be aware of confirmation bias as they are coaching or mentoring a person of their own creation, not necessarily the person in front of them.

Be aware of your privilege

Another way to be curious is for practitioners to raise their awareness of their privilege (explored in Chapter 3) in relation to everyday experiences or common school occurrences.

Through being curious about daily interactions and where a practitioner may or may not have privilege, a space can be created to find out more about the participant's lived experience so support and guidance can be provided.

Table 7.2 Example questions to raise awareness of privilege

Question	Your response	An example of where a person does not possess privilege
Do you require any additional support during meetings?		A person with autism may worry about what their mentor thinks of them if they request clear, concise written instructions and if they need to seek clarification on top of this.
		A person with a health condition may experience pain or extreme discomfort and require pain relief, a cooler temperature, a change of position etc.
Do you feel safe when walking down the school corridor?		A person with a disability or a chronic health condition may not feel safe or may endure pain if they feel they can't ask for reasonable adjustments or get them.
		A female teacher may be harassed by pupils as she transitions to another classroom.
Do you feel safe when travelling to school?		Some Black male teachers have shared how they have been stopped numerous times by the police because of the car they have been driving on their way to work.
		A teacher may not be able to drive and has to rely on public transport. They may feel unsafe as they travel to work, more so during winter, when it is darker earlier.
Do you feel assumptions are made about your interest in career progression?		Some South Asian teachers have shared how, because they wear the hijab, other staff assume they are not interested in career progression.
		A woman who has just returned from maternity leave is not approached about applying for a role she is more than qualified for but her less experienced colleague is.

Active listening

Curiosity is shown through active listening and this is when 'you not only hear what someone is saying, but you're also attuned to their thoughts and feelings' (Gallo, 2024). Teachers may find it more challenging to engage in this type of listening because we hear a multitude of voices every day and it can be hard to tune in to one voice. Mentors could additionally receive feedback from others about their mentee and this may result in more attention being paid to the needs of the person feeding back than those of the mentee. Minehart, Symon, Rock (cited in Gallo, 2024) share four listening styles:

- A task-oriented listener is focused on efficiency and shapes a conversation around the transfer of important information.
- An analytical listener aims to analyse a problem from a neutral starting point.
- A relational listener seeks to build connection and understand and respond to the emotions underlying a message.
- A critical listener typically judges both the content of the conversation and the speaker themselves.

If the practitioner knows their default listening style, they can then be intentional in using another style or styles that enable them to meet the needs of the participant and understand what is significant to them. Avoiding performative listening is imperative and if coaches or mentors are too reactive (e.g. complete sentences) or overly focus on how they will respond, they may miss out on an opportunity to truly hear what is being said and ask perceptive questions (Gallo, 2024).

Be intentional in creating a safer space

Feelings of safety can be impacted by how the participant see the practitioner interact with others. For example, if the participant notices their practitioner is critical of someone who shares a similar characteristic, they may not feel as able to be honest. If they notice their mentor or coach amplifying the voices of others (see Chapter 3), they may feel safer to speak out. Practitioners should not feel as though they need to be on guard but they do need to be conscious of which messages they are conveying to their coachee or mentee through their interactions with others.

Contracting

Research suggests that mentors and mentees have different perceptions of whether a safer space is provided in meetings: 'only one-third of mentees felt mentoring provided a safe space to discuss feelings, compared to two-thirds of mentors who believed this to be true' (National Institute of Teaching, 2023b). To create a shared understanding of safety, contracting should be the focus of the first formal meeting (see Chapter 6). This provides the participant with time to think about what allows them to feel safer and know that the practitioner values their perspective, contributing towards the development of trust. This could be communicated via email or during contracting, whatever enables the participant to feel more comfortable. When engaging in contracting, the practitioner should explain what contracting is and why it is taking place, as well as what to expect during mentor meetings or coaching conversations. It is better to over-communicate rather than assume there is a mutual understanding of why feeling safe matters. This is even more significant if a power dynamic is involved e.g. a senior or middle leader mentoring an ECT as there may be a real fear with being honest.

Example script for framing contracting

"We're going to spend some time contracting and this will allow us to agree on behaviours that will maximise the time we have together. I'd really value your honesty with this and I know this isn't always easy. Please know there is no judgement here and we can come back to this in future sessions if you don't feel comfortable sharing at this point."

Examples of questions to ask as the conversation progresses

- What helps you to feel comfortable in meetings?
- What helps you to feel you can be honest?
- For now, is there anything that you feel I need to know about you so I can better support you?

Contracting should be revisited or renegotiated in future sessions to maintain trust and a commitment to safer spaces. Asking for feedback is a useful way to facilitate this as this shows a willingness to improve to better meet the needs of the person you are working with. This demonstrates that you value what they can bring to the relationship and contributes to feelings of safety, as long as the feedback is then acted on. These questions are influenced by research on team psychological safety:

- How easy do you find it to speak your mind? Why might this be (Garvin et. al., 2008, cited in Edmondson, 2019)?
- How easy do you find it to ask for help? Why might this be (Nembhard and Edmondson, 2006 cited in Edmondson, 2019)?
- 'Have I done what I can to destigmatise failure (Edmondson, 2019)?'

In schools, time often prevents practitioners from being able to re-contract, as they want to ensure there is dedicated time for developing teaching practice; without this, however, professional growth may be limited. Indeed, if coaching or mentoring is not having an impact on practice, returning to contracting is an effective way to reset the relationship.

Provide the coachee/mentee with space to speak

For the participant to be able to be their whole self, they must know that their contributions are valued. Mentor meetings can be dominated by the mentor and this is understandable, particularly during the early stages of a teacher's career when they are developing their expertise. Nonetheless, they should still be provided for a space to speak so the practitioner can learn: what is influencing their mental model; what might affect personal and professional behaviours; and what their experiences as a member of the school community are. If participants are not 'enabled to share their experiences and practices, they often, especially if they experience particular challenges, revert back to their negative narratives instead of looking to the future' (Bentley, 2020 cited in Oberholzer and Boyle, 2024). Asking open-ended questions throughout is one way in which to do this. Some examples include:

- What are you most worried about right now?
- What could go wrong? How would you deal with this?
- What questions do you have?

To enhance this, the practitioner could remind the participant about why questions are being asked as this may encourage honesty or they might provide reflection time to show an appreciation of different processing needs. Being silent and appreciating silence is powerful because it provides the crucial time for reflection and processing. Even though it may be awkward, it shows the practitioner values the participant's unique perspective.

Gaslighting

Gaslighting (see Chapter 6) can be a very real part of the lived experience of historically marginalised groups. To develop trust, being aware of gaslighting means the practitioner can consider their response, especially when their participant shares aspects of their lived experience. For example, a person from an underrepresented group may feel they have to work twice as hard compared to those in dominant groups. A mentor may trivialise this concern, dismiss it or make the participant feel that it is solely due to a lack of competence. This makes the participant doubt themselves and hinders the development of trust. Coaches and mentors 'need to be open-minded, non-judgemental and curious and to accept what they hear about people's lived experience. Snap judgements can snap back at us' (Shah, 2025). Recognising and validating the individual's emotions has such power and demonstrates empathy and compassion. Statements such as: "I'm sorry to hear things are so challenging for you right now" ensure the participant feels listened to, valued and reduces any feelings of isolation.

Appropriate self-disclosure

Appropriate self-disclosure (see Chapter 6) may be helpful for the participant if the practitioner discerns feelings of isolation, doubt or helplessness. The practitioner may feel it is appropriate to: comment on their privilege; share a common lived experience as well as their experiences as a learner. For example, "I had a bursary, so I didn't have to work. We can discuss some ways of managing this together but what do you feel would be most helpful to you right now?" or "I used to be really nervous before presenting/teaching/leading because xxx. How does this relate to your experience?" This creates a space for the coachee or mentee to be vulnerable and articulate the support needed whilst granting power to the relationship, not the coach (Shah, 2022).

Adjust support and guidance whilst maintaining high expectations

Demonstrate commitment

'The essence of coaching is putting people first' (Palmer and McDowall cited in Shah, 2022). To do this, the participant needs to feel like they have your full attention. This means putting phones away, closing laptops, minimising distractions and switching off from other tasks. To coach or mentor with an ED&I lens means committing to the needs of the person you are working with. For example, it may help your participant to see resources in advance or be provided with time to make notes. Knowing the participant enables the practitioner to select the mentoring stance or coaching tools that will be most effective for them rather than feeling they have to rigidly stick to one approach.

In addition, the practitioner must show a commitment to themselves and consider who else is best placed to help the person they are working with. If the participant requires counselling, the practitioner could refer them to appropriate channels of support e.g. Mental Health First Aiders, employee assistance programmes or other external professional bodies. A coach or mentor must never work in isolation and must know who is in their team to support them e.g. the ITT or ECT coordinator, their line manager and members of their team. If there are concerns about the participant's professional growth or the amount of time the practitioner is spending working with the participant, they should speak to their line manager so the appropriate support can be provided to the practitioner and the participant. An ED&I lens does not mean reducing expectations, it means adjusting the support needed to thrive,

Feedback

Effective coaching (here we focus on instructional coaching) and mentoring need to foster accountability. One way to do this is through high-quality feedback. When providing feedback on lessons, avoid the stance of a 'judgementor', because, otherwise, feedback is influenced by the power dynamic at play and 'insights may be steeped in biases and fragile assumptions' (Sherrington, 2024). In practice, this looks like the practitioner having an irrefutable view of the lesson and dominating the conversation with little opportunity for the participant to speak and influence the direction of their professional growth. Sherrington states that feedback should be co-constructed with the participant sharing their thoughts about the challenges and possible solutions (Sherrington, 2024). This model is not just relevant for more experienced teachers; trainees are capable of sharing what they found challenging and possible solutions to address this.

Rachel Sewell, Director of Implementation at Steplab, shares another model of feedback where the participant is active in the process and the feedback meets the needs of the coachee, rather than the coach.

> **Case Study**
>
> Steplab's model of instructional coaching is a responsive coaching model. As the coach observes the lesson, they are looking for objective evidence based on what the teacher is saying and doing and what the pupils are thinking and doing. This allows the coach to remain curious and aims to remove observational bias. Based on what they have observed so far, the coach forms a hypothesis about the potential learning problems in the classroom. When they have this hypothesis, they then collect more evidence with the mindset of seeking to be proven wrong. The coach continues to collect evidence which supports or refutes their hypotheses and they decide on a potential goal and step to solve the most foundational learning problem. During the meeting with the coachee, lesson evidence is discussed and, in discussion with the coachee, the coach is looking for:
>
> 1. Shared awareness – did they notice the same things?
> 2. Their insight into how learning happens, allowing the coach to understand their existing mental models about learning problems in the lesson.
> 3. A shared decision about the right goal and step to work on in order to begin to solve the learning problem.
>
> The coachee is very much an active participant in this process, with the coach responding to their existing knowledge and needs, resulting in the coachee feeling their views are valued.

A lack of time can make this challenging and Sherrington mentions planning for the feedback conversation as you observe (Sherrington, 2024). The planning process should involve thinking about what can be effectively shared in the timeframe available and what could be shared with the coachee or mentee beforehand. A risk of instructional coaching is the coachee feeling they have to imitate the coach, minimising authenticity. The practitioner has to provide the building blocks of what the participant should aspire to practise but they must create space for autonomy by providing time for the participant to reflect and by giving them permission to practise in a way that reflects their emerging professional identity.

In order to avoid the stance of judgementor, feedback should be approached with care. For those from underrepresented groups, bias may come into action. For example, research shows that gender bias may be present with women more likely 'to receive kinder feedback that tends to be less precise and actionable' (King, 2023). Kim Scott's (2019) communication framework highlights the importance of caring personally and challenging directly, enabling honest feedback to be given while maintaining trust. Consideration of a person's characteristics and how feedback can be further adapted to meet their needs is helpful. For neurodivergent individuals, direct, actionable guidance may be required with a clear explanation about why the change is needed (Neal, n.d.). Again, avoiding assumptions of homogeneity is imperative. It is beneficial to demonstrate curiosity by asking about an individual's preferred way to receive feedback and by asking for feedback on your feedback. Consequently, the practitioner is able to see how the feedback is landing and can refine their approach accordingly.

Some studies suggest trainees can be largely unaware of their own privilege (Connolly, 2021 cited in Major and Briant, 2023). If we approach mentoring and coaching with an ED&I lens, the participant's privilege could mean that they are not aware of what affects feelings of belonging and safety in a classroom, chiefly for pupils from underrepresented groups. For example, they might assume that: everyone in a class has access to books or learning materials at home when setting homework; all children have visited local places of interest; or that all pupils will understand cultural references. Here, the mentor or instructional coach needs to help the participant to develop their person-centred knowledge by drawing attention to what could exclude some pupils and explaining why this might be the case. They then need to share what could be said instead to promote belonging. This does not tend to be a focus for lesson observations so, if it is noticed, it needs to be addressed at a suitable point during feedback.

Self-advocacy

Additional support may be needed for those who have to navigate 'the additional complexities presented by their diagnosis, as well as developing strategies for self-advocacy and engaging with their training from a strength-based perspective' (Lovatt and Davey, 2025). Even though Lovatt and Davey focus on students with a diagnosis of dyslexia, knowing how to self-advocate is a crucial skill for those from underrepresented groups. Nonetheless, there are risks involved in self-advocacy. For example, a person may:

- Feel it is safer to be silent so they are not perceived as a trouble-maker.
- Not have the confidence and self-worth to ensure their needs are met (Moe, 2021).
- Question how much support they will get if such support is not representative of their time within education as a pupil and/or as a teacher.

Self-advocacy is a learned behaviour, but it is not consistently and explicitly taught in schools. Pupils of colour (and then the adults they become) are:

> more likely to need to learn to self-advocate, given they are more likely to experience negative bias, stereotyping, lower expectations, and discrimination, both in and out of school. They need to be able to tell adults, especially White adults, that they are in fact worthy…
>
> (Duchesneau and Griffin, 2020)

Without consistent formal teaching of self-advocacy, individuals must see it modelled or have had the opportunity to practise it (Moe, 2021). A mentor can help to cultivate this skill. Firstly, a space can be provided for the person to articulate the value they bring and acknowledge their accomplishments e.g. start meetings with the participant sharing their achievements. This allows individuals to practise ensuring they are seen and heard for what they want to present and they see the value they bring to the school. If this is not articulated, it may not always be noticed by those in more senior positions.

Secondly, the practitioner can provide time for scripting or rehearsing conversations where they have to engage in self-advocacy. This could range from asking for reasonable adjustments to asking a more senior member of staff for further support or guidance. This could also include signposting helpful resources such as the video *Negotiation skills for women leaders in education* (Porritt, 2021).

Thirdly, the practitioner can be explicit in communicating the right to support. Our education system does not work for all within the school community so the reality of what self-advocacy looks like should be shared. For example, a person requiring reasonable adjustments needs to understand that for self-advocacy to have impact, they have to be tenacious, courageous and unapologetic in asking for what they need to be able to fulfil their role and responsibilities. Self-advocacy here may be a series of conversations with the person asking for the same support.

Fourthly, the practitioner should have a strong understanding of school systems and policies so they can give more informed guidance and, in facilitative coaching, this may involve switching to a more directive approach. For example, if an individual does not have access to insider information, they may have a limited awareness of business jargon e.g. honorariums or time in lieu. Consequently, they may not be able to advocate for themselves effectively or fully navigate internal systems and this may continue into their career. Trainees and early career teachers cannot, and should not, begin their teaching careers by viewing certain aspects of their identity negatively and, to do this, support is required.

For further discussion of reasonable adjustments, see Chapter 4.

Develop social capital

Another way to 'navigate these additional complexities' is through the acculturator stance, and developing social capital. Social capital can be defined as 'the extent and nature of our connections with others and the collective attitudes and behaviours between people that support a well-functioning, close-knit society' (What Works Wellbeing, 2022). Mentees may need to be directed to network with others, especially if visible characteristics mean they already feel isolated. For example, inviting the mentee to have lunch with the team or attend a staff social event. Introducing a mentee to someone who could support them based on an aspect of their identity is helpful e.g. a trainee with dyslexia might find it helpful to talk to a more experienced teacher with dyslexia about how they manage this in the classroom. These relationships matter and it may help to develop self-efficacy and self-advocacy as well as reducing feelings of isolation. It moves the mentee from '"legitimate peripheral" to full "participation" within the school community' (Hobson and Malderez, 2012).

Develop personal and professional skills

If mentors are to take the stance of an 'educator', they must go beyond the realm of limiting frameworks and consider if the participant would benefit from instruction on personal and professional skills, e.g. managing stress, self-regulation, challenging cognitive distortions, and this is required to foster high self-efficacy (Chan, 2008; Klusmann et al., 2008 cited in Beltman et al., 2011). It might involve the practitioner working with the participant on behaviours and skills outside of the classroom e.g. a teacher dealing with sexual harassment from pupils in shared spaces or providing guidance on managing workload to reduce feelings of stress.

Some may see this as 'hand-holding' or feel they are patronising the person they are working with. However, not all teachers, for example, have been taught effective time management, ways to deal with stress or how to apply such strategies to the many roles and responsibilities of being a teacher. When sharing strategies, asking the participant for their thoughts about what works avoids the practitioner from applying what works for them on the coachee or mentee. For example, a teacher with ADHD who is struggling with organisation may have tried lots of different strategies so more specialist support might be needed. Forming a teacher identity is a significant part of the trainee's experience (Steadman 2023, cited in Lovatt and Davey, 2025) and the provision of support outside of the taught curriculum may enable some teachers to thrive and remain within the profession.

If the participant experiences discrimination in the school setting, a relationship based on trust makes it more likely for the participant to share this with their coach or mentor. If the practitioner asks to talk about the participant's experiences outside of the classroom or as a member of the school community, the participant may be more willing to share. Sharing these experiences is a deeply personal choice and people may choose not to share for various different reasons e.g. they have not received help in the past. The mentor should be vigilant to the experiences of those from underrepresented groups; this vigilance means support can be provided even if prejudicial incidents are not disclosed. For example, Natasha, as a trainee and the only person of colour in her placement school, experienced racism from pupils in one of her classes. She never shared this with her mentor (and now regrets not doing so). Natasha would have appreciated: talking to someone about it; guidance on how she should have managed prejudicial behaviour aimed at her; and knowledge of what the school's response would be.

The practitioner should be knowledgeable about policy and know what is required to be reported. They should additionally appreciate that reporting an incident does not mean it is resolved and that the coachee or mentee might fear future interactions with the perpetrator(s). Empathy is shown here through statements and questions such as "I'm sorry that happened. Here are some options about what we could do. What is your preferred choice?" An overly empathetic or emotional response may not always help and may force the participant to revisit the incident through the practitioner's lens, influencing their thinking and their choice of future action.

> **Questions**
>
> 1. Reflect on the best coaching and/or mentoring experiences you have had. What did your coach or mentor do to help to establish trust and make you feel it was safer to be your authentic self?
> 2. What knowledge do you need to develop so you can offer more informed and personalised support to your coachee or mentee?
> 3. What barriers do you face when adopting an ED&I lens? How can these barriers be overcome and what support is required?

References

Amos, Z. (n.d.). *Coaching vs. Mentoring: What's the Difference?* Available at: Coaching Vs. Mentoring: 3 Key Differences & Examples | Radical Candor [Accessed 24 March 2025].

Beltman S., Mansfield, C., Price, A. (2011). Thriving Not Just Surviving: A Review of Research on Teacher Resilience. *Educational Research Review*, 6(3), 185–207.

Chambers, M, Warnes, M., Adams, E. (2025). *Developing Staff Professionalism through Leading a Culture of Learning.* Available at: https://my.chartered.college/impact_article/developing-staff-professionalism-through-leading-a-culture-of-learning/ [Accessed 28 March 2025].

Chartered College of Teaching (n.d.) *An introduction to instructional coaching*, Available at: https://my.chartered.college/early-career-hub/an-introduction-to-instructional-coaching/. [Accessed 24 March 2025].

Coaching the Shift Towards Organizational Health (2024). *The Iceberg Model of David McClelland.* Available at: https://www.coachingtheshift.com/en/ijsbergmodel-mcclelland-gedragsverandering [Accessed 14 March 2025].

Duchesneau, N., Griffin, A. (2020). *Self-Advocacy or Defiance in Protests? Depends: Are You White or Black?* Available at: https://edtrust.org/the-equity-line/self-advocacy-or-defiance-in-protests-depends-are-coachormentor-white-or-black/ [Accessed 20 February 2025].

Edmondson, A. (2019). *The Fearless Organisation Creating Psychological Safety in the Workplace for Learning, Innovation and Growth*. Hoboken, NJ: Wiley.

Frei, F., Morriss, A. (2020). *Begin with Trust*. Available at: https://hbr.org/2020/05/begin-with-trust [Accessed 7 January 2025].

Gallo, A. (2024). *What Is Active Listening?* Available at: https://hbr.org/2024/01/what-is-active-listening [Accessed 20 February 2025].

Goodrich, J. (2024). *What's the Difference between Instructional Coaching and Responsive Coaching?* Available at: https://steplab.co/resources/whats-the-difference-between-instructional-coaching-and-responsive-coaching/66d9c8990982810001156c58) [Accessed 20 February 2025].

Goodrich, J., Mccrea, P., Sims, S. (2024). *A Beginner's Guide to Instructional Coaching*. Available at:(https://steplab.co/resources/beginners-guide-to-instructional-coaching/66d9d0ea0982810001156c8f) [Accessed 20 February 2025].

Hobson, A., Malderez, A. (2012). Judgementoring and other Threats to Realising the Potential of School-Based Mentoring in Teacher Education. *International Journal of Mentoring and Coaching in Education*, 2(2), 89–108. Available at: https://shu.a.shu.ac.uk/7224/1/Hobson_and_Malderez_2013_Judgementoring_IJMCE_Post-print_draft.pdf [Accessed 15 November 2024].

King, M. (2023). *What's Really Holding Women Back at Work*. Available at: https://www.forbes.com/sites/michelleking/2023/08/02/whats-really-holding-women-back-at-work/ [Accessed 6 February 2025].

Lovatt, S., Davey, J. (2025). *Supporting the Professional Identity of Trainee Teachers with Dyslexia*. Available at: https://my.chartered.college/impact_article/supporting-the-professional-identity-of-trainee-teachers-with-dyslexia/ [Accessed 18 February 2025].

Major, E., Briant, E. (2023). *A Practical Guide for Teachers Equity in Education*. UK: John Catt from Hodder Education.

Maxwell, B., Hobson, A., Manning, C. (2022). *Mentoring and Coaching Trainee and Early Career Teachers: Conceptual Review*. Available at: https://www.researchgate.net/publication/366066070_Mentoring_and_coaching_trainee_and_early_career_teachers_Conceptual_review [Accessed 23 March 2025].

Moe, K. (2021). *Self-Advocacy: Improve Your Life by Speaking Up*. Available at: https://www.betterup.com/blog/self-advocacy?hs_amp=true [Accessed 25 March 2025].

National Institute of Teaching (2023a). *Mentoring and Coaching of Teachers What Can Research Tell Us?* Available at: https://niot.s3.amazonaws.com/documents/NIOT_mentoring_and_coaching_-_Key_Takeaways.pdf [Accessed 27 March 2025].

National Institute of Teaching (2023b). *Mentoring and Coaching Trainee and Early Career Teachers*. Available at: https://niot.org.uk/research-projects/mentoring_coaching_trainee_early_career_teachers [Accessed 26 March 2025].

Neal, B. (n.d.). *Temple Grandin Talks About Why Clear Feedback for Neurodivergent Individuals Matters*. Available at: Temple Grandin: Feedback for Neurodivergent Individuals | Radical Candor [Accessed 27 March 2025].

Oberholzer, L., Boyle, D. (2024). *Mentoring and Coaching in Education A Guide to Coaching and Mentoring Teachers at Every Stage of Their Careers*. London: Bloomsbury.

Porritt, V. (2021). Negotiation Skills for Women Leaders in Education. Available at: https://www.coachormentortube.com/watch?v=UTMeABj2dAg [Accessed 28 March 2025].

Scott, K. (2019). *Radical Candour How to Get What You Want by Saying What You Mean*. London: Pan Books and Pan Macmillan.

Shah, S. (2022). *Diversity, Inclusion and Belonging in Coaching*. Great Britain and United States: Kogan Page Limited.

Shah, S. (2025). *Mastering Inclusion*. Available at: https://www.linkedin.com/pulse/mastering-inclusion-salma-shah-pcc-h2gie [Accessed 28 March 2025].

Sherrington, T. (2024). *Lesson Feedback: Don't Send It, Don't Give It – Co-Construct It. Otherwise, It Won't Be Worth It*. Available at: https://teacherhead.com/2024/01/28/lesson-feedback-dont-send-it-dont-give-it-co-construct-it-otherwise-it-wont-be-worth-it/ [Accessed 21 March 2025].

Simkus, J. (2023). *Confirmation Bias in Psychology: Definition & Examples*. Available at: https://www.simplypsychology.org/confirmation-bias.html [Accessed 6 January 2025].

Sims, S. (2019). *Four Reasons Instructional Coaching Is Currently the Best-Evidenced form of CPD*. Sam Sims Quantitative Education Research. Available at https://samsims.education/2019/02/19/247/ [Accessed 24 April 2024].

Stokes, P., Fatien, D., Otter, K., Otter, P. (2020). "Two Sides of the Same Coin"? Coaching and Mentoring and the Agentic Role of Context. *Annals of the New York Academy of Sciences*.

Stonewall (2025). *Supporting Early Career LGBTQ+ People in the Workplace*. Available at: https://files.stonewall.org.uk/production/files/UPS-Resource-Final.pdf?dm=1738585603 [Accessed 27 March 2025].

What Works Wellbeing (2022). *Social Capital: Evidence Review and Synthesis*. Available at: https://whatworkswellbeing.org/projects/social-capital-evidence-review-and-synthesis/ [Accessed 27 March 2025].

Worth, J., McLean, D., Sharp, C. (2022). *Racial Equality in the Teacher Workforce: An Analysis of Representation and Progression Opportunities from Initial Teacher Training to Headship*. Available at: https://www.nfer.ac.uk/publications/racial-equality-in-the-teacher-workforce/ [Accessed 10 December 2024].

Creating a positive action programme

What is a positive action programme?

Under the Equality Act 2010, employers in England, Scotland and Wales can use positive action measures to help individuals who share a protected characteristic. It involves proportionate actions which are designed to: reduce disadvantage; meet different needs; and increase representation (Government Equalities Office, 2023).

For a positive action measure to be legitimate, it must demonstrate that it does not discriminate against others. For example, an employer could show that there is underrepresentation of women in leadership, and that this is not representative of the staff workforce. Even if such legitimacy exists, it does not mean that such interventions are always met positively. At the time of writing, there has been a backlash to ED&I work in America with some individuals from dominant groups feeling that such activity is unfair because they are not able to access the same opportunities or they are not worth the resource. This is why positive action measures require a completely transparent, data-informed rationale to minimise dissent as well as monitoring to gauge long-term feasibility. Crucially, a positive action measure must be underpinned by an overall strategic priority, most likely linking to recruitment and retention, so it is part of wider ED&I activity rather than a solution in itself.

Positive action, if it is in the form of an additional programme for those from historically marginalised groups, could be construed negatively by those it is aimed at. Participants may feel that it encourages deficit thinking, with more support having to be given, rather than a comprehensive review of systemic bias within an organisation. Worryingly, participants may then be perceived as being ED&I hires, there to fill a quota, rather than obtaining a role due to their talent and potential. It may cause participants to feel hypervisible, especially if the programme is aimed at people with invisible characteristics, as participants then have to navigate whether participation is worth the risk of disclosure of an aspect of their identity. Positive action programmes may be further problematic if there are assumptions of homogeneity with the intersectional identities of participants not being recognised.

Therefore, any positive action programme within an organisation should be carefully crafted to maximise impact and minimise harm to those from historically marginalised groups.

Planning a positive action leadership programme

We are going to share our learning from implementing Dixons Academies Trust's positive action programme: Accelerate. We'd like to thank Dixons Academies Trust for the opportunity to lead on the programme and showcase its work. This programme aims to increase representation at senior and middle leadership level of those from the global majority and it is part of a wider strand of work on representation. This is important so ED&I activity goes beyond isolated activity, e.g. diversifying the school website, and is part of wider ED&I recruitment work. For example:

- A review and adaptation of application and interview processes based on where bias is more at risk of occurring when making decisions (Tulshyan, 2022).
- Stakeholder feedback on marketing and communications.
- Changes to marketing and communication practices.
- Publishing an authentic equal opportunities policy statement (Tulshyan, 2022).

We recognise that a positive action programme focusing on the characteristic of race will not be applicable to all schools or trusts. However, the Accelerate programme for senior leaders has several components which could be applied to any school setting if the required resource is available. We will share how each component could be adapted on a smaller scale and it may be an intervention for all staff, to improve recruitment and retention, rather than a positive action measure. As you read this chapter, consider what could work in your setting and whether wider collaboration would provide greater opportunities.

For the purpose of brevity, as Accelerate is ambitious in scope, we are going to share an overview of each component and key learning in relation to the implementation plan headings shared in Chapter 2.

The problem

To develop a more nuanced understanding of the problem, data must be interrogated and it is essential to listen to and learn from potential participants of the programme. School workforce data may not present the necessary information to enable you to understand the current situation, especially if we consider intersectional identities. Thus, more data collection may be needed based on characteristics, viewpoints and experiences of the intended participants of the programme. If this is the case, it is essential to be clear and transparent about why this personal data is needed, how it will be used and how personal information will be protected (CIPD, 2019). Based on what data collection is permitted, more holistic data collection may be another strand of future ED&I activity. Here are some considerations when reviewing data:

- If participants prefer not to disclose a characteristic, how do you find out who should be part of the programme? Are any individuals potentially excluded if they don't disclose their race? For example, if a positive action measure focuses on race, those who are white passing may be excluded if assumptions are made on the basis of their skin colour.

- Is there consistency with how staff are identified as middle and senior leaders?

- Is the data available to find out about staff recruitment, retention and attrition figures based on the protected characteristic in comparison to the dominant group?

- Can you find out about staff career progression figures based on the characteristic in comparison to the dominant group?

- Can you find out any common concerns linked to being from a historically marginalised group based on feedback from exit interviews?

- Are you able to capture staff perceptions of recruitment and retention, including any feedback on advertising and recruitment processes?

From having access to this data, an evidence-informed rationale can begin to be developed. Nevertheless, more data is needed, using other mechanisms to capture feedback, to fully inform the rationale and enable specific interventions to be planned in more detail. To be able to listen to and learn from our senior leaders, we held a focus group where they could share their lived experience and their hopes and fears about a positive action programme. We then created a research-informed baseline survey which provided further insights into the lived experiences of those from the global majority, as well as the impact of intersectionality on challenges experienced in the workplace. The survey included evidence-informed statements based on experiences of those from the global majority (e.g. I have experienced microaggressions) and there was a Likert scale to capture views. We thought very carefully about how to introduce the survey and were explicit in sharing who would be able to access the survey data and how the data would be used. The aim of this was to encourage honesty and start to establish trust. The learning from this enabled us to clarify the problem and start to decide on the final outcomes for the programme. Moreover, we referred to some of this data during the Accelerate conference to highlight that participants were not alone in some of their experiences, thereby promoting connection. If a positive action programme is to help people, it is necessary that they inform and influence the planning.

Deciding on final outcomes

Backwards planning is vital to ensure coherence with the different strands of the programme as well as ensuring tangible outcomes. By engaging in a literature review and exploration of external programmes, we were able to craft the final outcomes. Significantly, they focus on both participant and organisational areas of growth. Here's an example of two of the programme outcomes:

- Participants develop broader leadership competencies.
- Trust leaders and principals increase their awareness of the lived experience of staff from the global majority.

By finalising our outcomes, we could then create the aims of the overall programme and start planning each component in more detail.

Intervention descriptions

Although thorough exploration gave us an understanding of some of the common challenges experienced by those from the global majority, we approached this learning with caution to ensure we were not unduly influenced by our own lived experience and did not make any assumptions of homogeneity. For example, as part of our reading, we understood that a common challenge is 'women of colour frequently experience more pushback when they negotiate or advocate for themselves as compared to white women and that most negotiation advice is futile until we address workplace bias' (Tulshyan, 2022). Within our focus group, knowing how to advocate was raised as an area of interest as well as some senior leaders wanting more opportunities to be able to raise their profile and develop their self-efficacy during job interviews. Therefore, external research combined with internal research allowed us to refine the content of programme components. External literature is not enough in itself, it must be corroborated by internal research so the positive action measure meets the needs of its participants.

Once we had decided on programme components, we had to consider the frequency and duration of each intervention and how this could be balanced against the competing priorities of senior leaders. The Accelerate conference (four hours in total) was a mandatory part of the programme because it enabled us to start discussions about the different aims of the programme and build a strong network. After this, participants were able to opt into the remaining components: group career coaching; stay conversations; mock interviews and training; and professional shadowing. Allowing for flexibility enabled us to engender commitment as the programme then met the individual needs of participants.

Accelerate conference

Attendance at a conference for participants was an essential launchpad for the programme and fully supported by principals. Through attending training organised by Diverse Educators as well as being founding members of Dixons Academies Trust's anti-racism group in 2020 (see the case study in Chapter 2), we knew that this space could be transformational if participants had the opportunity to share their lived experience in the workplace and understand the commitment from school leadership to seeing and hearing them as their authentic selves. In some ways, the conference was a form of an affinity group because it empowered members, amplified their voices and addressed common challenges whilst driving change within the organisation (The OR Briefings, n.d.). To engineer practical social support from the outset, we provided participants with the opportunity to raise awareness (see Chapter 3) and discuss questions such as:

- How do others treat you based on what you feel is your most visible characteristic? Consider both positive and negative interactions.
- Has this had any lasting impact?
- Do you feel that you need to act significantly differently at school compared to home?

We were keen to ensure the conference was a positive and empowering space for all and used co-constructed contracting to set the tone.

Trust leader Luke Sparkes introduced the conference, again demonstrating the commitment of the trust to increasing representation. During the introduction, we explained the title of the programme so participants understood it was about personal and professional fulfilment with the aim of increased staff retention and potentially career progression based on individual career goals. Another necessary part of the introduction was sharing other ED&I activity in the trust and its impact so far to show participants that this programme was part of a wider strand of work on representation.

During the conference, we focused on rethinking leadership image (Center for Creative Leadership, n.d.) and the impact of dominant images of leadership on professional behaviours. An example of this is engaging in code-switching, which is 'adjusting one's style of speech, appearance, behaviour, and expression in ways that will optimise the comfort of others in exchange for fair treatment, quality service, and employment opportunities' (McCluney et al., 2019). This led to discussions about authenticity and advocacy with practical tools for advocacy shared.

Research on role model effects show that they 'are theoretically stronger when multiple characteristics are shared' (Chung, 2000 cited in Gershenson et al., 2021) and they 'could help to raise achievement and attainment by inspiring students (Gershenson et al., 2021). This focus on inspiration is just as important for staff, especially if someone's experience within the education sector, as a pupil and member of staff, has been defined by an absence of representation. To highlight existing role models and the trust's commitment to becoming more representative, we knew a panel of speakers from the global majority was a must and adopted an intersectional lens when reaching out to CEOs, principals and equivalent leaders from the global majority in the education sector. We planned how we would chair the panel carefully so there were equal contributions from all speakers. This aspect of the conference proved the most inspirational, shining a light on the talent of those from the global majority within the education sector.

Other options

Trust leaders within Dixons Academies Trust have fully invested in this programme and we recognise that such a commitment may not be possible in all school settings. Other options to show the significance of representation include:

- Having an ED&I focus in the staff bulletin or an ED&I spotlight in staff briefing to share research digests on the importance of representation, role models and authenticity.
- Sharing research with senior leaders to raise awareness of factors affecting recruitment and retention for those with protected characteristics e.g. the problematic concept of professionalism as 'a Western hegemony has specifically privileged those who have the most proximity to Western and white culture, while disadvantaging those who are further from it' (Tulshyan, 2022).

Group career coaching

To plan group career coaching, we met with external coaches who provided expertise in relation to session content and shared how we could sensitively manage groups so all coachees felt seen and heard. We considered whether participants would prefer a coach from the global majority to better establish trust; however, feedback showed that this was not essential. Establishing a safer space was paramount for the four coaching sessions, especially as coachees did not know each other; time was factored in for this in the first coaching session. To structure the sessions, the Church of England Foundation for Educational Leadership (CEFEL) conversation framework is helpful and it has three stages: individual reflections; group dialogue; and consideration of action (Barrett, 2025). We wanted there to be the option for a more directive approach so relevant theory could be shared as well as useful guidance for coachees to be aware of in order to influence their career progression. Consequently, stimulus was used to promote reflection and discussion and actions were revisited in subsequent coaching sessions. Group career coaching sessions gave participants time to reflect on their professional growth and how they could thrive in their current role. In busy day-to-day lives, we do not have the luxury to engage in such thinking and participants found it helpful to take this time to invest in themselves.

Other options

- Coaches and line managers receive career coaching training so strategies can be applied during line management meetings or appraisal.
- Create a career progression reading list. Some areas of focus include: career goal visualisation; managing setbacks; and establishing a personal brand.

Stay Conversations

A stay conversation is a retention tool that aims to 'increase one's sense of purpose and commitment' and it takes place between a leader and 'high-potential and critical talent to reinforce their value and how much the organisation appreciates them and their strong future ahead' (Dagenais, 2020). When planning a stay conversation for Accelerate, we worked closely with HR and adapted their questions and guidance to meet the needs of Accelerate participants. For example, we included a question that linked to participants' feelings regarding being their whole self in the workplace. There can be a real fear around having such conversations and, to mitigate this, we produced guidance for trust leaders and principals and shared key points during a trust briefing. We ensured the process was completely transparent; participants could access the questions before the stay conversation and prepare their answers. Furthermore, the guidance shared with principals was included on the stay conversation proforma.

For a stay conversation to be successful, the leader should demonstrate 'empathy, advanced listening and targeted communication skills' (Dagenais, 2020). However, the participant must be able to advocate for themselves to ensure the stay conversation meets their individual goals. Group career coaching contributed to developing awareness of professional growth needs and the need for advocacy, with peers providing practical social support on how to do this.

Other options

- Pilot having a stay conversation (if this is not yet established in your school) and share learning with senior leaders.
- Line managers to access training on the value of acting as a sponsor.

Interview training and mock interviews

Supporting individuals with interviews is already established within our work across the trust. For example, all Dixons trainees have training on how to have an effective interview and have a mini mock interview with a member of the trust leadership team. One of the reasons Natasha incorporated this into the Initial Teacher Training (ITT) curriculum was to minimise the impact of not having access to insider information (see Chapter 7 for more information on this) and to develop self-efficacy. This became a component in the Accelerate programme for the same reasons, but with the additional aim of raising the profile of participants with trust leaders, countering any impact of affinity bias (see Chapter 4). Again, questions were shared with participants in advance and guidance for trust leaders and principals was created to ensure there was a shared understanding of purpose and process.

Other options

- Share interview questions with interviewees.
- Provide training for school leaders on affinity bias.

Professional shadowing

Professional shadowing, already a part of the professional growth offer across Dixons Academies Trust, was made explicit to Accelerate participants. Those from historically marginalised groups may have limiting self-beliefs, as we discuss in Chapter 7. Consequently, professional shadowing allowed them to see the realities of a role. This, in turn, contributed to the development of self-efficacy as it demystified the role. Participants were asked to select which role they would like to shadow and whether there was anything else we needed to consider when matching participants with the more senior member of staff. Here, the impact of intersectional identities was made apparent with some participants wanting to shadow more senior leaders with families in order to understand the personal and professional impact.

Other options

- Offer staff aspiring for headship the opportunity to meet those in more senior roles to find out more about the reality of a role.
- Provide opportunities for staff to get involved with high-profile work with a senior leader so the invisible work becomes more visible.

Deciding on implementation strategies

It is not possible for us to list all the actions we undertook to launch Accelerate; however, we will share some key learning points.

Advertising the programme

Initially, this began through pitching our programme to trust leaders and principals to explain the evidence-informed rationale for the programme and to outline the programme's components. It also developed person-centred knowledge by sharing the common lived experience of those from the global majority in the workplace. This was a crucial starting point in order to get leadership commitment and investment and make clear their role in some of the programme components e.g. stay conversations.

To reinforce leadership commitment, participants were personally invited to join the programme by two trust leaders. The programme was further advertised through a central bulletin for all academies within the trust to allow for transparency and ensure that any staff missing from the distribution list were aware of the professional development offer. We were keen to avoid staff being approached in person, and for it to be advertised in staff meetings, to avoid hypervisibility and people from the global majority being forced to explain themselves if they did not want to take part. We thought carefully about how to advertise the programme and were honest in explaining the rationale for this programme as well as highlighting the interplay between organisational learning and individual professional growth. Admittedly, being from the global majority helped us to think more deeply about our approach with the aim of including all and minimising feelings of discomfort.

Managing multiple components

As the Accelerate programme is ambitious in scope, managing different strands required administrative support and we recognise that this is not an option in all school settings. Moreover, dedicated time was needed to engage in thoughtful and inclusive implementation. For example, we: referred to the trust calendar to avoid organising events during pinch points; we found out when religious observances and celebrations were taking place to ensure we were not excluding participants; and we provided longer timeframes for each component to provide more flexibility for busy school leaders. As the programme needed collaboration with different stakeholders, it was vital to work backwards from scheduled events so there was timely communication and enough preparation time. Indeed, one of the joys of the programme was collaborating with and learning from a variety of stakeholders who were all invested in ensuring the programme was a success. Whilst it can be challenging to work at scale, initial time spent in creating an implementation plan, and then a more detailed project plan, created clarity around deadlines and promoted sustainability.

Creating a network

During the planning process, we knew we wanted to establish a network to bring more coherence to the programme as a whole and establish a sense of community. We decided this would be through a half-termly Accelerate research digest with the aim to inspire and empower participants. After the riots in England and Northern Ireland, in the summer of 2024, we realised that our response to national or international events affecting the global majority had to be more strategic so anyone leading on Accelerate knew this was part of the process. If such events are not acknowledged, with lived experience of some within the group is also dismissed.

Monitoring progress

This work is in its infancy and we are in year two of the programme. As a result, we cannot yet comment on the long-term impact of this work.

We can comment on some of the challenges of monitoring linked to data. Showing the impact of this programme by solely relying on the number of participants promoted is difficult because it is reliant on the number of vacancies available so it is not a reliable measure. Even if there is an increase in the number of people from the global majority in more senior positions, it may not address intersectional identities e.g. a balance between men and women from the global majority. To obtain qualitative data, the baseline survey was replicated and served as a programme evaluation tool to show the impact of Accelerate, and other associated ED&I activity, on personal and professional behaviours, experiences of belonging and perceptions of organisational support. Key findings have been shared with trust leadership, contributing to developing person-centred knowledge and organisational growth.

Another challenge of monitoring progress is based on the feasibility of the programme in the long term. This programme is dependent on the number of staff from the global majority in senior leadership roles and, for the programme to be viable, there must be a minimum number of participants. As the programme has already proved popular, it can only run based on what vacancies are available and who is then recruited. For that reason, for the programme to be feasible, and for the trust to continue to invest in it, the scope of the programme may have to be reduced or it may have to be offered biennially.

Evaluation feedback has really highlighted the impact of trust investment on individuals. For those who opted into many of the components, they have felt valued and seen and heard as their authentic selves. They have felt more equipped to advocate for themselves and appreciate their agency in shaping their professional growth. Creating a space for these conversations and for this training cannot be underestimated. Many of the participants have, in their words, "wanted to give back" and we have been able to amplify voices with participants being part of the middle leader Accelerate conference panel or facilitating sections of the Accelerate conference.

Questions

1. Which programme component is of most interest to you? Why?
2. How could this programme, a component of the programme, or one of the options shared, be implemented in your school?

References

Barrett, L. (2025). *Using Coaching Competencies within Group Dialogue to Enhance the Delivery of Leadership Development.* London: Impact Journal of the Chartered College of Teaching.

Center for Creative Leadership (n.d.). *What Is Authentic Leadership, and Why Does It Matter?* Available at: https://www.ccl.org/articles/leading-effectively-articles/authenticity-1-idea-3-facts-5-tips/ [Accessed 14 April 2025].

CIPD (2019). *Diversity Management that Works an Evidence-Based View.* Available at: https://www.cipd.org/globalassets/media/knowledge/knowledge-hub/reports/7926-diversity-and-inclusion-report-revised_tcm18-65334.pdf [Accessed 22 April 2025].

Dagenais, C. (2020). *The Stay Conversation: A Method for Keeping Your High-Performing Talent.* Available at: https://www.forbes.com/councils/forbescoachescouncil/2020/10/13/the-stay-conversation-a-method-for-keeping-your-high-performing-talent/ [Accessed 14 April 2025].

Gershenson, S., Hart C.M.D., Hyman, J., Lindsay, C., Papageorge, N.W. (2021). *The Long-Run Impacts of Same-Race Teachers. NBER Working Paper No. 25254. (JEL No. I2).* Available at: https://www.nber.org/system/files/working_papers/w25254/w25254.pdf [Accessed 13 April 2025].

Government Equalities Office (2023). *Guidance Positive action in the Workplace.* Available at: https://www.gov.uk/government/publications/positive-action-in-the-workplace-guidance-for-employers/positive-action-in-the-workplace#executive-summary [Accessed 11 April 2025].

McCluney, C.L., Robotham, K., Lee, S., Smith, R., Durkee, M. (2019). *The Costs of Code-switching.* Available at: https://hbr.org/2019/11/the-costs-of-codeswitching. [Accessed 11 April 2025].

The OR Briefings (n.d.) *Understanding Affinity Group Support in DEI Initiatives: A Comprehensive Guide.* Available at: https://oxford-review.com/the-oxford-review-dei-diversity-equity-and-inclusion-dictionary/affinity-group-support-definition-and-explanation/ [Accessed 13 April 2025].

Tulshyan, R. (2022). *Inclusion on Purpose an Intersectional Approach to Creating a Culture of Belonging at Work.* Cambridge, MA: The MIT Press.

Actions to take after ED&I training to enable lasting change

In Chapter 5, we drew on the mechanisms shared in the Effective Professional Development Guidance Report to explore how to plan an ED&I curriculum and subsequent training for staff and pupils (Collin and Smith, 2021). We will now focus on the final three mechanisms as part of the embedding practice group to demonstrate ways of ensuring lasting change. A focus on Guskey's model of evaluation then follows and this provides a broader lens for monitoring ED&I training. By merging this learning with the implementation plan (see Chapter 2), a sharper picture emerges of what monitoring and evaluation looks like in the ED&I space. Although this is our penultimate chapter, this hard thinking must occur during the implementation stage to ensure training is impactful and this thinking should be revisited and critiqued after training to ensure progress is monitored effectively. Such visible monitoring of progress may be needed more in comparison to other school interventions as there can be more resistance to ED&I interventions.

When deciding on mechanisms to embed practice and the depth of evaluation required, ED&I leads should consider the type of training taking place, its frequency and the extent to which it contributes to progress being made based on the strategic priority. For example, if ED&I training for pupils is embedded into PSHE, it is not feasible for extensive evaluation to take place after every PSHE lesson so interim monitoring points would need to be agreed. In contrast, training for teachers can be less frequent, but staff are more likely to be accountable for using new practices. Thus, if there is the necessary time and resource, more robust evaluation could occur. This chapter is most relevant to staff training, with the assumption that there is a strong leadership commitment to ED&I.

Embedding practice

This group of mechanisms supports participants to 'effectively embed practice to ensure that they continue to change their behaviour and improve their teaching' (Collin and Smith, 2021). To do this, the ED&I lead should know what the technique looks like and what opportunities exist for staff and pupils to engage in new practice. Within the ED&I space, there is another layer of complexity because it is impossible to anticipate when some techniques can be used e.g. to enable practice of a technique to challenge microaggressions, a microaggression must first take place and then be noticed and named as a microaggression. Therefore, a longer monitoring timeframe might be needed.

Providing prompts and cues

Providing prompts and cues can remind participants to 'carry out certain behaviours' (Sims et al., cited in Collin and Smith, 2021). In Chapter 5, we provide advice on revisiting learning and some of these strategies are relevant here. Other strategies include:

- Putting reminders in staff bulletins about what is expected and when it should take place.
- Creating a guidance sheet based on the technique which is emailed to staff.
- Producing display materials to remind pupils to speak up or of the difference between banter and discrimination.
- Emailing staff with data following on from the training e.g. the number of prejudicial incidents recorded.
- Sharing a video of the technique in action.

Encouraging self-monitoring

This mechanism requires participants to monitor and record their own performance. For pupils, an ipsative model of assessment is helpful to allow pupils to ascertain how their person-centred knowledge has developed and monitor their understanding and application of specific techniques e.g. knowing how to advocate for themselves in a conversation. Ipsative assessment is pupil-led with pupils comparing their learning between two points in time. It can focus on knowledge or skill development and a baseline assessment is needed (Palmer, 2022).

Such an assessment model is helpful in relation to ED&I as it allows pupils to engage in low-stakes reflection and monitor their learning. For example, pupils could have an ED&I learning journal which they complete at planned points based on a framework shared by the teacher. Staff could be asked to complete a reflection task after they have engaged in new practice. If this reflection can take place using an electronic form, results can be shared with the ED&I lead so leaders are more aware of where staff lack knowledge or need additional support to feel more confident delivering RSHE content (Ofsted, 2021).

Prompting context-specific repetition

The final mechanism involves teachers rehearsing and repeating behaviour in the same context as it would usually be delivered and repetition (at least twice) can support the embedding of practice (Sims et al., cited in Collin and Smith, 2021). Such practice lends itself to instructional coaching (see Chapter 7) but practice can be integrated into training. If there isn't time in training, practice could be the focus of a coaching cycle (if coaching is part of staff professional development) or department or phase meetings. There are some challenges with context-specific repetition and we have already referred to not being able to anticipate when certain techniques can be used. Discrimination can happen anywhere and at any time and its visibility depends on the person's ED&I lens.

Feedback is part of a practice cycle and contracting needs to be returned to before any rehearsal takes place. There may be real fears linked to performing ED&I techniques because they are not prevalent or explicitly taught. Treading into the ED&I space can feel deeply unfamiliar for some and cause them to feel completely outside of their comfort zone. Those who provide feedback need to have strong knowledge of the ED&I technique so feedback is high quality, consistent and appropriately nuanced. Relationships matter; if feedback is overly negative and critical it may prevent participants from changing their practice. See Chapter 7 for more on feedback.

As we mentioned in Chapter 5, a 'programme that features a mechanism from each of these areas represents a 'balanced design" (Collin and Smith, 2021). While featuring a mechanism from this area can be more complex, it allows new practice to be adopted more effectively so ED&I training does not become tokenistic.

Guskey's five levels for evaluating professional development

We will now explore how training can be evaluated to further enable lasting change across a school and this is most applicable in levels three to five of Guskey's evaluation model. These levels overlap with the progress and final outcomes columns in a completed ED&I implementation plan (see Chapter 2). Whilst Guskey's work focuses on evaluation based on staff professional development, some levels (e.g. levels 1 and 2) can be applied to specific ED&I training for pupils if the necessary time and resource for this can be provided. Prioritisation of monitoring and progress measures enable training to be impactful and ensures the monitoring measures are manageable for all involved.

Evaluation of ED&I training can predominantly focus on evaluating participants' responses. This is understandable, especially as the ED&I space provides a forum for contentious content, so an ED&I lead will want to know how such content has been received and where there may be resistance. This may remain a primary focus because, without participants being truly invested in ED&I, the desired impact of ED&I interventions may not be achieved. However, Thomas Guskey's five levels for evaluating professional development provides a useful reminder of what else should be thought about to allow for individual and organisational change (Guskey, 2016).

Guskey's five levels

1. Participant reaction

This is where you gauge how participants have responded to the training and whether they liked the experience and it is probably the most common way of retrieving feedback. To engage in this feedback, participants could be asked to complete a short questionnaire at the end of a training session. Questionnaire design can focus on: content; effectiveness of facilitation; level of enjoyment; and level of comfort. Within an ED&I space, it is helpful to learn about participants' feelings of safety.

Guskey cites some educators who dismiss this level of evaluation and refer to such questionnaires as 'happiness quotients' (Guskey, 2016). He emphasises that 'positive reactions from participants are usually a necessary prerequisite to higher-level evaluation results' (Guskey, 2016). While there is a focus on participant experience and comfort, within the ED&I space, this shows the commitment of the ED&I lead to creating safer spaces. Furthermore, understanding participant reactions provides a powerful reminder as to why we do this work as you see the difference it has made for an individual, even if it is not yet at an organisational level.

2. Participant learning

This level focuses on 'measuring the new knowledge, skills, and perhaps attitudes or dispositions that participants gain' (Guskey, 2002 cited in Guskey, 2016) and it could be through verbal or written reflections or a quiz where participants reflect on their understanding against statements. With pupils, this could form part of ipsative assessment. In order to do this, ED&I leads 'need to outline indicators of successful learning before activities begin' (Guskey, 2016). Within the ED&I space, measuring such learning may be complex, especially if the learning strongly challenges established bias. Therefore, questions or statements within level 2 activities need to be carefully crafted. For example, reflect on this statement: *I understand how my unconscious bias might affect daily interactions*. This suggests that the act of raising self-awareness is complete but this is unlikely to be the case due to changing identities and contexts. Moreover, the statement may be too provocative for participants who may not yet be ready to confront their bias. To limit resistance, the statement could be reshaped and changed to: *I understand what unconscious bias is and I am developing an understanding of how this might manifest itself in our school setting*.

Guskey states that 'careful evaluators also consider possible unintended learning outcomes, both positive and negative' (Guskey 2016). As practical social support is such a key component of ED&I training, there is more risk of unintended negative outcomes, especially if ED&I training is aimed at pupils and teachers do not feel equipped to support pupils effectively. During the planning process, there needs to be an awareness of this and how it can be mitigated. This is why ED&I work cannot be the work of one person; a diverse team is more likely to notice where, for example, stereotypes may be reinforced or deficit thinking is unintentionally promoted.

3. Organisational support and change

Organisational elements can sometimes hinder or prevent success, even when the individual aspects of professional development are done right (Sparks, 1996 cited in Guskey, 2016). Therefore, organisational processes and procedures need to be compatible with the new practices shared during ED&I training. Before training takes place, the ED&I lead will have thought about what progress looks like in the short-, medium- and long-term sections of the implementation plan and the required organisational support needed.

To maintain a commitment to ED&I, a meeting needs to take place with senior leaders overseeing the ED&I strategy after training. Evaluation should not be seen as an isolated activity and must again take place at strategic points to further monitor progress. Useful agenda items for this meeting include:

- Sharing any participant evaluation feedback and facilitator learning.
- Discussing whether enough resources were made available, including time for sharing and reflection (Colton & Langer, 2005; Langer & Colton, 1994 cited in Guskey, 2016).
- Deciding on what best practice can be shared and further enhanced.
- Agreeing on what further learning needs to be revisited and the time and resource needed for this.
- Revisiting the implementation plan and deciding on actions needed to monitor progress.

To monitor the progress in the medium and long term with school leadership, agenda items could include discussing:

- Any progress made in relation to the final outcomes on the implementation plan and any unintended outcomes.
- Actions that could be perceived as contentious and any stakeholder feedback needed to minimise any reputational risk.

- Deciding on next steps based on monitoring e.g. a script shared in a staff meeting outlining how staff should introduce content linked to a national or international cultural event.

- The planning and facilitation team for future training, including any data collection needed and any adaptations to the ED&I curriculum.

4. Participants' use of new knowledge and skills

This level allows ED&I educators to gauge whether new knowledge and/or skills are impacting practice. Within the ED&I space, some new knowledge and/or skills may not be readily visible or easy to anticipate. For example, training on understanding the lived experience of those in the school community may be more difficult to monitor if it is not linked to a more tangible action e.g. noticing and naming prejudicial incidents in school. Consequently, hard thinking is needed to think about associated actions linked to less visible traits and experiences and the longer timeframe needed to allow for progress.

With techniques where it is potentially easier to plan to monitor progress, such as lessons allowing for more diverse representation, learning walks could be used to ascertain the extent to which this has been embedded across the school and the further training needed to allow for the development of subject knowledge, teacher confidence and participant safety. Other ways to monitor progress include having the focus of the training as a set agenda item during: discussions with line managers; department or phase meetings; and coaching and mentoring.

5. Student learning outcomes

Any school ED&I interventions should be rooted in the difference it makes for the pupils that we serve. Guskey's final level makes this explicit with its focus on learning outcomes and how pupils benefit from teachers' professional development.

Within the ED&I space, it may be difficult to directly attribute ED&I interventions to increased attainment unless, perhaps, there is an explicit focus on increasing belonging of those who are school refusers or who are persistently absent. Guskey's model states that outcomes do not have to solely refer to attainment and could relate to behaviour or attitudes or any other final outcome as stated on the implementation plan. For example, this could mean: analysing the number of prejudicial incidents logged or analysing pupil responses based on feelings of belonging in whole-school ED&I surveys. Questions for such surveys could include:

- Do you feel listened to?

- Do you have a trusted adult you can talk to within school about any prejudicial incidents you have experienced?

- Do you value learning about the experiences of those within our school community?

Similar to level 2, there may be unintended outcomes and Guskey recommends looking at 'multiple sources of evidence' and interrogating its reliability and validity (Guskey, 2016).

Knowing what you are looking for in this level should act as a driver for effective ED&I implementation planning as evaluation becomes, 'a natural part of the planning process and offers a basis for accountability' (Guskey, 2016).

What further actions should the ED&I educator engage in after training?

Reflection based on facilitator learning and organisational support needed

In addition to Guskey's five levels of evaluation, it is beneficial for the ED&I lead to engage in self-reflection immediately after training so they can reflect on what worked well and what may potentially require further training or need to be addressed. If the ED&I educator has not planned or facilitated the training, they should meet with those involved so a debrief can take place. This then feeds into discussions with school leadership.

Reflection based on the creation of a safer space during training

As ED&I training allows participants to explore personal and contentious content, it is essential that the facilitator reflects on the learning environment created and feelings of safety for all participants. Such feelings may or may not be disclosed in questionnaires if participants are self-reporting so the facilitator's perspective is helpful as long as it is evidence based. It is helpful to reflect on:

- Who interacted with who, and why? Was anyone not included in conversations? Do you have any evidence about why this might be the case?
- Who was dominant during discussion? How do you know?
- Did anyone seem resistant to the content or less engaged? How do you know?
- Where did you feel there were strong emotions? What could have caused this?
- Was there any open challenge? How did you manage this? Could you have done this better? If so, who can support you?

Return to the implementation plan

Make changes to what needs to happen next based on stakeholder feedback and any progress made. Think about the medium-term and long-term progress goals and whether they need adapting and this should inform your discussion with school leadership. In ever-changing school environments, no action is certain so it is necessary to know what actions are your non-negotiables (with a clear rationale for this), where there can be flex and time and resource availability.

Prepare for future training

This allows the ED&I lead to think about any intersession activities as well as the next training session and any amendments needed. Based on the learning gained from evaluation so far, the ED&I lead should consider:

- Reworking the ED&I curriculum in consultation with school leadership so you are aware of the time commitment available.
- What ED&I concepts need to be revisited or introduced.
- What misconceptions or misinformation needs to be addressed.
- What listening and learning activity should take place and the involvement of any key stakeholders.
- What the ED&I educator needs to know and understand, including knowing what credible sources to draw on.
- Sharing best practice based on monitoring.
- Thinking about who could be involved in future training to widen the ED&I team and provide a diversity of voices and role models.
- Confirming what, if any, monitoring will take place.

What does this look like in practice?

To make this complex process clearer, we will share an example of what measuring progress can look like in practice. We encourage you to revisit the implementation plan in Chapter 2 and pay particular attention to the final two columns. The example we will share provides more detail about measuring progress after a training session based on this plan.

Example

Training aims

To support staff to understand:

- What unconscious bias is and how it manifests itself in the school setting.
- Understand how to tackle prejudicial incidents (policy and practice).

Table 9.1 An example of evaluating progress from training based on the strategic priority: pupils feel safe in school and feel able to speak up about prejudicial incidents, which has been the focus of the implementation plan in Chapter 2 and Chapter 5

Evaluation level	What?	When?
1. Participant reaction	A questionnaire for participants is shared with the aims of the session included at the top. Questions include:	End of training.
2. Participant learning	Which part of the training reassured you and made you feel more confident with noticing and addressing microaggressions with pupils? Why? (level 1)	
	Which part of the training would you have liked to spend more time on? Why? (level 1)	
	How could the facilitator have made the session a safer and more accessible space? (level 1)	
	What was the most important learning that you took away from the training? (level 2)	
	Which part of the training challenged or strongly influenced your thinking? (level 2)	
	A short baseline questionnaire is sent to staff before training with questions addressing:	
	feelings of safety in school; confidence with reporting incidents and it being acted on; confidence with knowing how to address prejudicial incidents. This will be revisited at the end of training and later in the year to further monitor progress.	
3. Organisational support and change (this is in addition to the implementation strategies in Chapter 2)	The ED&I lead requests time to meet with their line manager to finalise the actions needed following training and to confirm what time and additional resource is available.	After training.
	Time is provided for staff to complete reflection logs during staff briefing and discuss learning with peers – practical social support is provided.	Available to use after training.
	The ED&I lead works with the DSL to ensure there is increased specificity on the school management system so teachers are able to log prejudicial incidents more precisely and discuss what planned intervention should look like.	Within a month (date agreed in advance).

(Continued)

Table 9.1 (Continued)

Evaluation level	What?	When?
	Ensure such work is embedded into specific supervision for the DSL and pastoral teams receive additional training e.g. how to talk to pupils sensitively about their role in a prejudicial incident so they understand intent and impact and develop person-centred knowledge. A space should be provided for staff to raise concerns and receive support.	Within a month (date agreed in advance).
	School leaders attend a meeting to address any concerns from their teams with addressing prejudicial incidents and share any best practice. The ED&I lead then creates a one page FAQs document to share with all staff	Month after training.
4. Participants' use of new knowledge and skills	Create an opportunity for planned practical social support. In department/year/phase/ whole school meetings, staff discuss what is working well and areas of focus with a member of the senior leadership team. This stems from their reflection logs. Feedback is provided to the rest of senior leadership and the ED&I lead.	Next half-term after training.
	A 'speak-up culture' is demonstrated by the prejudicial incidents reported and the data dashboard produced.	Next half-term after training.
5. Impact on participant learning outcomes	Analysis of pastoral data as well as a review of feedback from any meetings with staff. Decisions made on further actions needed, including training.	Next term
	A baseline questionnaire is completed by all staff before the next training session and in the next term.	Next term
	Meet with leaders to review data and decide on next steps and any further training needed.	Next term and before the next training session
6. Facilitator self-reflection	Reflect on what worked well and areas of focus in relation to: explaining content; choice of activities and timing; what may need to be revisited; what the facilitator needs to do during the planning stage to feel safer and reflections of feelings of safety within the training space for participants.	Immediately after training

Challenges to monitoring progress

Scenario 1

What if some participants are positive about the training and make comments about it "being really good" or "you were so good" but follow it up with a statement such as, "Just to let you know we do diversity really well in our team."

1. What are areas of concern that you would want to flag?
2. What would be your next steps?

Recommendation

Manage your response to this comment. Whilst the praise provides a temporary boost, it does not show what the participant has learnt. It is vague and such comments could be seen as an attempt to show appreciation of the facilitator's efforts but not necessarily the content of the training. The ED&I lead should consider what evidence exists to support the staff member's claim and whether the pitch of the training was appropriate. If the ED&I lead feels that the school's ED&I priorities are still relevant, they should reflect on whether future training needs to clarify what diversity is and whether they need to gain a further understanding of how teams see diversity. Any misconceptions will need to be addressed. The ED&I lead should not be disheartened; within the ED&I space, there is learning and unlearning so such activity is a marathon, not a sprint.

Scenario 2

What if school leadership reduces the time and resources available?
What would be your next steps?

Recommendation

Discuss your concerns with your line manager and find out what other opportunities exist. Be aware that repeated conversations may be needed and tenacity is important here. Be prepared to act as an advocate for this work by being prepared for meetings and draw on the reasons for the ED&I intervention and the progress and impact so far. Be willing to compromise by knowing what your non-negotiables are. Meaningful ED&I work takes time and reviewing timeframes is not necessarily a negative as long as learning is revisited and returned to in the very near future.

If time or additional resource cannot be provided until a later point, creative thinking is needed. This should be in collaboration with others so opportunities can be found in other areas e.g. a staff briefing is dedicated to ED&I training every fortnight or there is a spotlight on ED&I in the staff bulletin and school newsletter.

Questions

1. Consider Guskey's five levels for evaluating professional development and implementation planning. What do you need to prioritise? Why?

2. In order to be able to prioritise this, what support is needed? What conversations need to take place and with whom?

3. What challenges might you have? How will you deal with them and who will support you?

References

Collin, J., Smith, E. (Education Endowment Foundation). (2021). *Effective Professional Development Guidance Report*. Available at: https://educationendowmentfoundation.org.uk/education-evidence/guidance-reports/effective-professional-development [Accessed 28 March 2025].

Guskey, T. R. (2016). Gauge Impact with Five Levels of Data. *Journal of Staff Development*, 37(1), 32–37. Available at: https://uknowledge.uky.edu/edp_facpub/62/ [Accessed 28 March 2025].

Ofsted (2021). *Research and Analysis Review of Sexual Abuse in Schools and Colleges*. Available at: https://www.gov.uk/government/publications/review-of-sexual-abuse-in-schools-and-colleges/review-of-sexual-abuse-in-schools-and-colleges#executive-summary-and-recommendations [Accessed 28 March 2025].

Palmer, R. (2022). *Assessing PSHE: Problems and Solutions*. Available at: https://blog.optimus-education.com/assessing-pshe-problems-and-solutions [Accessed 28 March 2025].

10 Protecting yourself as an ED&I educator

Being an EDI educator is deeply rewarding, but can also be incredibly complex. Those who take on this work may do so because individual experiences have led to a commitment to breaking down barriers for others and personal experiences of challenge have provided the insights needed to generate change. As explored in Chapter 3, lived experience is a strength in ED&I work and allows us to bring powerful perspectives to a team. However, it also means the work is highly personal. Although many roles within the education sector present difficulties and require a huge amount of dedication and time, working in the ED&I space holds an additional layer of challenge.

We reflected multiple times on how best to structure this chapter, as we want to avoid generating feelings of helplessness by focusing solely on the challenges of the role. We have chosen to include a broad range of potential experiences, ensuring an honest and realistic reflection of what ED&I leads may encounter. The chapter will alternate between problems and solutions, but we are by no means suggesting that there is a 'one-size-fits-all' approach, or that there is one fixed solution for each issue explored. Readers should consider the full range of suggestions and select those that they feel are most appropriate.

Emotional tax and emotional labour

Emotional tax refers to the need to be on guard to protect against bias linked to protected characteristics and the associated effects on wellbeing and ability to thrive at work (Brassel et al., 2022). Catalyst (2022) found that 61% of employees from marginalised racial and ethnic groups in Australia, Brazil, Canada, the United Kingdom and the United States indicated that they are on guard to bias and discrimination on their teams. Intersectionality saw an increase in this percentage, with 74% of LGBTQ+ and 84% of trans and non-binary employees from marginalised racial and ethnic groups being on guard to bias in their teams.

This hypervigilance can develop for a variety of reasons. It may come from historic or ongoing prejudice both in and outside of the workplace, generating consistent anxieties around repeat experiences. It may also come from being a visible minority in the workplace. Things like affinity bias can prevent us from feeling as though we wholly belong in a team, with fears developing around others' perceptions of who we are. In the worst cases, daily experiences of workplace discrimination may be a reality in workplace cultures where microaggressions and inappropriate comments are allowed to go unchallenged. If we are exposed to such things daily, we may find ourselves perpetually braced for the next negative interaction or experience.

Emotional labour, as described by Hochschild (2012), is the term given to the effort people put into managing their feelings to present a certain image, especially in jobs that involve interaction with others. This means presenting as being in control of our emotions to create a specific and pleasant experience for those that we work with. The role of an ED&I lead is not only to steer a strategy or to ensure things run smoothly but also ultimately to educate others around a range of lived experiences, often including those to which we have a personal connection. Due to this, the role involves extremely high levels of both professional and personal responsibility. Any personal connections to the role, combined with the fact that issues surrounding ED&I are often systemic and ever-present in society and the media, mean that ED&I leads do not have the luxury of simply 'switching off' outside of the workplace. It is not unlikely that the very issues we are confronted with in the workplace may also appear when out in public, and even more so when watching the news or accessing social media.

Constant exposure to ED&I-related issues can cause extreme levels of emotional fatigue which, left unchecked, are more than likely to result in burnout. Professor Maslach and Jackson (1981) defined burnout as 'a syndrome of emotional exhaustion and cynicism that occurs frequently among individuals who do "people-work" of some kind', with significant symptoms being 'increased feelings of emotional exhaustion', 'the tendency to evaluate oneself negatively' and feeling unhappy and dissatisfied with workplace accomplishments. To maintain credibility and adhere to what is deemed as professional behaviour, ED&I educators are likely to feel obligated to hide these feelings in the workplace. This is made even more challenging since informing others is a fundamental part of the role, and the feelings and reactions of others are often at the centre of our thinking. We are often tasked with developing explanations that involve reliving difficult experiences and so we are forced to repress any emotions that we are feeling ourselves. In presentations and meetings, we may feel a huge range of emotions without the audience recognising these in our voices, faces or body language as we prioritise delivering to others in a way that is engaging, palatable and encourages understanding.

Practical steps for individuals

Set personal boundaries

Setting boundaries is essential for self-preservation and steps can be taken to do so both within and outside of the workplace. Although burnout can feel sudden, there are likely to be indicators in the lead-up to this and it is important to be in tune with yourself to recognise when things are becoming difficult. Time management is a crucial skill in any professional role; in ED&I work, however, where emotional labour is significant, it becomes even more essential. Structuring time effectively can help prevent burnout, particularly when engaging with emotionally heavy material. For example, researching lived experiences can be deeply impactful but also emotionally exhausting. It's easy to spend hours reading distressing statistics and case studies to educate others, but this can take a serious toll. After such intense work, it's unlikely you'll feel refreshed or ready to move seamlessly into the rest of your day. Instead of trying to absorb everything at once, build in time for reflection and pace yourself. Rather than attempting to research all protected characteristics in one sitting, set manageable goals. For instance, commit to identifying five key insights about a specific characteristic for the day; once you reach that goal, stop. You can always return to it later, but breaking tasks into smaller, measurable steps provides a sense of progress and completion – preventing the cycle of endlessly searching for the "best" research, which can ultimately lead to information overload.

There will be challenging days and prioritising your wellbeing outside of work is essential. If you have been left feeling emotionally drained or under pressure during the day, be mindful of how you spend your time afterward. Ask yourself whether watching the news or reading ED&I-related articles will be helpful, or if it will only add to the emotional weight you are carrying and hinder your ability to recharge. You might feel that a particular article could support your work, but it is important to take the time to pause and consider how much you'll genuinely absorb when already exhausted. Instead of pushing through, bookmark it and come back to it when you have the mental clarity and capacity to engage with it fully. Blocking out time for recovering and giving yourself space to rest is just as important as the work itself.

Set professional boundaries

Sometimes, we simply have to say 'no'. When workplace expectations exceed your capacity, it's healthier to push back than to keep pushing forward at the expense of your wellbeing. Since ED&I roles are often a relatively new addition to many schools and trusts, there may be little organisational clarity around what realistic expectations should look like. By openly communicating what is feasible within your workload, you not only protect yourself from burnout but also help shape a more sustainable and clearly defined role – benefiting both you and the organisation in the long run. This is, of course, easier said than done and a useful strategy can be to de-centre yourself. As an ED&I lead, your goal is to foster greater workplace inclusion and help shape the organisation into a better place for everyone. It can be helpful to remind yourself that, while you currently hold the role, someone else may take it on in the future. Being honest about what is a realistic workload isn't just about self-preservation – it also ensures that those who follow in our footsteps aren't set up for failure. If unsustainable expectations go unchallenged, the role may become unmanageable, ultimately undermining the long-term impact of ED&I efforts. Setting clear boundaries now helps to create a more sustainable and effective foundation for the future.

Reduce feelings of isolation

It is often the case that just one individual in an entire organisation is tasked with leading on ED&I. Not only is this a huge responsibility to carry, which brings its own challenges, but it can also be incredibly isolating. In most school settings, roles naturally involve a sense of commonality and shared experience. Heads of department, for example, can relate to one another regardless of subject area and, within trusts, there is often even an extended network across a range of schools, providing further opportunities for collaboration and a wider range of colleagues to connect with. ED&I leaders, however, often operate without a direct counterpart, despite our work feeding into multiple areas of school life. This can create a sense of isolation, making it harder to find the same level of collaborative support that many other roles benefit from in the workplace.

Practical steps for individuals

Find a network

Various strategies are recommended for managing workplace stress and these often include things like mindfulness, involvement in physical activity and taking breaks. Although such recommendations can be supportive, it is important to remember that our lived experiences are real, impactful and cannot be managed away using surface-level strategies. In order to overcome the emotional weight of navigating experiences linked to our characteristics, it is important to be able to be able to unpick them and to seek support and advice. Whilst things like professional coaching and even therapy can be incredibly useful, they can often involve further emotional labour where our experiences are not truly understood by the person to which we are speaking. For example, it would be unhelpful to have to explain the pressures of being confronted with ableism or racism in the workplace to a professional with no prior experience or understanding of these characteristics. For this reason, seeking a network of people with shared experiences can be extremely beneficial in terms of being truly understood.

In some cases, as in our own, you may be fortunate in being able to find such a network within your own organisation. Although we work in the same academy trust, we are based in different schools and did not initially work alongside one another. ED&I initially became part of each of our roles in slightly different capacities – Natasha through designing and leading on the ITT programme, and Funmi through leading on Anti-Racism and ED&I across the trust, with an emphasis on culture and curriculum.

Although we had previously shared experiences through an Anti-Racism group, we only started working closely together when coordinating an ED&I training programme for leaders across our trust. Although as teachers delivering to large groups has been a fundamental aspect of our role for many years, we quite quickly began to realise the pressures of planning and delivering training in the sphere of ED&I. Of course, many people experience nervousness prior to public speaking and facilitation; for us, however, there was an additional layer of thought processes and questions throughout the process: *How might people react to the topics we hoped to explore? What if we were to become visibly emotional upon discussing our lived experiences? Most significantly, what if overt bias were to manifest from the audience during the sessions – how would we navigate this?*

Additionally, our intent on being data-focused, in addition to framing our work sensitively to an audience made up of a vast range of characteristics, meant that we engaged in extensive reading and research on themes that were often personal to us. Over time, we began to open up to each other about the emotions we experienced and, often, our shared experiences of ED&I-related burnout. Our meetings would often begin with a check-in about our thinking and feeling, in which we offered support to one another – things that so often are not the initial focus in workplace interactions. Identifying shared experiences allowed us to recognise a safer space in one another and this has been instrumental in our ability to persevere in our ED&I work.

We recognise, however, that not everyone is able to benefit from shared experiences in the workplace in this way. This can be for a range of reasons, ranging from poor workplace relationships to external or personal factors preventing educators from wanting to divulge our personal experiences and hidden characteristics to colleagues. In cases such as this, it can be helpful to source external networks and mechanisms for support. Fortunately, there are organisations dedicated to fostering inclusivity and support. DiverseEd, for example, a UK-based network and platform provides a vast network for educators focused on ED&I but also offers a wealth of resources for educators. The collection of blogs published by the DiverseEd network can be incredibly beneficial for educators who are not yet ready to be open in reaching out to others – through reading experiences that resonate and identifying shared experiences, we can reduce feelings of isolation and loneliness without having to speak out before we are ready to do so.

Practical steps for the organisation

Be proactive in sourcing support

Supporting ED&I leads requires acknowledging the unique pressures they face. While workplace stress is common, ED&I leads navigate these challenges alongside additional emotional and professional burdens. It's important to recognise that asking for help isn't always easy, so consider how you can proactively support them. Professional coaching can be highly beneficial, especially when provided by those with experience in ED&I work. Rather than waiting for the employee to seek support, take the initiative to source coaching as soon as they step into the role – removing the added burden of them having to identify their struggles, request help, and arrange coaching on their own time or at their own expense.

In some cases, supervision, rather than coaching, may be more beneficial for employees. Coaching supervision is a 'reflective and collaborative process between a coach and a supervisor that supports ongoing professional development and effectiveness' (Daniel and Bramall, 2023). In the ED&I planning space, for example, the EDI educator would discuss their training plan with the supervisor who would then provide further guidance, training or support. This not only contributes to the professional growth of the EDI educator but also acts a safety mechanism for them. Supervision does not require immediate actions; it encourages hard thinking in a safer space where ideas are discussed in partnership. Supervision may be more helpful here rather than mentoring or coaching, even though there are overlaps. Mentoring tends to be hierarchical, with less experienced colleagues adopting the advice from superiors. This can create an imbalance of power through which the ED&I educator may be more inclined to adopt their superior's ideas rather than standing by their own. Supervision creates a space for the EDI educator to talk through and sense-check their decisions.

Build collective responsibility

Recognise that ED&I work should not be solely reliant on one person and take steps to ensure the responsibility is shared across the school or trust. Although the ED&I lead will likely be responsible for conducting the initial research and establishing steps forward, it is essential that employees across the organisation are held accountable for embedding these. Clear expectations should be set for all leaders and teams to contribute towards ED&I efforts, reducing the perception that it is the role of one person only. Continuously frame ED&I as a shared mission and outline the ways in which all members of the team should contribute to this, using the knowledge and skills that are required for other parts of their role. For example, where an absence of representation for various characteristics has been highlighted, HR leads should be tasked with implementing strategies for improvement, curriculum leads should identify key areas in which their own subject can be diversified, and so on.

Tenacity fatigue

Being the sole voice for ED&I requires immense tenacity, but it can also lead to significant fatigue. In meetings, discussions and daily interactions, we often feel the weight of being the consistent advocate for equity. This role involves constant repetition—reinforcing the same messages again and again – which can be frustrating. While ED&I leads may wonder why an ED&I perspective isn't naturally embedded in decision-making, others may start to see us as negative and disruptive, or even as troublemakers. This resistance often stems from a deep-seated fear of change. People can perceive equity for others as a personal loss, as if progress for one group must come at the expense of another.

As ED&I work challenges long-standing systems and norms, it is often met with defensiveness, reluctance and discomfort. Due to this, there may be barriers at every stage and overcoming these barriers can feel exhausting. This can be especially challenging in organisations that prioritise *presenting* as inclusive over making the meaningful changes needed to achieve true equity. In such cases, ED&I leads are likely to be championed for suggesting superficial changes, such as the celebration of cultural events and history months, but are likely to face animosity where deeper, structural changes, such as rights for equal pay, or changes to recruitment policies, are brought to the table.

In many roles, advocating for oneself and reinforcing one's ideas are perceived as leadership qualities and are likely to result in progression over time. In ED&I work, however, the very same qualities may be perceived as being resistant to organisational policy, the result of which can mean being perceived as the wrong fit for a team. Dr. Kecia Thomas coined the term 'Pet to Threat' to describe the common experiences of women of colour in predominantly white workplaces. This framework explains how women of colour are initially welcomed and celebrated – seen as an organisational 'pet' – but then, as they gain confidence and assertiveness, they are increasingly seen as resistant and enter the phase of being perceived as a 'threat' (Thomas et al., 2013; Thomas, 2024). As well as causing emotional harm, when left unchallenged, such negative perceptions from others can have an impact on an EDI educator's career progression. Being consistently perceived as a disruptor may lead to an employer's reluctance to consider individuals for promotion or even for experience in wider areas.

Practical steps for individuals

Learn to embrace conflict

Conflict often carries negative connotations, making it something many instinctively want to avoid. It's easy to interpret tension as a sign that you've done something wrong, but in the context of ED&I work it is important to reframe this perspective. Conflict often arises when people are not aligned, particularly when there is resistance to challenge or change. However, by appointing an ED&I lead and investing in training, an organisation is already acknowledging that a misalignment exists – hence the need for learning and development in this area.

The norms that have been established and maintained within a school or trust exist because those in dominant positions of power have upheld them over time. Therefore, when conversations about change take place, it is natural for defences to be raised. Leonardo and Porter (2010) criticised avoidance of conflict as an attempt to 'side step the issues, as well educative aspects of anger and frustration, necessary for a beneficial and truly liberatory dialogue on race to take place'. Our role as ED&I educators is to dismantle and adapt existing systems for the benefit of all, rather than just some. For people that have benefitted from the existing systems, change may feel uncomfortable, and this discomfort may lead to resistance. In fact, if there is no resistance at all, it may indicate that the discussions are not truly challenging the status quo in a meaningful way. In generating healthy conflict as ED&I leads, you are doing exactly what your role requires of you.

Defer to others

The responsibility for ED&I must be shared and it is important to recognise where others can support in amplifying the work. Prior to speaking in large meetings, it can be useful to request one-to-ones with those chairing to bring their attention to key messages, particularly where you are conscious that there may be pushback. Having one-on-one discussions about contentious topics is often more productive than addressing them in large-group settings. This approach fosters constructive criticism rather than creating an overwhelming 'all against one' dynamic. In school leadership meetings, for example, sharing information with the head teacher in advance can allow you to sense-check contentious areas and to agree to share responsibility for delivery. This can serve to reduce the burden of responsibility within meetings.

Practical steps for the organisation

Ensure collective responsibility for ED&I

The responsibility of advocating for ED&I should not rest solely on the ED&I lead. Leaders within the organisation must actively take ownership of this work and embed it into their own practice to demonstrate that inclusion is a collective, strategic priority rather than an individual pursuit. There is a strong case for the ED&I lead to be line-managed by the principal or executive leadership team. Given that some individuals may be resistant to change, it must be clear that ED&I is not just an isolated initiative but a fundamental organisational priority. Regular line management meetings should allow the ED&I lead to communicate key insights, enabling senior leaders to take forward messaging themselves. This not only reinforces institutional commitment but also helps distribute responsibility, reducing tenacity fatigue and ensuring that meaningful change is driven from the top.

Due to the contentious nature of ED&I work, there is perhaps more of a need to manage reputational risk, both for the school and for the individual leading on ED&I. Those leading on any ED&I activity should consider any risks during the implementation process and through the process of listening and learning to key stakeholders within the school community. Of course, there may be unintended outcomes or unexpected responses to how an ED&I intervention is received. The ED&I lead needs to be confident that school leadership will support them and that there will be a considered response to negative statements or misinformation. They also need to be confident that they will be supported if they have to deal with an overtly discriminatory responses, and feeling safe here is a prerogative.

Challenge bias

In Chapter 2, we explore the importance of raising self-awareness and the concept of unconscious bias. It is essential for organisational leaders to be vigilant as to where bias is perpetuated and to challenge this where necessary. There is a significant connect between employee satisfaction and prompt responses by senior managers to inappropriate behaviour (CMI, 2024). Within meetings, leaders should pay attention to the ways in which people are responded to and identify patterns. Reflect on whose confidence is praised and whose is questioned. Question whose research is well-received and whose is disregarded. Where you identify potential biases manifesting, take action to encourage self-reflection within teams.

Hypervisibility

Hypervisibility refers to the excessive attention or scrutiny placed on individuals due to their identity, often based on gender, sexuality, race, disability and other protected characteristic. It magnifies differences, making individuals stand out in ways that can be isolating, exhausting or even harmful (Oxford Review, 2025). Anyone can become hypervisible in their role, but for ED&I educators – especially those with protected characteristics – the intersection of who we are and the issues we advocate for makes this even more likely. Holding protected characteristics can, at times, lead people to assume that you are in the role purely for personal gain, or out of animosity towards those with certain characteristics, rather than out of a commitment to meaningful change for everyone. Instead of recognising your expertise and workplace competencies, people may reduce your presence to your identity, seeing your advocacy as self-serving rather than as part of a broader mission for equity. This perception can undermine your credibility, making it harder to be recognised as a leader working towards systemic improvements that benefit everyone. This can occur when working with pupils, as well as with staff. For example, Owen Jones, director of education at the charity *Hope not Hate*, which delivers anti-discrimination workshops, said he had seen boys in four school surround female teachers who mentioned being feminists, saying 'they must hate men'. As a result of this, the charity avoids sending women to deliver sexism workshops because of safety fears (Belger, 2022).

The impact of hypervisibility can be magnified when one person is made the 'face' of ED&I. This means that every conversation, presentation or initiative is led by the same person, reinforcing the misconception that the work is driven by a personal agenda. This can create uncomfortable feelings of being a symbolic representative for ED&I, making us feel like the face of the movement rather than part of a collective and meaningful effort. Over time, this can also lead to disengagement from others, as they may see the work as an individual pursuit rather than a shared responsibility.

Example

Scenario 1

Two women of colour delivered a training session in a school with a predominantly White British teaching body. Aware of the potential risks and resistance that can arise when discussions focus heavily on race – a challenging but familiar reality – they took deliberate steps to ensure a broad representation of protected characteristics. In doing so, they also made themselves particularly vulnerable by sharing aspects of their own hidden characteristics. Despite these efforts, feedback collected after the session included comments suggesting that a wider range of characteristics should be covered, rather than an emphasis on race. This prompted a mix of emotions, including disappointment that the careful research and lived experiences shared had not been fully acknowledged, and frustration that, even when efforts were made to minimise their own perspectives as women of colour, any references to these experiences were still perceived as excessive.

Scenario 2

Within an organisation, two individuals were regularly involved in activities, presentations and conferences related to ED&I. On one occasion, a representative visited a school to run focus groups with pupils about their experiences. The school subsequently requested one-on-one sessions with staff to discuss their perspectives on the ED&I strategy, which was accepted as a valuable opportunity to gather staff voices and inform future improvements. During these discussions, some staff members shared constructive reflections and asked questions about the strategy, which were welcomed. However, one individual responded with immediate confrontation, framing the ED&I work as a personal agenda rather than an organisational policy.

Practical steps for individuals

Highlighting bias

Despite challenging bias being a fundamental part of the role, this can be extremely difficult to do when the bias is directed personally. When reflecting on scenario 1, for example, the facilitators could have followed up with the head of the school to thank them for the audience's engagement, whilst also sharing their reflections on some of the feedback received. This could have provided a valuable learning opportunity for some of the school staff. Although this may be challenging, constructive feedback can help to further highlight the complexities of ED&I work and the unconscious biases that can shape perceptions. Engaging in this dialogue may encourage deeper reflection among staff and reinforce the importance of embracing all aspects of inclusion, even those that may feel uncomfortable.

Step away from hostile interactions

Hostility and discrimination should never be accepted as 'just another part of the role' for ED&I leads. The ED&I should not feel a personal responsibility to help the staff member to understand the ED&I strategy. If a person is hostile, an ED&I lead needs to have the confidence to end the conversation and seek organisational support. It is important that the burden of justifying an organisational strategy should not fall solely on one individual.

Practical steps for employers

Make careful decisions surround facilitation

Organisational leaders should be intentional about who is facilitating ED&I discussions. It is not fair for women to be the sole voices advocating for women's rights, for example. When individuals from underrepresented groups are always the ones speaking on these issues, it can put them in difficult positions, reinforcing assumptions that ED&I is a personal agenda rather than an organisational priority. In some cases, it may even lead to accusations of a "victim mentality".

A more effective approach is to have a diverse range of facilitators, particularly individuals who can acknowledge their privileges in relation to certain issues and who may be less likely to face hostility – for example, men discussing gender equity. Of course, the data and lived experiences must still be gathered in consultation with those directly affected, and ED&I leads play a crucial role in this process. Employers should take the initiative to ensure a range of voices are involved in facilitation, reinforcing that inclusion is an organisational commitment – and is perceived as such – and not just the responsibility of those with lived experience.

Establish and amplify discrimination policies

Scenario 2 highlights the importance of organisations having a clear and well-communicated process in place so that staff know exactly what to do when faced with hostility. No individual should have to navigate such situations alone, and there must be systems of support and accountability to ensure that ED&I leads can carry out their roles without being subjected to personal attacks. Raising awareness surrounding behaviours that are, and are not, acceptable can also support in preventing staff from participating in discriminatory behaviours in the first instance.

Overcome feelings of failure

ED&I work is, in many ways, idealistic. This is not because it lacks merit but rather because in undertaking this work, ED&I educators are seeking to address systemic inequalities that have been entrenched for centuries. The very existence of ED&I roles is evidence of a deficit. Matthias (2024) describes the term itself as 'oxymoronic' – it does not deal with equality but with inequality, not with diversity and inclusion but with their absence.

Many other roles in education have established frameworks. For example, safeguarding leads operate under KCSIE, heads of department follow the National Curriculum, and so on. This is not at all to suggest that such roles operate without significant challenge, but there is at least clear guidance to be followed. ED&I work, however, lacks a concrete blueprint. For the work to be successful, a shift in mindset is required and this is incredibly challenging to achieve. Encouraging those around you to broaden their horizons and to think differently is a gradual process – the slightest shifts may occur without being immediately visible. This lack of immediate, tangible outcomes can make the work feel disheartening; the progress is often invisible, and the impact is rarely instant. For this reason, it can be easy to feel a sense of frustration and even failure.

However, it is important to remain grounded and to recognise that long-term change takes time. History has shown that change is slow. Centuries after the Suffragette movement, for example, gender equality remains an ongoing battle. The very existence of the Equality Act (2010) acknowledges that inequality is persistent – the necessity of this law is a recognition that equity will always be resisted by some. The reality is that no individual can single-handedly transform the world, but this does not render your work meaningless.

Practical steps for individuals

Document incremental change

Rather than focusing on what hasn't been achieved, it is essential to be intentional in recognising what *has*. What may seem like small steps to us can be far more significant than we first realise. Shifting our mindset to acknowledge this can help sustain motivation and reinforce the value of our work. For example, securing ED&I as an agenda item – even if the discussions that follow are difficult – is a success in itself as it ensures that others are prompted to reflect. Providing a safer space for individuals to share their lived experiences, even when those experiences are painful to hear and immediate solutions are not available, creates an opportunity for people to feel heard – perhaps for the first time. This not only deepens your own and others' understanding of the human impact of inequality but also lays the groundwork for meaningful, long-term change. Recognising these steps as progress is crucial because systemic transformation is built on sustained, intentional efforts, not just immediate, visible outcomes. These incremental changes matter and documenting them – even by listing small wins at the end of each day or week – can maintain motivation.

Capture feedback

It is natural to want to push consistently for more evidence of progress;, in doing so, however, there may not be the appreciation of progress already made. This is why it is important to seek the perspectives of those around you – their insights can highlight changes you might have overlooked. This can be achieved through formal mechanisms, such as surveys at the start, midpoint, and end of the year, allowing you to track shifts in experiences over time.

However, it can also be as simple as having a conversation. Asking people what they feel has changed can make you aware of progress you may have dismissed as minimal. Often, what seems small to us – such as a shift in language, a newfound confidence in speaking up, or a sense of confidence and belonging where there wasn't one before – can be deeply meaningful to others. A simple 'How do you feel now?' at the end of a conversation with someone that has reached out to you can reveal a significance in ED&I work that may otherwise have overlooked.

As idealists, it can be easy to feel disheartened when change doesn't happen as quickly or visibly as we hope. However, it's important to remember that ED&I work is not about personal sense of progress – it is about the experiences of others. Rather than measuring success solely by what is seen, take the time to listen to others, understand their perspectives, and recognise that change, however gradual, is happening.

Questions

ED&I leads:

1. Reflect on your experience in post. How often did you accept feelings of burnout as a normal part of the role?
2. Which practical steps will you prioritise going forwards?

Employers and line managers:

1. How often have you taken the time to consider the unique challenges faced by those leading on ED&I within your organisation?

References

Belger, T. (2022). Schools See Rise in 'Incel' Extremism Prevent Referrals. Available from: https://schoolsweek.co.uk/schools-see-rise-in-incel-extremism-prevent-referrals/

Brassel, S., Shaffer, E., Travis, D.J. (2022). Emotional Tax and Work Teams: A View from 5 Countries. Available from: https://www.catalyst.org/research/emotional-tax-teams-key-findings/

Chartered Management Institute (2024). *Walking the Walk: The State of Equality, Diversity, and Inclusion in UK Workplaces.*

Daniel, R., Bramall, S. (2023). Supporting Teacher Wellbeing through Coaching Supervision. Available from: https://chartered.college/2023/05/24/supporting-teacher-wellbeing-through-coaching-supervision/

Hochschild, A. R. (2012). *The Managed Heart: Commercialization of Human Feeling.* 3rd edn. Berkeley, CA: University of California Press.

Leonardo, Z., Porter, R. K. (2010). Pedagogy of Fear: Toward a Fanonian Theory of 'Safety' in Race Dialogue. *Race Ethnicity and Education*, 13(2), 139–157. Available from: https://doi.org/10.1080/13613324.2010.482898

Matthias, P. (2024). Language Inclusivity Is Not Always Inclusive. *Times Higher Education.* Available from: https://www.timeshighereducation.com/campus/language-inclusivity-not-inclusive

Maslach, C., Jackson, S. E. (1981). The Measurement of Experienced Burnout. *Journal of Organizational Behavior*, 2(2), 99–113. Available from: https://doi.org/10.1002/job.4030020205

Oxford Review (2025). Hypervisibility – Definition and Explanation. Available from: https://oxford-review.com/the-oxford-review-dei-diversity-equity-and-inclusion-dictionary/hypervisibility-definition-and-explanation/

Thomas, K. M. (2024). The Persistence of Pet to Threat. *Forbes*, 13 January. Available from: https://www.forbes.com/sites/keciathomas/2024/01/13/the-persistence-of-pet-to-threat/

Thomas, K., Johnson-Bailey, J., Phelps, R., Tran, N. M., Johnson, L. (2013). *Women of Color at Midcareer: Going from Pet to Threat.* 10.5040/9798216002536.ch-014

Webber, J. (2025). The Hidden Cost of Leading EDI: How to Avoid Burnout While Driving Change. LinkedIn. Available from: https://www.linkedin.com/pulse/hidden-cost-leading-edi-how-avoid-burnout-while-driving-jason-webber-nkk5e/

Final thoughts

If you decided to read this book, you most probably recognised that ED&I work is highly complex. Our intention in writing was not to simplify ED&I or to reduce it to a tick box list. Rather, we encourage readers to embrace this complexity – the multiple forms that ED&I work can take open up endless pathways of opportunity for change in schools, trusts and wider society.

To leaders, we urge you to move further beyond simple compliance with equalities law and to consider what is required to begin to develop a sense of belonging for all within your school or trust. There is no quick solution to this and accepting the potentially long road is a fundamental aspect of committing to ED&I work that is authentic, rather than performative. If you are unsure where to begin, we urge you to remember the power of listening and learning. This involves drawing upon existing expertise but, more importantly than this, really *hearing* the staff and pupils in front of you. It may feel challenging as a leader to admit where you lack knowledge but in the sphere of ED&I this is important – your vulnerability will demonstrate to others that they can be too. In the words of Bell Hooks (1999), 'honesty and openness is always the foundation of insightful dialogue'. Although taking feedback may not feel like a significant step to you, for anyone that has felt unable to speak for any reason, your encouragement of feedback may be the first opportunity they have ever had to speak out, which can be monumental. In fact, we encourage you to embrace 'small' steps. So long as your ED&I work is a long-term investment, these will grow into something much bigger.

For those without leadership responsibilities, always remember the difference you can make. Your personal power is significant. Whether it is through developing your person-centred knowledge, being more aware during interactions with colleagues or pupils, or challenging bias where you recognise it, you have the power to make change. In the words of Alice Walker (in Martin, 2004) 'the most common way people give up their power is by thinking they don't have any'.

For anyone alone in driving ED&I work, our message is *keep going*. We know this work is challenging but you began because you recognise its, and your, importance. You will face challenges and that is testament to the level of change you are aspiring for. In the words of Audre Lorde (1984), 'I have come to believe over and over again that what is most important to me must be spoken, made verbal and shared, even at the risk of having it bruised or misunderstood.'

Do not, however, minimise the importance of protecting yourself. Your perceptions of progress will fluctuate and some days you may feel like giving up. Remember 'courage doesn't always roar. Sometimes courage is the quiet voice at the end of the day saying, "I will try again tomorrow"' (Mary Anne Radmacher, 2022).

References

Hooks, B. (1999). *All About Love: New Visions.* New York: William Morrow.
Lorde, A. (1984). *Sister Outsider: Essays and Speeches.* Trumansburg, NY: Crossing Press.
Martin, W.P. (2004). *The Best Liberal Quotes Ever: Why the Left is Right.* Naperville, IL: Sourcebooks.
Radmacher, M. A. (2022). *Courage Doesn't Always Roar.* Available from: https://www.goodreads.com/quotes/38657-courage-doesn-t-always-roar-sometimes-courage-is-the-little-voice [Accessed 6 May 2025].

Index

Pages in **bold** refer to tables.

active listening 154–155
affinity bias 78
Afro hair 82
Agarwal, P.: children and identity 63; error management theory 57
age 14–15

bias 57
burnout 191

case study 36–41, 50, 66–68, 82–84, 91–92, 95, 111, 150, 160
coaching: facilitative 115, 148; group career 172–173; instructional 148, 159
code-switching 171
cognitive load 110
collective responsibility 48–49, 197
community 35–36
compassion 66, 109, 128, 140
confirmation bias 153–154
contracting: in coaching and mentoring 156–157; when delivering training 133–135
co-planning 102–104
Crenshaw, K. 56–57
cultural events 93
culture fit 78
curiosity 138, 152–154
curriculum: avoiding harmful narratives 88; diversification of 83–84, 123; ED&I training design 104–109; learner safety 85–88

DEIB 9
Department for Eduction (DFE) 35
disability: language of 5; Equality Act definition of 15–16
discrimination 13–14
Diverse Educators 35, 194
diversity 10
Dixons Academies Trust: case study on anti-racism group 39–40; positive action programme 168–178

ED&I: landscape 8–28; lens 78–79
EDIJ 9
Education Endowment Foundation (EEF) 42
emotional labour 190–191
employee resource groups (ERGs) 39–40
Equality Act (2010) 13–23
equality objectives 25
equity 9

facilitation 102–104, 200
families: connecting with 94–95; potential barriers **95**
feedback: coaching and mentoring 159–161; evaluation 180–182, 202; professional development 118–119; safer spaces 143
focus groups 38–39
frontloading 86
fundamental British values 28

gaslighting 158
gender-fluid 24
gender identity: Equality Act (2010) 23; language of 5
gender reassignment 16–17
goal-setting 115
governors 49–50

Halo Code 82
Hope not Hate 199
hypervigilance 190–191
hypervisibility 198–199

IDEALS framework: models of **121–122**; outline of 120
identity 55
implementation plan 42–43; example **44–47**; example of an ED&I training curriculum **106–109**; evaluation 184
inclusion and belonging 4, 11–12
Inclusiveness Index 8
Initial Teacher Education and Training (ITE/T) 26–27
intent-impact gap 86–87
intergenerational trauma 56
intersectionality: example activity **61**; explanation of 56–57
interview 173–174
ipsative assessment 181

Kara, B. 59, 83
Keeping Children Safe in Education (KCSIE) 25–26

Lander, V. 26–27
language 5
LGBTQ+: case study 66–69; experiences 12; *see also* non-binary; sexuality and sexual orientation; gender identity; gender reassignment
listening 34–40, 50, 95, 117
lived experience: of authors 1–3; definition of 56

Macfarlane, R. 83–84
marriage and civil partnership 18

Maternity Teacher/ Paternity Teacher Project (MTPT) 35
MENCAP 35
mentoring: definition 146–147; informal 147; reverse 147–148
microaggression: explanation of 69–70; forms of 69, **70–71**; responding to 72–73; self-reflection on 74–75
microinclusions 74

National Curriculum 83
National Foundation for Educational Research (NFER) 35
non-binary 24

Ofsted: report on a rapid review of secual abuse in schools 38–39
Osivwemu, O. 49–51

performativity 52
perspective-taking approach 105, 113
'Pet to Threat' 196
policies and statements: caution around 52; review of 79
positive action programmes 19
pregnancy and maternity 18–19
prejudice-related incidents 79–80
privilege: awareness of 154, **155**; example case study 66–69; explanation of 65–66, 68
professional development 109–112
professional shadowing 174
protected characteristics 13–24
PSHE 99
psychological safety 127
Public Sector Equality Duty (PSED) 24–25

race: Equality Act definiton of 19–20; language of 5; and mental health 26
racial literacy 85
reasonable adjustments: complexities of 89; legalities of 15
religion or belief 20–21
representation 10–11
responsibility 48–49
role-models 88, 113, 171
Runnymede Trust 35

safeguarding 25–26
safer spaces: in the school building 90–92; in training 127–128, 130–133
Sanusi, A. 49–51
self-advocacy 161–162
self-disclosure 135–137, 158–159
self-reflection: explanation of 58; structured activity 59–63
sex: Equality Act (2010) definition of 21–22
sexuality and sexual orientation: Equality Act definition of 22–23; example case silence 90, 128–129, 140, 142; language of 5
Smith, H. 26–27
speak-up culture **44–45, 186**
statutory duties 12–26
stay conversations 173
Stonewall 17, 23, 35, 88
study 66–68

supervision 195
surveys 36–37; example survey questions **37**

Teachers' Standards 27–28
techniques 116–119
tenacity fatigue 196
tolerance 28
thresold concepts 55–58
training: cascading of 50–52; planning of 120–124
trauma 26, 56, 67–70, 140

unconscious bias 57
uniform 81–83

vulnerability 51, 58, 60, 128, 135–140

'woke' 6
women's health 91

For Product Safety Concerns and Information please contact our EU representative GPSR@taylorandfrancis.com
Taylor & Francis Verlag GmbH, Kaufingerstraße 24, 80331 München, Germany

www.ingramcontent.com/pod-product-compliance
Lightning Source LLC
Chambersburg PA
CBHW080412170426
43194CB00015B/2784